The approach to fiction:

Good and bad readings of novels

Douglas Hewitt

Rowman and Littlefield
Totowa, New Jersey

First published in the United States of America 1972
by Rowman and Littlefield, Totowa, New Jersey

ISBN-0-87471-127-4
73-150315

Printed in Great Britain by
Western Printing Services Ltd, Bristol

Contents

	Acknowledgements	vii
1	A declaration of intent	1
2	A partnership in mediocrity: *The Way We Live Now*	13
3	The conventions of realism: the shared world	45
4	The conventions of realism: the unshared world	67
5	The logical prison: *Little Dorrit*	85
6	Interpretation and over-interpretation	105
7	Reinterpretation and misinterpretation	129
8	Entertaining ideas: *Crotchet Castle*	147
9	Novels of ideas and ideas in novels	163
10	Tense and baggy monsters	183
	Index	195

Acknowledgements

The greater part of Chapter 6 appeared in *The London Review*, no. 1, Winter 1966, and of Chapter 8 in *Essays in Criticism*, xx, no. 2, April 1970, and I tender my thanks to the editors for permission to reproduce what first saw the light in their journals.
  As for other acknowledgements—I am reminded of the words of Proust: 'A book is a great cemetery in which, for the most part, the names upon the tombs are effaced.' I hope that not all my ideas are dead, but I am well aware that much of what I say in this book commemorates what I have been told, or have read, or have been stimulated to think by the arguments of others. Colleagues, friends, students, other writers (categories far from exclusive of one another) have taught me much and it gives me very great pleasure to thank them.

D.H.

Oxford, 1972

'Though criticism cannot boast of being a science, it ought to aim at something like a scientific basis, or at least proceed in a scientific spirit. The critic, therefore, before abandoning himself to the oratorical impulse, should endeavour to classify the phenomena with which he is dealing as calmly as if he were ticketing a fossil in a museum. The most glowing eulogy, the most bitter denunciation have their proper place; but they belong to the art of persuasion, and form no part of the scientific method.'

Sir Leslie Stephen: *Hours in a Library*

'. . . there is no whole to any analogy, we use as much of it as we need; and, if we tactlessly take any analogy too far, we break it down.'

I. A. Richards: *The Philosophy of Rhetoric*

I

A declaration of intent

Each novel can be seen as a unique work which creates the taste by which it is judged; novelists obtain the appropriate responses from their readers by establishing the right expectations—usually in the first few pages and often in the first few words.

This is true, but readers come to the novels with certain expectations and writers confront their virgin paper with certain expectations; sometimes those of the readers are inappropriate and it is arguable that those of some writers have been a hindrance to them. Moreover, it is in the nature of readers and critics to make generalizations about fiction. In practice, therefore, novels are not always considered as unique creations and thus we have histories of the novel, treatises on the novel and society, the technique of the novel, the decline of the novel and so forth.

It is an oddity of literary criticism that the common generic name for all the novels ever written is the singular of the component members of the class—'the Novel'. We do not talk thus of 'the Poem' and 'the Play'. The usage may be no more than a harmless peculiarity, influenced perhaps by a feeling that 'fiction' has too many associations which are insufficiently scholarly. But it is often symptomatic of a misleading assumption that we can discuss all novels in the same terms, that there is a unity of development, and that the same critical procedures can be applied to works as diverse as *Ivanhoe* and *Moby Dick* and *The Brothers Karamazov* and *Tristram Shandy*.

Nor is this assumption confined to ephemeral criticism. A writer as acute as Ian Watt feels able to say in *The Rise of the Novel*: 'It would appear, then, that the function of language is

1

much more largely referential in the novel than in other literary forms', and 'the world of the novel is essentially the world of the modern city'.* If we were to substitute 'novels' for 'the novel' in these two generalizations we might feel less satisfied; observably, language is used more or less referentially in a higher proportion of novels than poems, and far more novels are set in towns than elsewhere. But the use of 'the novel' encourages us to feel that there is one, right, central fictional tradition, from which *Wuthering Heights*, say, and *Moby Dick*, diverge.

In taking realism as the norm, Ian Watt is within the main English tradition. There are others, though most have a shorter history. A very influential one has been established by critics who combine a desire to treat novels as though they were lyric poems with an urge to establish patterns of symbols, myths and archetypes. The limitations of this method, too, are not only seen in its wilder excesses—the burying of novels under evidences of unrestrained ingenuity—but by the number of works with which it shows itself patently unable to deal.

In practice, maintaining the right to make some generalizations but trying not to subsume all novels under 'the Novel', we often move towards a rudimentary kind of genre criticism. We recognize that there are different kinds of novels by attaching to some of them descriptive adjectives ('realistic', 'allegorical'), by using descriptive phrases ('novel of ideas'), or, especially for minor and rather special forms, adopting popular labels ('thriller', 'science fiction'). As early as 1785 Clara Reeve pointed out the need for one very important distinction:

> No writings are more different than the ancient *Romance* and modern *Novel*, yet they are frequently confounded together, and mistaken for each other. (*The Progress of Romance*, i, 7)

and defined the difference thus:

> The Romance is an heroic fable, which treats of fabulous persons and things.—The Novel is a picture of real life and manners, and of the times in which it is written. The Romance in lofty and elevated language, describes what never happened nor is likely to happen.—The Novel gives a familiar relation of such things,

---

* I should like to stress that throughout this book I have normally chosen examples of what seem to me to be critical errors from the work of critics to whom I feel myself indebted. It is common ground that there are bad critics. My point is that certain surprising misconceptions are found in the writings of good ones.

as pass every day before our eyes, such as may happen to our friend, or to ourselves. (i, 111)

One of the obvious weaknesses of much genre criticism is its tendency to harden classifications into exclusive categories; easily labelled works are often not the most interesting, so a lot of time is wasted haggling about which side of a boundary to place the better ones. In the discussion of fiction a further disadvantage is often produced by commitment—sometimes unconscious, sometimes polemical—to one particular genre. Clara Reeve's terminology, for example, weights the scale rather obviously, for most of us, in favour of 'the Novel'. The claims of Lukács and others for the realistic novel of society as the only way of dealing adequately with our awareness of ourselves as social beings (and consequent blurrings of the use of 'realistic' as a descriptive term for subject matter or for technical method or for a supposed inevitable union of both) underline the problem which this sort of criticism is bound to face.

Implicit in all such discussion of categories is the question, which has taken up so much critics' time, of the relationship between novels and 'real life'. Suggestions about the nature of this relationship have ranged, at various times, from an extremely simple 'documentary' view to the claim that there is no 'real life' and that the question is thus not a useful one. The extreme documentary view obliges us to exclude from the category of novels rather a lot of works which we all agree to be novels and it leads logically to the view that when sociology was born the novel began to die; it is not, I think, now held by anyone who has any real interest in fiction. Of the other extreme it can only be said that, though there is a perfectly reputable philosophical tradition which supports it, yet the novelists with whom I am mostly concerned in this book and their readers certainly believed—and believe—that there is a real life, largely publicly shared, outside books. Our novelists have certainly been men *pour qui le monde extérieur existe.*

John Harvey suggested in *Character and the Novel*, that realistic novels need to be talked about in terms of mimesis, and 'romances' are better talked about in terms of their autonomy. If one had to make a choice this rough-and-ready distinction is probably the best, but I would greatly prefer not to have to make the choice. It is true that everything in a novel can be referred

3

both to something outside the book (for language is a public referential system) and also to other things within the book (for the most rudimentary novel is a system of correspondences), and realistic novels demand more discussion in terms of the former and 'romances' more discussion in terms of the latter. But even the most resolutely realistic novel is an autonomous structure of words, and the words of even the least realistic refer to objects, ideas, human characteristics, which we share before we begin to read the book.

I wish to propose in this book a way of considering novels, a model, which will enable me to do justice to the fact that different novels affect us in different ways, without involving us in tedious demarcation disputes, and which will at the same time do justice to the sense that the relationship between novels and life is not basically different in different kinds of works. We should be able to make some general statements without being led to make the wrong ones.

First, however, it is important to make clear the kind of status which I want my suggestion to have—the kind of status which I believe is possible for any such models. I believe that all categories, all theories of fiction, all generalizations, if they are to be useful, must be recognized as being provisional and for convenience only. The human mind (including those human minds which create novels) is untidy; there seems no reason why it should be possible to produce tidy classifications and systems for fiction and attempts to do so normally lead us farther and farther away from the books about which we are trying to talk. If our generalizations enable us to get closer to individual works, to make useful distinctions, to clear muddles out of the way, they justify themselves. There are, no doubt, an unlimited number of models, of ways of generalizing about novels, and they are of varying degrees of use. Some will do a modest job of work but will not take us very far. If we said, for example, that some novels are long and some are short, that they thus have different characteristics and it is futile to ask of one kind what the other gives, this might serve some limited purpose; but if we pressed it far we would find it a lot more trouble than it was worth. Some —this is true, I think, of the categories which I shall use in this book—will take us a good deal farther and enable us to elucidate a considerable number of muddles. If we push any of them too far we end up either misrepresenting individual works for the sake of a scheme or becoming so scholastically abstract that we replace the works by labels. When Northrop Frye, for example, says that within his fifteen categories of novels *A la Recherche du Temps Perdu* is a Novel-Confession-Anatomy, *Don Quixote* a Novel-Romance-Anatomy, and *Ulysses* a Novel-Romance-Confession-Anatomy, I cannot envisage any discussion of these works in these terms which will be other than totally destructive of the effects of the books or actually unrelated to them. Either the critic twists the books to fit them into their slots or he rises into a metacriticism in which the titles stand for types which are hardly individualized but bear different labels.

My hypothesis then is provisional, for use. I have found it helpful, when considering the relationship between a novel and the lives we lead and to which the novel seems to have some relevance, to conceive the relationship under the figure of metaphor. The relationship between a novel and life is akin to that between the two parts of a metaphor (the 'vehicle' and the 'tenor' in I. A. Richards's terms). I include simile within this term, for here there is no need to distinguish between them. It is, however, very useful to consider the different ways in which different metaphors work on us and how far this may help to enlighten us about the different ways in which novels function.

I imagine that some such view is widely shared and I believe that it is worth pursuing the speculation some way, for two reasons in particular—first, because discussion of the realistic mode has often been in terms of mimesis which suggests that the relationship is more direct and more logical, and, second, because when we talk of novels being 'metaphorical' we have often been so concerned with 'romances' that we have forgotten that the figure of metaphor may usefully be applied to all novels.

Ostensibly, metaphors assert a resemblance between one thing and another (similes, of course, actually make this assertion by their syntactical form). When we describe blossom as falling like snow or speak of a carpet of flowers we seem to be doing little more than increasing the vividness of our description by indicating a visual resemblance. But it is only with the most straightforward and rudimentarily descriptive metaphors that we could be satisfied for a moment with this account of what is happening. When Burns says 'My love is like a red, red rose' it is quite clear that indicating a resemblance is hardly in question. She is not scarlet, she is not composed of a number of petals, she is not

5

a few inches across and one of many virtually identical blooms on the same thorny stock. What we are doing in our response to this is basic to all metaphors; we are transferring the feelings which are aroused by the metaphor—beauty, fragrance, desirability—to the object to which the metaphor refers, the lady, and recognizing that they illuminate the poet's feelings about her. Because language is in its nature metaphorical, being so largely composed of dead and dying metaphors, we perform this apparently rather complicated feat of transference with the greatest ease and, indeed, without realizing what it is that we are doing. This is not, however, always true; there is enormous variety in the ways in which metaphors affect us, and I suggest that the same is true of the metaphorical relationship of novels to life.

Just as certain metaphors achieve their effect by a sense of closeness, of perceived similarity, so certain novels—the ones which we commonly call 'realistic'—function metaphorically in the same way. There is a strong element of the descriptive, of obvious appropriateness; just as an inadequate idea that a metaphor is a likening of one thing to another is most likely to be asserted unthinkingly in such cases, so a simple idea of the novel as a fictional document is most likely to be accepted in discussion of these novels.

Straightforward metaphors of this kind include, of course, the majority of the daily, half-dead ones—the carpets of flowers and the shields which politicians promise us against inflation—but some of the most obvious metaphors are among the most powerful. When Mark Antony says: 'the long day's task is done,/And we must sleep', the aptness of the image is obvious; it is sanctioned by tradition; the mind has to make no leap of connection. The context and the form—the rhythm of the lines— make it appear the most perfect and complete statement possible. Similarly, the best realistic novels appear in some senses perfectly obvious; they appear to require no interpretation; there often seems very little need to say anything about them. It is perhaps more important here than in the discussion of other kinds of works to be clear that we do not read such novels primarily as documents. There may be documentary elements in them (just as there may be informative elements in metaphors) but basically what is happening when we respond is that certain feelings are aroused in us by the novels and we then find (to put matters simply) that these feelings are relevant to the life that we know.

Of the best novels we feel that they reveal things to us, that in some way which may have nothing to do with 'information' we 'know more about life' after we have read them. This is one of the reasons why the 'relevance' of novels cannot be at all easily discussed in terms of the closeness of the created life in the novel to our own particular experience nor their convincingness in terms of their historical accuracy. The social experience of Tolstoy's characters is in many ways remote from ours and it is obvious that his portrayal of the feelings of the Russian peasantry is far from historically accurate. But his metaphor is internally consistent and, in transferring to our lives the feelings aroused by the novel and finding them convincing and relevant, we are not transferring them as 'information' which we then feel obliged to check against such other facts as we may obtain from, say, our knowledge of Russian history.*

Some straightforward metaphors may, of course, appear hackneyed because we feel that the writer is using them as clichés; they are not merely lacking in obvious originality but also in that vividness which makes us feel that the perception which they express is a genuine one. An analogous effect in fiction is produced by those novels where the writer seems to have accepted a theme and a form which represents not a personal vision but a stock response.

Metaphors may also appear as dead metaphors; that is, though their form may be metaphorical they are accepted as non-metaphorical direct statements. Analogous to this is the novel whose effect on us is entirely in terms of documentation, sociological reporting. It is not difficult to think of honest, well-researched realistic novels of which we might say that they are good documents but dead metaphors. They may provide interesting information, they may tell us a good deal about the lives which people lead, and they may even comment intelligently on them, but the work does not impress us as being a work of art, a whole with sufficient complexity, sufficient achieved form, to function as a metaphor. Throughout, its reference is continually outwards to social observation, to the frame of mind appropriate to sociology or history or journalism, and its effect is therefore virtually exclusively documentary.

Cases such as this provide a good example of one of the minor

* But see Chapter 9 for a discussion of those places where Tolstoy tempts us to precisely this destructive action. Not even Tolstoy is perfect.

uses of my metaphor model. This model is not intended to provide standards of judgment which could take the place of the kinds of discrimination by which we normally judge the success of novels. But it may sometimes provide an illuminating way of expressing a dissatisfaction (or a satisfaction). It may, for example, express what sometimes seems an almost puzzling lack of interest which we feel in some novels which are decently written accounts of plausible relationships between well-observed characters within a convincing plot—a lack of interest which is a much stronger adverse judgment than we make about some other works where the flaws are greater and more obvious.

So far I have been concerned with metaphors which make their effect by an obvious appropriateness and with novels which are analogous to them. But not all metaphors are of this nature. Some surprise us and require a leap of association. We do not immediately have the same sense of inevitable rightness, of apparently effortless appeal to the great central certainties. Energy is created by their very strangeness, sometimes, indeed, by their very yoking together of contraries. Such is Macbeth's: 'pity, like a naked new-born babe,/Striding the blast'. There is no simple sense in which pity is like a naked, new-born babe as there is a simple sense in which death follows life as night the day. Our first impression may be one of strangeness. But the associations of the image—helplessness succeeded immediately by immense power created by the perception of helplessness—corresponds to a profound and very striking awareness of what pity is and does. Moreover, the sudden leap from helplessness to the power of 'striding the blast' corresponds to Macbeth's appalled sense of the powers which he will not be able to control. Such metaphors are revelatory and they gain much of their power from the energy with which we have to meet the linking of apparently dissimilar things. Proust describes one of their effects very strikingly: '[The novelist] fuses a quality common to two sensations, extracts their essence and, in order to withdraw them from the contingencies of time, unites them in a metaphor, thus chaining them together with the indefinable bond of a verbal alliance.'

The effect of a novel like *Wuthering Heights* is akin to this. Just as the quotation from *Macbeth* links dissimilar things together and surprises and convinces us that the link has enlarged our perceptions, so Emily Brontë presents happenings and relationships and speeches which are very different from those of our daily life and then convinces us that the feelings called up in us by them are relevant to our own experience—not that we and the people we know behave and talk like Catherine and Heathcliff or live in a world of such polar opposites as Thrushcross Grange and Wuthering Heights, but that the total complex of feelings which Emily Brontë projects through the novel is central to our experience. Dickens's grotesques, symbols, parodies, foreshortenings, operate in the same way, and so do the varied technical methods employed by Melville in *Moby Dick*. Much of the energy generated—the energy which is called out in us and thus gives the novel conviction—is a product of the jump which we make in connecting our own experience and the formalized and inventive work.

I have used the terms 'surprise', 'strangeness', 'jump', and I believe that this corresponds to an inherent characteristic of metaphors and novels of the kind which I have described; but, of course, once our minds are engaged by the metaphors and the novels the element of strangeness recedes into the background. Once caught up, we read the works in their own terms and we shall only notice the strangeness if we begin to misread or if we talk with people who are misreading—such as, for example, people who are endeavouring to respond to *Wuthering Heights* as if it were a realistic novel and thus obliging us to be consciously aware of the high degree of stylization of the work.

There are, however, also metaphors whose effect depends on a conscious awareness that we are yoking together dissimilars. An obvious example of this is Donne's famous 'stiffe twin compasses'. Their effect always includes a good deal of conscious intellectual awareness; we come to see an appropriateness in the image, but we remain aware of our own intellectual processes in making the connection. A similar effect is achieved by some novels; I think this is true of the novels of Samuel Beckett, for example, of Melville's *The Confidence Man*, and, in a more extreme way, of the novels of Ronald Firbank. My list of examples is deliberately varied in importance and in seriousness because there is no necessary connection between these qualities and the nature of the relationship between the novel and our lives, any more than there is between the kind of metaphor and the significance of the work in which it appears. But, just as certain obvious metaphors may affect us as dead metaphors and certain realistic novels as inert documents, so some deliberately surprising metaphors may seem only frigid conceits and some novels whose effect I have likened to them may be only exercises in frivolous ingenuity. Here we feel that we cannot be bothered to make the jump which connects them to our experience or, in some cases, are so busy trying to connect the parts of the metaphor that we lose the sense of a whole which can be thus related to our own lives.

One of the characteristics of metaphors is that we do not normally push them too far. I said that when we think of the poet's love as being like a red, red rose we allow feelings about fragrance, beauty and desirability to come into our minds and to transfer themselves to the love for which the rose is a metaphor. It is also true that we do not allow into our minds feelings about greenfly, pruning and the need for manuring (all of which, for someone with a garden, may arise when the word 'rose' is encountered). Similarly, we do not reflect, of Antony's speech, that after sleep we must rise again for another long day's task, nor, in Macbeth's, so visualize the baby as to identify it as a male or a female child. We are all familiar with the situation in which the writer loses control of his metaphor or when, because of unfamiliarity with the conventions within which he writes, or because of freakish personal associations, we lose control of it ourselves and misread the work. But normally—to an extent which is quite extraordinary—we do not; we realize what associations of the image are in keeping. This is achieved partly by the directing power of convention, partly by the context, and partly by the control exercised over one part of the metaphor by the other parts.

We know how to 'take' novels in much the same way as we know how to 'take' metaphors; we gain a sense of what is 'in keeping'; and we are also familiar with situations when this sense of keeping breaks down and we begin to pursue undesirable associations or to ask unwanted questions. Here, too, a sense of the convention within which the writer is working is of paramount importance. When we misunderstand a novel we most often do so because we do not realize what kind of book it is. Charlotte Brontë's misplaced attempt in her introduction to *Wuthering Heights* to assert to polished readers that the picture of 'unlettered moorland hinds and rugged moorland squires' was a consequence of her sister's rustic upbringing is an example of this. The novelist also controls our responses by the structure of the book, by establishing a narrator or authorial *persona*, by all the varied methods by which different parts of the book control one another—by, in short, establishing a set of norms, a sense of unity.

My purpose in this book is to consider a number of ways in which our response to novels is controlled, both by what happens in the books and by what conventions exist, so that we 'take' the books aright. Though most, if not all, of what follows in succeeding chapters has been written with my metaphor model in mind, I have not hesitated to diverge from it, to make other kinds of distinctions, to pursue arguments where they lead without anxiously bringing them back to a model which I do not set up as a comprehensive 'theory of the novel'. I hope that much which I have to say may be of interest to a reader whose cast of mind is such that my metaphor model is unhelpful to him.

I shall discuss three nineteenth-century English novels: Trollope's *The Way We Live Now*, Dickens's *Little Dorrit* and Peacock's *Crotchet Castle*. Formally they are very different from one another: *The Way We Live Now* may reasonably and for convenience of discussion be called a realistic novel, *Little Dorrit* a symbolic novel and *Crotchet Castle* a novel of ideas. Each is concerned to a considerable extent with the 'condition of England' question and the works by Trollope and Dickens both bear some relationship to the same historical facts—Mr Melmotte and Mr Merdle derive from their authors' feelings about the same railways speculator. Each will be discussed in the terms which seem most useful and the terms vary very much from book to book. I follow my chapters on each of the novels by a series of speculations about the critical procedures which I and others have followed in approaching them, discussing such matters as the characteristics of the tradition of realism and some of its inherent tensions, the meaning of the term 'interpretation' when applied to fiction and the possibilities of overinterpretation, reinterpretation and misinterpretation, and the precarious nature of 'ideas' in fiction and the criteria of right response to them.

In this introductory chapter it remains only to say that a man who offers to discuss the art of fiction in such large terms must know that he will often state the obvious. The state of criticism of fiction is such that a critic who says, for example, 'the task of the novelist is to create credible characters' will appear to some of his readers to be uttering literary blasphemy, to others refreshing and long-delayed novelty, and to others flat platitude. My task could, perhaps, be described as defining the appropriate contexts for platitudes.

2

A partnership in mediocrity:
The Way We Live Now

The title of Trollope's *The Way We Live Now* defines the novel very thoroughly; not merely are we told that this will be a general picture of contemporary life, but the form of words emphasizes the implicit alliance of writer and reader, hints at some contrast with a more satisfactory age, and, finally, has about it a directness not entirely free from the pedestrian.

The phrase is echoed twice in the book and, though I do not suggest that Trollope is given to subtle effects of echo and correspondence, it is worth noting that on each occasion it points to those aspects of contemporary life which are the central concern of the book. When Lady Monogram is explaining to Georgiana Longestaffe the rules of social decorum which will not allow her to invite Georgiana's fiancé, the Jewish financier Brehgert, to dine, she says:

> 'There's the butcher round the corner in Bond Street, or the man who comes to do my hair. I don't at all think of asking them to my house. But if they were suddenly to turn out wonderful men, and go everywhere, no doubt I should be glad to have them here. That's the way we live, and you are as well used to it as I am. Mr Brehgert at present to me is like the butcher round the corner.' (Vol. ii, 90. All references are to The World's Classics double volume.)

Lady Monogram has just explained why she can receive Mr Goldsheiner, who has married Lady Julia Start and 'got himself in', and her whole conversation with Georgiana is haggling about what she will do in return for tickets to the reception given by Melmotte, one of the wonderful men who go everywhere. The way we live now, in short, is a matter of social ambition, money and snobbery.

It is right that the other use of the title phrase should concern love and betrayal, for it is in relationships of love and marriage that the theme is largely worked out. Trollope comments at the beginning of Chapter LXX on Felix Carbury's threat to confront Paul Montague with his knowledge that Paul has engaged himself to Hetta while still having a liaison with Mrs Hurtle:

> There is no duty more certain or fixed in the world than that which calls upon a brother to defend his sister from ill-usage; but, at the same time, in the way we live now, no duty is more difficult, and we may generally say more indistinct. . . . There is a feeling, too, when a girl has been jilted,—thrown over, perhaps, is the proper term,—after the gentleman has had the fun of making love to her for an entire season, and has perhaps even been allowed privileges as her promised husband, that the less said the better.

The love affair of Hetta and Paul is (apart from that of Ruby Ruggles and John Crumb) the least socially heterogeneous of those on which Trollope spends much time. Paul Montague is a 'gentleman' and distantly related to Hetta, though he is involved in the financial manoeuvres of Melmotte and is the lover of Mrs Hurtle, who is not merely suspect as an American but also manifests that piratical spirit of which Melmotte is the most enterprising representative. The other courtships are ones which cut across the accepted lines of class division: Paul and Mrs Hurtle, Lady Carbury and Mr Broune, Sir Felix and Marie Melmotte, Lord Nidderdale and Marie, Georgiana Longestaffe and Mr Brehgert. They are all marked by mercenary calculation, of varying degrees of heartlessness, by the gentry, combined with assumptions of innate superiority.

It might seem that a theme of this kind would be better presented by the method of the scene from which my first quotation is taken than by the method of the second. The interplay of characters offers scope for subtlety and the possibility of complexity of presentation. Here, for example, we are aware that Georgiana knows perfectly well the rules of society which Lady Monogram is telling her and we recognize Lady Monogram's pleasure in paying off old scores by spelling out her reasons. The dogmatic address to the reader, whose mental activity is relatively circumscribed, seems altogether less flexible. Yet Trollope chooses to present much of his novel by plain statement, speaking apparently in his own person. It would be as well to consider why he does so and what effects are achieved by this method.

At first sight, certainly, the degree of dogmatism is so great and the relationship sought with the reader so direct that his method appears to admit little uncertainty, little ambiguity and little subtlety. 'Let the reader be introduced to Lady Carbury, upon whose character and doings much will depend of whatever interest these pages may have,' the book begins, and continues, within a few lines: 'Something of the nature of her devotion may be learned by the perusal of three letters which on this morning she had written with a quickly running hand.' Trollope is clearly willing to risk making his characters appear puppets by creating a closer relationship between narrator and reader than that between the reader and his image of the characters. This is seen at its most extreme at the beginning of the second chapter: 'If the reader does not understand so much from her letters to the three editors they have been written in vain'—written by Trollope for the reader's benefit, that is, not by Lady Carbury for her correspondents'. Such a reminder that here is a writer telling a story to his reader is of a piece with Trollope's odd habit of calling his baker Mixet, his African traveller Dr Palmoil, and his lawyers Messrs Slow and Bideawhile.

Such obvious breaches of the apparent logic of the story are fairly rare, but the motive for them, as for Trollope's narrative method in general, is clear—the establishment of an implicit relationship of trust and near-equality with the reader. The direct addresses, present throughout the novel, serve to define the expected reader, whose attitudes, beliefs and prejudices are worked upon by the issues of the book. In so doing, of course, they also define, within a partnership of honest mediocrity, the narrator, whose numerous overt reflections are, as I hope to show, far from identical with the effect of the whole book.

The implied reader is a man of the 'middling sort'. 'Were I to buy a little property, some humble cottage with a garden,—or you, O reader, unless you be magnificent,—the money to the last farthing would be wanted, or security for the money more than sufficient, before we should be able to enter in upon our new home' (i, 325). The reader is clearly not expected to be magnificent, not an Auld Reekie nor a Melmotte. But equally he is not a Ruggles, for of one of the womenfolk of that class Trollope says, in a passage which defines to perfection a prevalent mid-nineteenth century attitude to the working class: 'If she be good-looking and relieved from the pressure of want, her thoughts soar into a world which is as unknown to her as heaven is to us, and in regard to which her longings are apt to be infinitely stronger than are ours for heaven' (i, 170). The unknown, heaven-like world is the social situation of the readers and the narrator.

Trollope, in short, asserts an identity of social background with his readers and claims only that rather greater knowledge of the world which permits him to say: 'Most of my readers will not probably know how a man looks when he comes home drunk at six in the morning.' His psychological summings-up, couched in a plain, trenchant, basically unfigurative language, appeal to moral values which seem equally shared and equally taken for granted. Of Sir Felix he says:

> He liked to be kindly treated, to be praised and petted, to be well fed and caressed; and they who so treated him were his chosen friends. He had in this the instincts of a horse, not approaching the higher sympathies of a dog. But it cannot be said of him that he had ever loved any one to the extent of denying himself a moment's gratification on that loved one's behalf. His heart was a stone. (i, 17–18)

In less moralizing passages the impression at which he aims is of judicious and balanced common sense, unsurprising but convincing, going a little—but only a little—beyond the powers of the reader whom he has postulated. Such is his shrewd comment on the advantages of oral confessions of infidelity over written ones.

> A man may desire that the woman he loves should hear the record of his folly,—so that, in after days, there may be nothing to detect: so that, should the Mrs Hurtle of his life at any time intrude upon his happiness, he may with a clear brow and un-daunted heart say to his beloved one,—'Ah, this is the trouble of which I spoke to you.' And then he and his beloved one will be in one cause together. But he hardly wishes to supply his beloved one with a written record of his folly. And then who does not know how much tenderness a man may show to his own faults by the tone of his voice, by half-spoken sentences, and by an admixture of words of love for the lady who has

filled up the vacant space once occupied by the Mrs Hurtle of his romance? But the written record must go through from beginning to end, self-accusing, thoroughly perspicuous, with no sweet, soft falsehoods hidden under the half-expressed truth. (ii, 243)

We come early, then, to accept the narrator as reliable, common-sensical, not stupid, but ordinary, even commonplace. The tendency of the whole book, however, is to explore and to modify the assumptions and standards which are assumed as shared between the writer and the reader. The effect is not the extreme one of achieving irony by using a narrator who is shown to be wrongheaded. The dogmatic statements of the beginning are correct so far as they go, but the book affects us as revealing Trollope, in the course of telling his story, being obliged to show situations, people, moral dilemmas for which they are not altogether adequate.

Most of the more marked discrepancies between what I have called the 'partnership in honest mediocrity' of Trollope the narrator and the implied reader and the effect of the whole book are caused by passages of dramatic presentation—those between Paul and Mrs Hurtle, for example, or between Roger Carbury and Father Barham, or Nidderdale and his father. The effect could be briefly described as the spectacle of a man of decent, worthy, conventional, but limited, standards who is obliged by his honesty and openmindedness to recount events which do not altogether tally with his expectations and which, indeed, sometimes cast considerable doubts upon the adequacy of his values, who, as the book progresses, goes some way towards admitting this, and, perhaps, leaves us questioning them more than he does.

The theme of the novel as it develops in the first few chapters seems to be the decay of values on the part of 'Society'—especially London Society—which embraces an utterly unworthy Melmotte in an attempt to acquire his money either by joining him in business or by marrying his daughter. Against this stand as touchstones of old and admired values—the way we lived once—Hetta and Roger Carbury, the country gentleman. Several characters express such a view of decadence. Lady Pomona Longestaffe's regretful verdict is that 'Things are changed'. Trollope speaks of Melmotte's Conservative supporters as 'honest good men, men who really loved their country, fine gentlemen who had received unsullied names from great ancestors'. With some irony at the customary presentation of youthful rakes, we are told: 'And then, even into the Beargarden there had filtered, through the outer world, a feeling that people were not now bound to be so punctilious in the paying of money as they were a few years since' (ii, 229).

But, whatever may be said, it is certainly not merely a decadent section of society which courts Melmotte. His triumphal progress is assisted by all the powers in the land. The note is struck very early in the book when he gives a ball; the Marchioness of Auld Reekie meets the Countess of Mid-Lothian at it, having come because she has heard that the Duchess of Stevenage will be there. As a reward for giving the dinner to the Emperor of China, Melmotte is admitted to an entertainment at Windsor Park; he can choose whether to be adopted by the Liberals or the Conservatives and, in describing the choice of him as candidate, the various powers which ally themselves with him are catalogued: 'There was the popular element, the fashionable element, the legislative element, the legal element, and the commercial element. Melmotte undoubtedly was the man for Westminster' (i, 326). The Church of England is charmed by his gift to the Curates' Aid Society; the Church of Rome, in the person of Father Barham, hopes to claim him as a Catholic. It is fitting, therefore, that the list of guests prepared for his dinner should be representative. It is presented by Trollope in a strain of satirical farce which is reminiscent of Dickens:

> Royalty had twenty tickets, each ticket for guest and wife. The existing Cabinet was fourteen; but the coming was numbered at about eleven only;—each one for self and wife. Five ambassadors and five ambassadresses were to be asked. There were to be fifteen real merchants out of the city. Then great peers,—with their peeresses,—were selected by the general committee of management. There were to be three wise men, two poets, three independent members of the House of Commons, two Royal Academicians, three editors of papers, an African traveller who had just come home, and a novelist;—but all these latter gentlemen were expected to come as bachelors. (i, 328)

The truth is that Melmotte has not corrupted those who hang round him. He has merely discovered that

> He could thus trade either on the timidity or on the ignorance of his colleagues. When neither of these sufficed to give him

undisputed mastery, then he cultivated the cupidity of his friends. He liked young associates because they were more timid and less greedy than their elders. (i, 217–18)

Those who show up worst in the relationship are those whom we would expect to be most firmly rooted in traditional values— Lord Alfred Grendall, for example, who is ironically referred to when acting the flunkey as 'the duke's nephew', never separates himself from his master until that master is ruined, at which point Trollope's verdict is: 'Lord Alfred was one of those who knew when to leave a falling house' (ii, 112).

Nor is there any reason to believe that this relationship between the gentry and the world of finance is a new one, nor its exploitation by the ruling classes. Young Nidderdale may have compunctions about trying to marry Marie, but his father, the Marquis of Auld Reekie, speaks with the accumulated wisdom of age when he warns his son against visiting Marie after her father's crash: 'Don't you go and make a fool of yourself . . . This is just one of those times when a man may ruin himself by being soft-hearted' (ii, 336). When Felix Carbury reflects that it is an understood bargain that he provides rank and position and Marie provides money, he is not expressing any new and decadent code of behaviour; he is merely parroting the traditional view. This is set forth in detail at the beginning of chapter LVII in relation to Nidderdale:

> It had been an understood thing, since he had commenced life, that he was to marry an heiress. In such families as his . . . it is generally understood that matters shall be put right by an heiress. It has become an institution, like primogeniture, and is almost as serviceable for maintaining the proper order of things. Rank squanders money; trade makes it;—and then trade purchases rank by re-gilding its splendour. The arrangement, as it affects the aristocracy generally, is well understood, and was quite approved of by the old marquis—so that he had felt himself to be justified in eating up the property, which his son's future marriage would renew as a matter of course. (ii, 59)

The case of Georgiana Longestaffe is, in relation to this tradition, an interesting one. Stupid and selfish though she may be, her plight is a genuine one. She must marry and she must marry money. When, speaking of her projected visit to the Melmotte's, she says: 'I must go. It's the only chance that is left', she is expressing herself somewhat melodramatically, but she is not far from the truth. If her family thinks that she is at fault, it is not because she is mercenary but because she has been insufficiently realistic in her previous expectations. She is allowed to go to London to stay with the Melmottes so that she may make a financially satisfactory marriage. Here, however, the double standard of judgment, which extends beyond the narrower aspects of sexual morality, comes into play. Grasslough and Nidderdale, who are quite prepared for marriage with Melmotte's daughter, treat her with a want of respect; Lady Monogram, who will intrigue for tickets to the Melmottes' reception, explains why the rules of social decorum oblige her to treat Georgiana coolly. She is the victim of that hypocrisy which is elsewhere summed up so succinctly: 'From the beginning of the Melmotte era it had been an understood thing that no one spoke to Madame Melmotte' (ii, 107). Finally her own greed prevents her from marrying 'an old, fat Jew' who is kinder, more honest and more honourable than any of her own set, and we are left in no doubt that the outcome is, for Mr Brehgert, a most fortunate deliverance. It cannot really be said that the old county family of Longestaffe comes well out of its encounter with the world of finance.

Trollope's way of seeming to share conventional attitudes with his readers and then being obliged to produce surprises is very clearly seen in his treatment of the relationship between Georgiana and Mr Brehgert. Initially he speaks with that disparagement of alien groups which finds its classical expression in anti-semitism. That Fisker and Mrs Hurtle are American is enough to make them suspect, but a great deal more emphasis is placed on the Jewishness of some of the others. Madame Melmotte, described as having 'the Jewish nose and the Jewish contraction of the eyes' is referred to as 'that Jewish-looking woman' or 'the Bohemian Jewess'. Cohenlupe is 'a gentleman of the Jewish persuasion'. This last phrase alone would be enough to justify the assumption that Trollope is inviting the reader to adopt the attitude of sly and lofty disparagement which is the characteristic English middle-class form of anti-semitism. When Mr Brehgert, the 'old, fat Jew' of Mr Longestaffe's description, appears, he seems to fit the stereotype and the way in which he is described is the stereotyped jeer:

He was a fat, greasy man, good-looking in a certain degree, about fifty, with hair dyed black, and beard and moustache dyed a dark purple colour. The charm of his face consisted in a pair of very bright black eyes, which were, however, set too near together in his face for the general delight of Christians. (ii, 91)

(It is worth noting that the contrast between Mr Brehgert and the Gentiles who despise him is not between the dyed and the undyed; Mr Longestaffe, too, had 'hair and whiskers carefully dyed'. But this would hardly be enough to undermine the readers' prejudices about the bad taste and lack of probity of Jews: Mr Brehgert's whiskers sound rather badly dyed.)

Trollope, however, having allowed the averagely prejudiced reader to assume that his prejudices are shared by the novelist, produces a number of surprises. Georgiana, reflecting on the numbers of 'decent people' who have married Jews, knows that:

Jew, Turk, or infidel was nothing to her. She had seen enough of the world to be aware that her happiness did not lie in that direction, and could not depend in the least on the religion of her husband. Of course she would go to church herself. She always went to church. It was the proper thing to do. As to her husband, though she did not suppose that she could ever get him to church,—nor perhaps would it be desirable,—she thought that she might induce him to go nowhere, so that she might be able to pass him off as a Christian. She knew that such was the Christianity of young Goldsheiner, of which the Starts were now boasting. (ii, 92–3)

In a novel in which, as I hope to show later, the conventional forms of religion are contrasted with real, even fanatical, belief, it is, I think, significant that Georgiana notes that one great obstacle to Mr Brehgert's acceptance by her family is that he is a practising Jew: 'How could she tell parents such as these that she was engaged to marry a man who at the present moment went to synagogue on a Saturday and carried out every other filthy abomination common to the despised people?' (ii, 93)

Lady Pomona, in a passage of rich stupidity which is perhaps the funniest thing in the book, makes her own Christian opposition to the proposed marriage:

'It's unnatural. It's worse than your wife's sister. I'm sure there's something in the Bible against it. You never would read your Bible, or you wouldn't be going to do this.'

'Lady Julia Start has done just the same thing,—and she goes everywhere.'

'What does your papa say? I'm sure your papa won't allow it. If he's fixed about anything, it's about the Jews. An accursed race;—think of that, Georgiana;—expelled from Paradise.'

'Mama, that's nonsense.'

'Scattered about all over the world, so that nobody knows who anybody is. And it's only since those nasty Radicals came up that they have been able to sit in Parliament.' (ii, 263)

The climax of the relationship comes in chapter LXXIX, 'The Brehgert Correspondence' and with Georgiana's resolve, which symbolizes perfectly the whole situation not only of Georgiana but of the gentry in their dealings with the commercial classes throughout the book: 'But she would keep the watch and chain he had given her, and which somebody had told her had not cost less than a hundred and fifty guineas. She could not wear them, as people would know whence they had come; but she might exchange them for jewels which she could wear' (ii, 279). She is not, in the event, permitted to do so because of the insistence of her sister who, bent on revenging herself for previous slights undergone when Georgiana seemed to have the advantage of her in the marriage market, asserts the claims of the family honour.

There remains a coda, in the form of an interview between Mr Longestaffe and Brehgert, which makes the final comment on the mixture of prejudice, stupidity and hypocrisy which composes the Longestaffe attitude—and which, I suggest, Trollope could confidently expect to find in a large number of his readers. Brehgert triumphs within the terms in which he has been presented throughout. He never ceases to be a fat man with badly dyed whiskers, but his mind is clear and he is both firm and good-natured. Refusing to accept Longestaffe's embarrassment as that of a superior who is too gentlemanly to discuss a mistake which has been overcome, he ends on a note which is positively epigrammatic. To Longestaffe's suggestion that 'on so delicate a subject the less said the soonest mended' he replies: 'I've nothing more to say, and I've nothing at all to mend' (ii, 362).

In brief, then, there is no warrant in the happenings within the book for the view that society, in taking up with Melmotte and his like, is decadent. Society is only too happy to make use of him in the way in which it has always done. Moreover, in the crucial matter of the Longestaffes and Mr Brehgert, integrity, good manners, and (the quality of dye on whiskers apart) even good taste are represented rather by the Jewish upstart than by the county family.

The most thoroughgoing denunciations of these corruptions comes from Roger Carbury and it remains for us to consider Trollope's presentation of him, for he seems to approximate more closely than any other character to those moral and social values whose disappearance in London are mourned both by Lady Pomona Longestaffe and by the narrating author.

For Hetta he is the touchstone of right and wrong: 'I always feel that my cousin Roger is a rock of strength, so that if one did whatever he said one would never get wrong. I never found any one else that I thought that of, but I do think it of him' (i, 361). He is marked off from most of the rest of his class by fulfilling a useful social function. Trollope makes the point, which is perhaps more obvious to the twentieth-century reader, that the root trouble with the Beargarden set is idleness; the paralysing boredom of Sir Felix and his cronies is well caught; they have nothing to do with time but kill it. Their elders are either busy wasting their inheritances in the belief that the younger generation will marry money or trying to recoup their fortunes by fastening upon Melmotte. Lady Carbury, exceptionally, works hard at her writing, but her books are worthless and her marriage to Mr Broune allows her to accept this. Roger, on the other hand, runs one farm, fulfils his duties by attending meetings on church matters, and looks after his tenants to an extent which allows John Crumb to regard him in a paternal light. He explains to Hetta the beliefs behind this and they are the traditional ones of the landowner:

> 'He owes a duty to those who live on his land, and he owes a duty to his country. And, though it may seem fantastic to say so, I think he owes a duty to those who have been before him, and who have manifestly wished that the property should be continued in the hands of their descendants. These things are to me very holy.' (ii, 473)

It might seem that he can speak for a worthier way of life which he himself describes as 'old fashioned', which could be expected to have a greater appeal for the public of Trollope's age, when the radicalism which Roger abhors had made fewer inroads than it has since done, and which would justify him in saying that Melmotte's position 'is a sign of the degeneracy of the age'.

But Trollope goes to considerable lengths to call in question many of his values. In a minor way he draws a parallel between Roger's attitudes and those of Mr Longestaffe. It is impossible to think of Roger apart from Carbury Manor; in so many ways it sums up Roger's situation and his claim upon our sympathies. It is an old-fashioned house, less splendid than others in the county, not very comfortable, modest in its outward appearance, but it has 'that thoroughly established look of old county position' (i, 129). It is only a few pages before this passage that Mr Longestaffe's town house has been described in similar terms and with the plain statement that Mr Longestaffe gives it a similar symbolic value:

> . . . it was the old family town house, having been inhabited by three or four generations of Longestaffes, and did not savour of that radical newness which prevails, and which was peculiarly distasteful to Mr Longestaffe. Queen's Gate and the quarters around were, according to Mr Longestaffe, devoted to opulent tradesmen. Even Belgrave Square, though its aristocratic properties must be admitted, still smelt of the mortar. Many of those living there and thereabouts had never possessed in their families real family town-houses. (i, 119)

Such a similarity between the values of Roger and those of a man who, in his dealings with Mr Brehgert, for example, is seen to place prejudice before feeling and intelligence and to do so because of his sense of his inherent position, might be taken as an insignificant resemblance, even a coincidence, were it not that Trollope follows the two chapters which deal most extensively with Roger's 'old fashioned notions' (chapters XIV and XV) by the rather surprising chapter XVI, 'The Bishop and the Priest'. Father Barham, apart from his hope that he may claim Melmotte as a Catholic, has no function in the novel except that of helping, with the Bishop, to define Roger's character more thoroughly and to suggest a wider frame of moral reference than would otherwise exist within the novel. This widening begins in chapter XVI.

Trollope's description of the Bishop of Elmham, who is to be Father Barham's opponent in the discussions at Roger's table, is sharp; it blends hints of emotional and spiritual complications with irony in a manner which surprises any reader who has assumed too thoroughly that the bluff man-to-man narrating manner is a guarantee against all disturbance. Trollope praises the bishop's domestic and social virtues, and then goes on:

But I doubt whether he was competent to teach a creed,—or even to hold one, if it be necessary that a man should understand and define his creed before he can hold it. Whether he was free from, or whether he was scared by, any inward misgivings, who shall say? If there were such he never whispered a word of them to the wife of his bosom. From the tone of his voice and the look of his eye, you would say that he was unscathed by that agony which doubt on such a matter would surely bring to a man so placed. And yet it was observed of him that he never spoke of his faith, or entered into arguments with men as to the reasons on which he based it . . . he was never known to declare to man or woman that the human soul must live or die for ever according to its faith. Perhaps there was no bishop in England more loved or more useful in his diocese than the Bishop of Elmham. (i, 148–9)

For Father Barham, by contrast,

The dogmas of his Church were . . . a real religion, and he would teach them in season and out of season, always ready to commit himself to the task of proving their truth, afraid of no enemy, not even fearing the hostility which his perseverance would create. (i, 150)

Roger, contrasting the two, 'felt that the bishop's manner was the pleasanter of the two' (i, 151).

The scene is set for a number of disputes about religion in which Barham, who has the lack of taste to assume that religion is more important than social decorum and that Erastianism is a fit subject for attack, is met by the bishop with courteous evasiveness and progressively alienates Roger, who grows 'tired of his pet priest'. Lady Carbury, in her own discussion with Barham, produces the arguments of Roger and the bishop at a lower level of intelligence and with more of a comic effect:

'They [bishops] are so much respected everywhere as good and pious men!'

'I do not doubt it. Nothing tends so much to respect as a good income. But they may be excellent men without being excellent bishops. I find no fault with them, but much with the system by which they are controlled. Is it probable that a man should be fitted to select guides for other men's souls because he has succeeded by infinite labour in his vocation in becoming the leader of a majority in the House of Commons?' (i, 177–8)

Roger finds it necessary to put an end to the argument and,

though Lady Carbury is both stupid and insincere, it cannot be said that the bishop or Roger himself would be able to refute Barham's case more convincingly. Lady Carbury has remarked that infidelity is 'worse than anything'.

> 'I don't know that it is worse than a belief which is no belief,' said the priest with energy;—'than a creed which sits so easily on a man that he does not even know what it contains, and never asks himself as he repeats it, whether it be to him credible or incredible.'
> 'That is very bad,' said Lady Carbury.
> 'We're getting too deep, I think,' said Roger . . . (i, 178–9)

It is worth noting that Roger concludes the discussion with the same phrase as that with which Mr Longestaffe endeavours to silence Mr Brehgert and which is, as an expression of a certain assumption of good manners, so signally refuted:

> 'I don't like hearing my Church ill-spoken of,' said Roger.
> 'You wouldn't like me if I thought ill of it and spoke well of it,' said the priest.
> 'And, therefore, the less said the sooner mended,' said Roger, rising from his chair. (i, 179)

I am not suggesting that Trollope has deliberately made a point of seeing that Roger and Longestaffe, at such widely separated moments in the book, make the same answer. Such is not Trollope's method and he may well never have noticed the repetition. But both comments are the most natural ones from such men in such circumstances, and in each case they represent an attempt on the part of a traditionally-minded gentleman to resist an effort by an outsider—in one case an impoverished Roman priest and in the other a rich Jewish banker—to challenge comfortable assumptions about behaviour, in particular the belief that certain matters ought not to be talked about because no gentleman would wish to discuss them.

It is inevitable, therefore, that by the end of the book Roger, bothered by rumours that he is a likely convert to Roman Catholicism and irritated by Barham's proselytizing, should oblige the priest to cease his visits unless he will stop talking about religion—a condition which he knows to be unacceptable. Roger is, as an humane man, made unhappy by his action, but it appears to him as inevitable.

His attitude towards Mrs Hurtle, another threat to the established order, is similarly compounded of orthodox pieties and
evasiveness. When Paul Montague tells him that, in no circumstances, will he marry her, he seems to reproach him—'You
will get out of it, honestly if you can; but you will get out of
it honestly or—any other way.'—but then, by a shift to a
tendentious metaphor, agrees: 'If you make a bargain with the
Devil, it may be dishonest to cheat him,—and yet I would have
you cheat him if you could' (i, 369).

In equating Mrs Hurtle with the Devil, Roger speaks, we must
suppose, for moral and social orthodoxy. She is a fallen woman;
though Trollope treats her relations with Paul with a reticence
greater than he does similar situations elsewhere in his novels (in
John Caldigate, for example), such a remark as 'I have given you
all that I can give' is clear enough indication that she has been
his mistress. As such, she and Paul are judged by society upon
very different terms—a double standard of morality which is
expressed most neatly by Roger when, seeing them together at
Lowestoft, he says to Paul, 'And what must you be, to be here,
in public, with such a one as she is?' (i, 437). The indignity for
Paul lies in allowing himself to be seen in public with a woman
who has allowed herself to become his mistress. That such a
double standard is unjust has been made clear by Trollope very
early in the book—and in a context which shows it as atrociously
unfair: 'Henrietta had been taught by the conduct of both father
and mother that every vice might be forgiven in a man and in a
son, though every virtue was expected from a woman, and
especially from a daughter' (i, 15).

But Mrs Hurtle is not associated with the Devil merely because of her lack of chastity; even if we choose to assume that
she is not in fact Paul's mistress but has merely allowed herself
to be compromised in the world's eyes, she is still almost as
abhorrent to orthodoxy. For if we think of her, as we are bound
to do, in contrast to Hetta, it is clear that the double standard is
concerned not solely with chastity but also with the whole
conception of what is truly feminine behaviour.

Hetta is the model of feminine modesty. Her attitude towards
marriage is characterized as 'a girl's usual enthusiastic affection
for her chosen lord' (ii, 241), but when Marie Melmotte asks her
whether she was not justified in being willing to run away with
Felix—'Don't you think that if a girl loves a man,—really

loves him,—that ought to go before everything?', Hetta 'felt quite certain that under no circumstances would she run away with a man' (ii, 108–9). Certainly, her action in visiting Mrs Hurtle is, by her own standards, bold, but it is presented by Trollope with some irony: 'That afternoon Hetta trusted herself all alone to the mysteries of the Marylebone underground railway, and emerged with accuracy at King's Cross' (ii, 385). Mrs Hurtle, by contrast, in Paul Montague's words, 'had seen so much of drunkenness, had become so handy with pistols, and had done so much of a man's work, that any ordinary man might well hesitate before he assumed to be her master' (i, 446–447). It is on this lack of femininity that he bases his rejection of her—not so much on any specific acts, for he is unwilling to say that she ought not to have defended herself against assault, but on a general unwomanliness of outlook and temperament. She herself points out to him, when she shows him the unsent letter in which she threatens to horsewhip him and he says that no woman should behave thus, that it is convenient for the gentlemen if women behave in the way which is felt to be womanly—'Shall a woman be flayed alive because it is un-feminine in her to fight for her own skin?' (ii, 8). Her own verdict upon her incompatibility with Paul is one with which it is difficult to disagree: 'It had been one of the faults of her life that she had allowed herself to be bound by tenderness of feeling to this soft over-civilised man. The result had been disastrous, as might have been expected' (ii, 379).

Here, in considering the interplay between what the narrator tells us and what he shows, we must beware of attributing to Trollope intentions which would have horrified him and which he would not have expected to be effective with his readers. Mrs Hurtle's genuine and passionate love for Paul, her independence of judgment, the fact that 'the idea of being tame was terrible to her', her frank admission of sexual passion, are likely to make a greater appeal to us than to our counterparts of the 1870s. We are also less favourably inclined to a view of marriage which is expressed in terms of 'her chosen lord' and more willing, perhaps, to accept 'soft over-civilised man' as a just description and not merely the expression of Mrs Hurtle's resentment. There is probably meant to be more tension, less onesidedness in the situation than we may feel if we read the novel as if it were a modern one. But there is an equally great temptation for the present-day reader—that of assuming that our bold attitudes could never have been held by Trollope and presented by him to his readers, that because he was writing in the 1870s he must have intended Paul's rejection of Mrs Hurtle and his marriage to Hetta not merely as the inevitable effect of temperament and social pressure, but also as a thoroughly desirable emotional and moral conclusion.

But it would be unwise to take too simple a view of Trollope as subscribing to the more puritanical aspects of Victorian thought and assuming that his readers would be similarly timid. The plot of *John Caldigate* turns on the question of whether Caldigate has committed bigamy by marrying Hester Bolton although he has already married 'Mrs Smith' in Australia. There is no question but that he has lived with her, yet he is intended to retain our sympathy and Hester's love. We might here invoke the double standard of morality, but this cannot be done in the interesting case of *The Belton Estate*. Clara Amedroz, the heroine of that novel, is set between two claimants to her hand, and she first chooses the cold, correct Captain Aylmer. He bids her end her acquaintanceship with Mrs Askerton when it is revealed that that lady left her husband under the protection of Colonel Askerton and lived with him as his wife until the death of her husband freed them to marry. Clara refuses, and her progress to her other suitor, the impulsive and warm Will Belton, is marked by her accepting the hospitality of Colonel and Mrs Askerton. Her move from the wrong suitor to the right one, from dutiful affection to warm love, from the Aylmers' house where she is a guest to the house which she will share with Will, goes via the cottage of someone who has been denounced as a fallen woman.

Trollope could not take sympathy for Mrs Hurtle for granted as easily as a writer could do now, but there is no reason to conclude that he thought it impossible to induce such feelings in his readers. His way of presenting her fits very well into his general strategy of seeming to share with his readers rather conventional and commonplace attitudes and then being obliged by the events he chronicles to admit what may be more uncomfortable. Nowhere is this more clear than in the last chapter in which she makes any significant appearance, chapter XCVII, in which is described her last, agonizing meeting with Paul. This ends: 'I think Mrs Pipkin was right, and that Mrs Hurtle, with all her faults, was a good-natured woman.' Even after making allowances for the high value which Trollope puts on good nature, we feel this to be a judgment of quite extraordinary inadequacy. It therefore draws our attention to the limitations of the narrator's frame of reference by showing how much of our feelings about Mrs Hurtle must lie outside the overt moral judgments of the storyteller. The chapter which concludes with this anticlimactic judgment and chapter XCI, the previous one in which she appears, are particularly fine and project with great force those qualities in Mrs Hurtle which earn our sympathy and our admiration, but which hardly find a place in the code of, say, Roger Carbury. In both chapters she displays not only her love for Paul but also her penetration into the natures of those who are now her adversaries. Of Paul she says to Hetta: 'he cannot be ill-natured although he can be cruel', and the comment appears not only brilliantly true of Paul but also in key with so much which is at the heart of the book's concern for the realities of forms, politenesses, the gentlemanly code. Of Hetta she says to Paul: 'the baser your conduct had been to me, the truer you were in her eyes', and we do not doubt the truth of what she says. She knows what she is fighting against and how hopeless is that fight—'you had allowed yourself to be talked out of your love for me by English propriety even before you had seen her beautiful eyes'. Above all, she impresses us because she speaks with the note of real loss, of uncompromising pain, which convinces us of an intensity of feeling which is so lacking in most of the personages in the book, which is, in a sense, what is lacking in the whole society which rejects those who intrude into it.

We can hardly avoid comparing her with the other lover who is made unhappy by Hetta's love for Paul—Roger Carbury. He, too, has a painful scene, after which he cannot talk of love again. In point of gentleness and self-abnegation he has the advantage over her, but do we not feel some uneasiness at such a passage as this?

> 'And still you will be all the world to me,' he continued, with his arm round her waist. 'As you will not be my wife, you shall be my daughter.'
> 'I will be your sister, Roger.'
> 'My daughter rather. You shall be all that I have in the world. I will hurry to grow old that I may feel for you as the old feel for the young. And if you have a child, Hetta, he must be my child.' (ii, 407)

The promised transformation of Roger's love into parental and grandparental affection only avoids being positively distasteful because from the start we have felt in it no urgency of sexual passion. In Mrs Hurtle it is the strength and constancy of such passion, even to her own harm, which we admire.

It is, of course, as I have said, difficult to decide just how conscious Trollope may have been of the full effect of these sections of the book. I suspect that Roger's mawkish leavetaking is so much in the fictional convention of the good but disappointed lover that he would not share our uneasiness nor expect his readers to do so. But the fact that, after Paul's farewell to Mrs Hurtle, we do not again see the happy lovers Hetta and Paul, except very perfunctorily in the last chapter, is surely an indication that he knew that as a couple they are not very interesting.

Those qualities of vigour, intensity, will, which Mrs Hurtle possesses and which are so lacking in those who are or who become her adversaries, are almost the monopoly of the characters who challenge the established order of society. Partly, it is clear, this is Trollope's intention. The weak dissipation of Felix and the Beargarden set, relieved though it is by the ineffective good nature of some of them, the spiritless pride of Georgiana Longestaffe, the timid snobbery of Lady Monogram, the vacillations of Paul Montague are carefully presented. So are the religious zeal of Father Barham, the firmness of Mr Brehgert and the brutal self-reliance of Melmotte. But in part the contrast between the effects of different people is due to Trollope's writing more convincingly about some characters and some actions than about others, and this, presumably, is an indication of what he felt about most deeply and believed in most thoroughly. Among the weakest passages by far are those which are intended to express the strong, good feelings which might temper the near-monopoly in vigour of the wicked and the socially unacceptable. Such is Roger's declaration of love to Hetta:

> 'Do not coy your love for me if you can feel it. When you know, dear, that a man's heart is set upon a woman as mine is set on you, so that it is for you to make his life bright or dark, for you to open or to shut the gates of his earthly Paradise, I think you will be above keeping him in darkness for the sake of a girlish scruple.' (i, 185)

We have only to set this against Mrs Hurtle's outbursts or those touchingly awkward ones of Marie when she is in love with Felix, to see how fustian it is. Here, I think, Trollope may not have been aware of his inability to make Roger's feelings convincing. But elsewhere he sometimes gives signs that he recognizes his inability to make such passages ring true; this is surely so in the ironic reported speech in which he handles Paul's declaration to Hetta of that love which is to play so large a part in the story:

> Paul Montague of course had very much to say in answer to this. Among the holy things which did exist to gild this everyday unholy world, love was the holiest. It should be soiled by no falsehood, should know nothing of compromises, should admit no excuses, should make itself subject to no external circumstances. If Fortune had been so kind to him as to give him her heart, poor as his claim might be, she could have no right to refuse him the assurance of her love. And though his rival were an angel, he could have no shadow of a claim upon her,—seeing that he had failed to win her heart. It was very well said,—at least so Hetta thought,—and she made no attempt at argument against him. (ii, 150)

But we do not find such unconvincing rhetoric nor such ironic evasion when we come to Mrs Hurtle, nor to Father Barham, nor to Mr Brehgert, nor to Mr Melmotte. Whenever Trollope writes of the strongminded, of those for whom conviction or will —even self-will—is dominant, he is at his most effective. It is in his dealings with Augustus Melmotte himself that we see most clearly impressiveness going against the apparent moral grain of the book. Throughout the novel Melmotte stands out as a continuously convincing and interesting character. Trollope is particularly successful in catching in his speech a note which individualizes him without appearing in any sense a formula or caricature, which gives an outward form to the alternation in his nature between bullying and a kind of heavy reasonableness. He also ensures that Melmotte's presence gains weight because we continually see the impression which he makes on those around him. Other people, too, are defined by the reactions of others to them, but with Melmotte we feel, more than with the others, the constant energy which he directs upon his surroundings and which makes even those who are not immediately concerned with his actions acutely conscious of his presence. Both these qualities are seen particularly well in chapter LIV, 'The India

Office', when Melmotte insists on being presented to the Emperor of China—a scene, incidentally, where we are likely to feel that there is something to be said for his argument:

> Mr Melmotte put up his hand and stopped him. 'I'm not going to stand this kind of thing,' he said. The old Marquis of Auld Reekie was close at hand, the father of Lord Nidderdale, and therefore the proposed father-in-law of Melmotte's daughter, and he poked his thumb heavily into Lord Alfred's ribs. 'It is generally understood, I believe,' continued Melmotte, 'that the Emperor is to do me the honour of dining at my poor house on Monday. He don't dine there unless I'm made acquainted with him before he comes. I mean what I say. I ain't going to entertain even an Emperor unless I'm good enough to be presented to him. Perhaps you'd better let Mr Wilson know, as a good many people intend to come.' (ii, 39)

Paradoxically, however, he attains his full stature when his attendants fall away. The scenes which we are likely to remember most vividly are those during the long ten days' lull between the dinner for the Emperor and his suicide, when, abandoned by his hangers-on, alone and yet the centre of attention, he walks about London on the day of the election, goes to the City and keeps his own counsel, and makes his two visits to the House of Commons. But by this point in the book he is not merely a figure who dominates, he also displays qualities which may earn admiration even though they are seemingly outside the overt moral frame of reference of the book. Will, courage, self-knowledge—all these he has in abundance, so that he achieves a kind of coarse dignity which catches our imagination more than anything else in the book. Without burking the fact of his criminality, Trollope presents him in terms which demand respect:

> Perhaps never in his life had he studied his own character and his own conduct more accurately, or made sterner resolves, than he did as he stood there smiling, bowing, and acting without impropriety the part of host to an Emperor. No;—he could not run away. He soon made himself sure of that. He had risen too high to be a successful fugitive, even should he succeed in getting off before hands were laid upon him. (ii, 105)

> A grandly urbane deportment over a crushed spirit and ruined hopes is beyond the physical strength of most men;—but there have been men so strong. Melmotte very nearly accomplished it. (ii, 293)

Such passages go far to turn him into, if not a hero, at least a villain-hero. His own expression is stoic: 'What's one man that another man should be afraid of him? We've got to die, and there'll be an end of it, I suppose' (ii, 114). It is appropriate that the image which Trollope uses twice in chapter LXXXIII—'Melmotte Again at the House'—should be a Roman one: 'It was thus that Augustus Melmotte wrapped his toga around him before his death!'

It is a measure of his impressiveness—of however deplorable a kind—that the seventeen chapters which separate his death from the end of the book should appear so largely an anticlimax. But they are an inevitable anticlimax, for the novel is not an account of the rise and fall of Augustus Melmotte but of the way we live now. Even if we did not know that Lady Carbury was originally intended to be the central figure in the book, we would still suspect that Melmotte caught Trollope's imagination and arrogated to himself a larger share of the life of the novel than was originally intended. But we might not realize just how great a change came over the book. Trollope's preliminary notes for the book (printed in Appendix IV of Michael Sadleir's *Trollope: A Commentary*) consist of a list of characters with descriptions of their natures and some indication of plot. That of Lady Carbury concludes—'The chief character'; Roger Carbury is 'Hero of the book'; Melmotte does not even have a description to himself; he appears only as Marie's father—'Augustus Melmotte, great French swindler'. Nevertheless the book remains essentially a panoramic study of society; Melmotte has come to dominate much of the book as he dominates large areas of the society which it depicts, but the others have lives of their own and their private feelings and social relationships have not all been absorbed into their relationship with Melmotte. Thus, at the moment of his suicide, the lives of those surrounding him—just like the lives of any group of real people at any one specific point in time—have not come to any satisfactory point of rest—satisfactory, that is, not necessarily for them as people but for the observer, the reader. Marie is still in love with Felix; Roger and Paul are still at odds over Hetta, Mrs Hurtle has not abandoned the hope of marrying Paul, Lady Carbury's financial problems are still far from solved, Sir Felix is still a burden to his mother.

What we find in the last seventeen chapters, therefore, is the separating out of the various groups which have been brought into relationship largely by Melmotte. In the earlier parts of the novel the narrative usually moves forward in sections of several chapters at a time—chapters XVI–XXI, for example (a section, incidentally, which overruns a serial division), or chapters XXXVII–XL. Trollope may move from one group of characters to another but he does so by means of narrative passages which link the groups together. But at the end each chapter deals with a separate group of people and the following chapter usually has no immediate connection with it. Thus chapter XCIV marries off John Crumb and Ruby Ruggles, XCV marries off Sophia and Georgiana Longestaffe, XCVI recounts the dissolution of the Beargarden set, XCVII describes Mrs Hurtle's last meeting with Paul Montague, XCVIII sends off Marie, Mme Melmotte, Fisker, Croll and Mrs Hurtle to America, XCIX marries off Lady Carbury and Mr Broune and ships Sir Felix off to Germany, and C marries off Paul and Hetta.

It is easy to exclaim against this that it is clumsy, that it dissipates our interest, that it is totally lacking in form, that it is, in fact, an extended version of that last chapter, so common in nineteenth-century fiction, in which we are given a summary of the later careers of those characters who were not present in the penultimate chapter. All this is true. But it is important to realize that this long and fragmented anticlimax is there because of the existence of a real dilemma. Any novelist who wishes to show a society made up of smaller groupings, themselves made up of individuals, and not merely of conflicting or cooperating masses, will have to face this problem. It is as crucial for George Eliot or for Tolstoy as it is for Trollope and I shall discuss it generally in my next chapter. Trollope's way of dealing with the problem may not be the most satisfactory imaginable but for him it seems inevitable. With his essentially uncatastrophic view of life, his concern for slow shifts of power, for the continuity of experience and the need to come to terms with circumstances, he is bound to want to follow his characters after the dramatic climax.

Akin to the problem of how to end the novel is that of how to combine the various centres of interest throughout the book, how to maintain a sense of continuity, how to pick up the threads of one plot when we return to it from another. This, too, is not a problem peculiar to Trollope, and I shall discuss it generally in my next chapter. Trollope's way of tackling it is simple. He is transparently clumsy. 'Fisker,' he says, 'had started, as the reader will perhaps remember, on the morning of Saturday 19th April, leaving Sir Felix at the Club at about seven in the morning', or 'We must now go back a little in our story,—about three weeks,—in order that the reader may be told how affairs were progressing at the Beargarden', or 'When Hetta Carbury received that letter from her lover which was given to the reader some chapters back', or, most transparently of all, 'Any reader careful as to dates will remember that it was as far back as in February that she had solicited the assistance of certain of her literary friends . . .'

This sort of clumsiness, like the formlessness of the conclusion, seems, if not deliberate, at least consciously accepted. Having chosen to place an authorial narrator firmly in the novel, Trollope sees no reason why he should not use him in as obvious a fashion as may be convenient. He knew of other, less direct ways of telling a story; he begins *Is He Popenjoy?* with a discussion of the possibility of beginning vividly *in medias res* and explains why he decides against it in terms of possible muddle. He would probably have thought similarly about alternatives to his obvious method of picking up threads. The narrator is there; let him work. Moreover, as I have stressed, the relationship between the narrator and the reader is of the essence of *The Way We Live Now*; whether the choice is conscious or not, the effect which Trollope achieves is often that of a sober account by a man too artless to tell anything but the truth. It is interesting to observe that this kind of relationship can survive the giving of obviously 'invented' names like Slow and Bidewhile to minor characters (which is, we might say, akin to the kind of jocular naming which is common among very ordinary people), but could not, I feel sure, survive a form of much greater subtlety and complexity than Trollope has chosen.

Trollope does, indeed, fail to make use of—even at times he seems deliberately to avoid—elements which we tend to think of as effective in novels. Surprise, in general, he eschews. We do not participate in Melmotte's decision to kill himself, yet it is an entirely credible action; it could have come as the kind of surprise which, in retrospect, we feel to be likely. Trollope prevents this by his comment on Melmotte's appearance at the House of Commons: 'It was thus that Augustus Melmotte wrapped his toga around him before his death!' and repeats the image a couple of pages later. It is typical of his method that he practically never ends a serial instalment on any note of suspense. The titles of the chapters might have been designed to prevent dramatic excitement: '"I Do Love Him"', 'Mr Cohenlupe Leaves London', 'Hetta Carbury Hears a Love Tale'. Trollope even seems on occasions to go to some lengths to avoid the most effective way of producing a climax. Could deliberate avoidance of the dramatically effective go farther than his dealing with the proposed elopement of Sir Felix and Marie? At the end of chapter XLIX, before the time has come, as the story unfolds, for Marie to set out, he says: 'At three o'clock in the morning, Sir Felix had lost over a hundred pounds in ready money. On the following night about one he had lost a further sum of two hundred pounds. The reader will remember that he should at that time have been in the hotel at Liverpool' (i, 467). He returns to Sir Felix, after describing Marie's journey to Liverpool, and tells in detail of his gambling and drunkenness and of his failing to catch the train for Liverpool. There is a certain amount of irony about Marie's journey to join the lover who will not be there to meet her, though it is very muted irony and Trollope makes little of it, but the splitting of the description of Sir Felix's defection—a brief summary in anticipation of Marie's journey and a more detailed account after it—serves to replace a potentially effective dramatic scene by an altogether flatter narration.

Trollope rarely writes major dramatic scenes and he particularly avoids scenes in which a number of trains of events come to a simultaneous climax. Often, indeed, as in the example which I have just given of Sir Felix's aborted flight, he seems deliberately to avoid any density of effect; his instinct is to separate out the issues and to deal with them singly. Apart from such public scenes as the banquet, Melmotte's two visits to the House of Commons, and the initial ball, most of the significant scenes are encounters between two people only, or passages of solitary reflection. This does not seem to be because of any specific incapacity; on the rather few occasions when he does show the interplay of a group of people he does so without any sign of strain; the scenes in the boardroom may be cited as examples or the vivid chapter XCVI which tells of the last meeting of the Beargarden set. The reason for Trollope's choice of method seems rather that, concerned though he is with society, he sees it as composed of individuals who develop slowly, reconcile themselves to a fate which they partly control and partly endure and with which they must come to terms in private. Specifically he is concerned with people making up their minds. States of painful indecision, often protracted, are of particular interest to him: Lady Monogram uncertain as to whether to go to the reception, Melmotte as to whom to buy off with the money which remains, Sir Felix as to whether to elope with Marie, Lady Carbury as to what to advise him, Roger as to whether to be reconciled with Paul, Georgiana as to how to answer Mr Brehgert's letter, Mrs Hurtle as to which of her three letters to send to Paul. Some of these uncertainties are about trivialities, some about matters of fundamental consequence; in some the decision matters, in some it makes no difference what is decided; but all of them take time. Together they go far towards giving a central unifying conception to the book.

This essentially undramatic outlook is largely responsible for the novel's being so much more effective as a whole than it seems in detail. One aspect of this is that Trollope's prose is generally unexciting. It is somewhat more varied than we often remember, and it has more sharpness, more of an occasional epigrammatic quality, for example, than our memories usually give it credit for. When we cast our minds back over the book we tend not to recall the description of the Prince who 'made a few words go a long way, and was well trained in the work of easing the burden of his own greatness for those who were for the moment inflicted with it' (i, 42), nor the description of Lord Alfred Grendall who 'looked aristocratic, respectable, and almost commercial' (i, 343), nor the conclusion of the meeting at which the floating of the company is announced:

> People out of doors were to be advertised into buying shares, and they who were so to say indoors were to have the privilege of manufacturing the shares thus to be sold. That was to be their work, and they all knew it. But now, as there were eight of them collected together, they talked of humanity at large and of the coming harmony of nations. (i, 90)

But our memories are right thus to subdue these incidental felicities to an impression of a narrative tone which we would call—were the word not likely to be taken as pejorative—ordinary.

Similarly, Trollope does not focus the meaning of his subject or explore its implications by metaphor or by scenes which achieve the force of symbols. The language throughout tends to be unfigurative; the only image of note is that of speculation and betting as applied to politics, social life (especially in the matter of Melmotte's reception), and, very often, for the marriage market. At times we have the impression of deliberate avoidance of anything which might savour of the symbolic. When Hetta visits the Melmottes after the reception, the scene is described thus: 'Within the hall the pilasters and trophies, the wreaths and the banners, which three or four days since had been built up with so much trouble, were now being pulled down and hauled away. And amidst the ruins Melmotte himself was standing'. (ii, 164) The scene seems to demand development, emphasis; it is a complete symbolic expression of Melmotte's situation. But it is kept at the level of factual description; the symbolic overtones are so faint as to be practically inaudible when the passage is read in context. It is buried in the middle of a paragraph which tells us what Melmotte has been doing before and what he proposes to do later in the day. It is hard not to believe that here we have a deliberate avoidance of what would seem to most novelists an obvious and legitimate effect, in the interest of dedication to the hard facts of the matter. Similarly, we feel that, although Trollope may produce a superficial and conventional effect by calling his lawyer Bideawhile, it would be grotesquely out of keeping to let our minds wander over Mr Melmotte's name, wondering how he is related to Maturin's Melmoth the Wanderer, or to observe any effect of irony in the fact that the destination of the railway, to which so much devotion is expressed, is Vera Cruz.

Trollope never moves far from the ordinary, the down-to-earth and the total effect of the book is rooted in this. His narrator starts by assuming a partnership with the reader in conventional values and unsurprising perceptions, and takes us by sober and conscientious exploration of his subject to a position which is considerably less dogmatic and far more flexible. Trollope has often been described as a novelist of common sense, but it is a common sense unusually openminded and unusually critical of the received values to which he seems naturally drawn.

There is, of course, in such an account of the effect of the novel an ambiguity which can hardly be avoided. There has, indeed, throughout my account of the book been a certain ambiguity, centring round the word 'narrator'. It might be briefly defined as the impossibility of deciding whether Trollope intends to give the effect of the narrator being obliged to admit the impressiveness of Mrs Hurtle, say, or the inadequacy of Roger when confronted by Father Barham, or whether he is himself unaware that we respond as we do. Without entering upon a lengthy discussion of the 'intentional fallacy', I would say that I do not believe that it matters much which we decide. But it is hardly possible to avoid some mention of the question, and this for two reasons. First, Trollope commented freely on his own work in his *Autobiography* and elsewhere, taking a view of literary creation which suggests that for him it was an almost wholly conscious activity and, moreover, one of a singularly straightforward kind. Secondly, the form of this novel, with its moralizing commentator, rests for much of its effect upon the sense of the man who is telling the story. To claim, as I do, that the narrator comes to admit feelings which Trollope himself is on record as denying exposes me more plainly than in most discussions of this kind to the charge of reading effects into the book which are not there.

It is not difficult to show that the actual effect of the book is, in a number of places, rather different from what Trollope appears to have thought. Few readers, for example, would be willing to place Mrs Hurtle, as Trollope does, among his list of 'the wicked and foolish people'. But the case of Father Barham is surely the most striking. When Mary Holmes wrote as a Roman Catholic to protest against the depiction of Father Barham, Trollope replied, pointing out his favourable portrayal of Roman Catholic priests elsewhere but indicating that Barham is based on an actual priest whom he had befriended, of whom he says: 'he would never desist for a moment from casting ridicule and opprobrium on my religion, though I would not on any account have hinted a slur upon his. I was obliged to drop him. He made himself unbearable' (*The Letters of Anthony Trollope*, ed. Bradford A. Booth, 332). This justification of Roger Carbury's viewpoint and actions hardly tallies with the effect of the book, in which Barham does not ridicule Roger's religion but where he certainly gets the better of his opponents in the arguments in which he takes part.

To speak of Trollope's intentions is to suggest something more fixed and consistent than one's knowledge of human nature justifies. It has often been observed that novelists, when functioning as novelists as distinct from retrospective or prospective commentators on their own works, may be less conventional and more openminded, more willing to be disturbed by the beliefs of those outside their own social group, than they are in their daily life. Trollope may be giving expression in the book to an uneasiness in his feelings about his religion and his relationship with the model for Father Barham which he never admitted to his correspondent or to himself. He may well have been reacting in the same way in his portrayal of Mrs Hurtle. Just how conscious he may have been of this and the degree of consciousness at different times and in different moods seems of little importance.

Our responsibility as readers is not to Trollope's own conception of the book (which may well have varied from time to time), but to its total effect. This it is which should prevent us from interpreting it by emphasis on isolated passages read in the light of preconceptions alien to the whole. We should not elaborate a symbolic fable in which Melmoth the Wanderer points the way to what he claims is the True Cross nor hail Mrs Hurtle as a heroine from the world of D. H. Lawrence. But I do not believe that it is any such misrepresentation to assert that the strength of the book comes from our sense of a down-to-earth narrator, telling the story in the plainest way he can, even at the cost of some clumsiness, and, through his openness to experience, reaching depths of perception of which we would not initially have thought him capable and which he only intermittently admits. How else should we account for the surprising manner in which, towards the end of the book, he reflects upon the circumstances under which a suicide is declared insane?

> If the poor wretch has, up to his last days, been apparently living a decent life; if he be not hated, or has not in his last moments made himself specially obnoxious to the world at large, then he is declared to have been mad. Who would be heavy on a poor clergyman who has been at last driven by horrid doubts to rid himself of a difficulty from which he saw no escape in any other way? Who would not give the benefit of the doubt to the poor woman whose lover and lord had deserted her? Who would remit to unhallowed earth the body of the once beneficent philosopher who has simply thought that he might as well go now, finding himself powerless to do further good upon earth?

Such, and such like, have of course been temporarily insane, though no touch even of strangeness may have marked their conduct up to their last known dealings with their fellow-mortals. . . . Just at this moment there was a very strong feeling against Melmotte, owing perhaps as much to his having tumbled over poor Mr Beauchamp in the House of Commons as to the stories of the forgeries he had committed, and the virtue of the day vindicated itself by declaring him to have been responsible for his actions when he took the poison. . . . But we none of us know what load we can bear, and what would break our backs. (ii, 356–7)

This is the same narrator who, at the opening of the book, summed up the characters of Lady Carbury and her son so briskly and with so little a sense of complexity; but he has thought more deeply since then; he has come to see the possibility of putting himself in Melmotte's place and he is a good deal more bitter about 'the virtue of the day'. There are times in the earlier part of the novel when the reader suspects that it should rightly be called *The Way They Live Now*, but by the end it is clear that *We* is the right word.

'*Je suis un homme pour qui le monde extérieur existe.*'

Théophile Gautier

'Imitations produce pain or pleasure, not because they are mistaken for realities, but because they bring realities to mind.'

Samuel Johnson: *Preface to Shakespeare*

3

The conventions of realism: the shared world

I have referred to *The Way We Live Now* as a realistic novel and assumed that this would not be misunderstood. But since I want, in the next two chapters, to discuss some of the manifestations of realism and to speculate about some of its implications, it seems necessary to say what I mean by the term. Any definition must be rough-and-ready. 'Realism' has had too violent a history for anyone to expect his own definition to meet with complete agreement from anyone else and, as I wish to show, realism is a convention which, like all conventions, is never found embodied in a pure state; we always use it with a sense of approximation.

My own use of the term, the one which I believe to be most helpful in discussion, is strictly confined to the techniques of novels. I call Trollope's novel realistic because his interest is in a society which we believe to be like that which he and a considerable number of his contemporaries knew, and he depicts this society by showing us the actions and describing the thoughts and feelings of plausible characters conceived at the level of daily life. One manifestation of this is that he takes good care to make his characters talk in a way which gives the impression of being how such men and women talked in real life, so that when Roger Carbury grows implausibly rhetorical about love we feel this as a flaw. The rhetoric of Catherine Earnshaw or Captain Ahab, by contrast, is in keeping with *Wuthering Heights* and *Moby Dick* which, though there may be passages in them which are realistic, are not as a whole realistic novels.

This painstakingly unoriginal definition is a limiting one. It goes no farther than Sir Leslie Stephen's rather early use of it in 1874 in *Hours in a Library* where he says that Crabbe's scenery 'is as realistic as a photograph'. But the great battles which have raged around the concept of 'realism' have not been concerned with this limited, technical sense, and many of its colloquial uses are tendentious. Echoes of long battles between Romantics and Realists still play around us. The adjective 'stark' is still likely to be attracted to the term. There must be few of us who have not found ourselves using 'realistic' as a term of praise rather than of definition. One obvious reason for this is that most bad novels purport to be realistic but break the convention within which they are conceived. Trapped by his own inadequacies, the bad novelist shuffles in a gross coincidence or unconvincing change of heart. Damning him for being 'unrealistic', we are likely to give the term 'realism' a sense of the praiseworthy which it does not deserve outside the specific comment.

The most potentially misleading use of the term derives, I think, from the historical association between the formal convention and certain kinds of subject matter and social attitudes. The great realistic novelists of the nineteenth century—Balzac, Tolstoy, George Eliot, for example—dealt at large with society and they were critical of the nature of that society; the claim is often made that realism is pre-eminently the convention within which the writer can convey a 'true' picture of society and, conversely, that the conveying of such pictures is the proper business of realism. Arguments of this kind—in which some of the novelists themselves took part—tend very often to be about the relative values of different kinds of novels and, implicitly or explicitly, about the values of the societies in and about which the novels were written. Such arguments are distressingly often circular or suggest—as discussions of Zola's *Le Roman Expéri-mental* do, or many of the central ideas of Lukács—that literary criticism is some other preoccupation in masquerade.

Such arguments, of course, have their use; if we are concerned with the history of critical concepts it is vital to remember them. But for my purpose they are likely to be very misleading. Realism, in any technical sense which can be of use to the critic, is clearly not the only way in which society can be depicted and criticized with conviction. Dickens's very effective dealing with the administrative system of England in *Little Dorrit* is achieved by the unrealistic means of parabolic exaggeration, allegory and grotesque symbolism. It is hardly too much to say that those characters whom Dickens presents, formally, in the most realistic way tend to be at bottom stock mid-nineteenth century senti-mental and melodramatic stereotypes, while he deals with social facts, ascertainable as such by reference to blue books and the like, in terms of symbolism and grotesques.

By 'realistic', then, I refer to a formal convention. Like all conventions it is the result of compromise between various demands. But we often talk as though it is not a convention at all, as though it were a way of presenting a direct picture of a series of typical and lifelike experiences. As soon as we try to define it, however, we realize how many questions we are usually begging—how far we take for granted highly conventional and often highly complex features. Discussions which take it as something more than a technical term—which are concerned with it as a method of achieving social and psychological truth—seem particularly unaware of this. Some of the ways in which we often talk about the effect of novels point to the questions which we are begging.

My own statement of what I mean by 'realistic' is couched in terms of 'depicting' and 'showing' and I have just taken over from common usage the word 'picture' as applied to a novel; this is a very usual way of talking and it indicates how readily we make use of dead metaphors about visual effects to describe the effect of verbal communication. The most celebrated and often-quoted equation of this kind is Stendhal's epigraph, taken from Saint-Réal, for chapter XIII of *Le Rouge et le Noir*: '*Un roman: c'est un miroir qu'on promène le long d'un chemin*', and his later use of it as a tongue-in-cheek justification for depict-ing wicked people, but the notion of the mirror in the roadway as a useful image for the realistic novel has been widespread. The fallacies in the equation are obvious, but it is worth pointing them out because, even if we know when we think about it that we are not using the image as a literally accurate description, there is a tendency for unexamined assumptions which fit in with the fallacies to linger in the mind.

There are two main ways in which the image of the mirror is inappropriate to the effect of a novel—one concerned with the manner in which non-verbal phenomena are presented in terms of words and one with the inevitability of form. First, the mirror reflects a chair as a chair and a face as a face, while a novel presents objects in a sequence of words from which—in the case of a human face, for example—it would be impossible to reconstruct the actual appearance of what is supposedly mirrored. Second, a mirror reflects something which is there already, while a novel does not exist until it is written; the image leaves out of account which road you choose, at which point on it you start and finish, in which direction you point the mirror and whether, from time to time, you cover it up.

In this chapter I shall discuss a few of the implications of two inevitable tasks which the novelist must perform. He must continually give an account in words of phenomena which are not themselves verbal and he must, by the act of choice, give some shape to his work. Both these tasks are, of course, essential for all novelists; the first, indeed, is basic to all speech and writing. But the dealing of realistic novelists with these problems is worth particular attention. Characters, objects, places in realistic novels are meant to be recognizable, akin to those which we actually know, existing at the level of daily life; the aim of a realistic novelist is, one might think, to make us forget the interposing medium. The form of realistic novels must not appear to exclude the contingent elements of daily life; the aim might seem to be 'natural', to have no form.

Language

The clearest example of how phenomena which are not verbal are presented in words is the way in which a novelist introduces and describes a character. It is striking that those characters of whose 'reality' we are most persuaded, even those of whose physical presence we are most assured, are often known to us first by those qualities which, in our acquaintance with real people, we know—if we ever do—last: their deepest and most basic feelings. But they are commonly lacking in the most obvious qualities of the people we know in life. We get to know them, as it were, back to front, and sometimes we never have any grasp at all of the most elementary facts about them. What colour are Anna Karenina's eyes? How did Tertius Lydgate do his hair? How tall is Gilbert Osmond? Was Elizabeth Bennet's voice high or low? In reality these are the kind of things which we notice first; in fiction we often have a strong sense of the reality of the character and, indeed, know him better than we can know anybody in real life, without being able to answer such questions. Sometimes this is because the writer has not told us;

sometimes we have been told but have not registered the information, for our ability to visualize from description is extremely limited, so that most description of characters seems a waste of time. We remember characteristics which are of symbolic significance or which are used as a kind of repeated motif—Mr Verloc's heavy-lidded eyes or Papa Karamazov's fleshy Adam's apple—but how many of my readers who are familiar with *Anna Karenina* can answer my first question—what colour are Anna's eyes? They are, in fact, bright grey, and we are told so on her first appearance. I do not think we know about Elizabeth Bennet's voice.

The language in which novelists try to convince us of the reality of people and places and objects functions in a complex and varied way. We register some of what we are told in a straightforward way, some in a symbolic manner because it seems an index to character; some seems essential, even though we do not remember it, because it functions as a guarantee of reliability. It assures us that the writer knows; Defoe displays this most clearly; he often seems to be saying 'I can tell you all these details, so I can't be lying'. Sometimes—more often than we think—the effect of description is largely the experience of the passing of time. We would feel it inappropriate to have a significant character appear without an introduction of some length; this is why descriptions which we do not remember often only *seem* a waste of time. Most important, in describing what we may not be able to visualize or may not remember, the writer is establishing a tone, defining his viewpoint, often asserting his *bona fides* as a presenter and, in the process, defining the desired reader.

When we look back on a novel and talk about it, we extract that which is memorable, that which can be discussed in terms of some abstraction. When we are reading it we are experiencing a series of moment-by-moment experiences, some of which we will hardly recall afterwards but which are crucial in establishing our relationship with the book and our sense of the existence of the people and the happenings of which it treats.

Let us consider at some length one 'introduction' of a character. A good example for this purpose is the first long paragraph of *Middlemarch*, since the very beginning of the first chapter (apart from the *Prelude*) introduces Dorothea Brooke, a character whose sufficient reality few readers will be disposed to doubt.

I have numbered the sentences for ease of reference, but I would ask the reader to look at it first as a passage of connected prose.

(1) Miss Brooke had that kind of beauty which seems to be thrown into relief by poor dress. (2) Her hand and wrist were so finely formed that she could wear sleeves not less bare of style than those in which the Blessed Virgin appeared to Italian painters; and her profile as well as her stature and bearing seemed to gain the more dignity from her plain garments, which by the side of provincial fashion gave her the impressiveness of a fine quotation from the Bible,—or from one of our elder poets, —in a paragraph of today's newspaper. (3) She was usually spoken of as being remarkably clever, but with the addition that her sister Celia had more common-sense. (4) Nevertheless, Celia wore scarcely more trimmings; and it was only to close observers that her dress differed from her sister's, and had a shade of coquetry in its arrangements; for Miss Brooke's plain dressing was due to mixed conditions, in most of which her sister shared. (5) The pride of being ladies had something to do with it: the Brooke connections, though not exactly aristocratic, were un-questionably 'good': if you inquired backward for a generation or two you would not find any yard-measuring or parcel-tying forefathers—anything lower than an admiral or a clergyman; and there was even an ancestor discernible as a Puritan gentle-man who had served under Cromwell but afterwards conformed, and managed to come out of all political troubles as the pro-prietor of a respectable family estate. (6) Young women of such birth, living in a quiet country-house, and attending a village church hardly larger than a parlour, naturally regarded frippery as the ambition of a huckster's daughter. (7) Then there was well-bred economy, which in those days made show in dress the first item to be deducted from, when any margin was required for expenses more distinctive of rank. (8) Such reasons would have been enough to account for plain dress, quite apart from religious feeling; but in Miss Brooke's case, religion alone would have determined it; and Celia mildly acquiesced in all her sister's sentiments, only infusing them with that common-sense which is able to accept momentous doctrines without any eccentric agitation. (9) Dorothea knew many passages of Pascal's *Pensées* and of Jeremy Taylor by heart; and to her the destinies of man-kind, seen by the light of Christianity, made the solicitudes of feminine fashion appear an occupation for Bedlam. (10) She could not reconcile the anxieties of a spiritual life involving eternal consequences, with a keen interest in guimp and artificial protrusions of drapery. (11) Her mind was theoretic, and yearned

by its nature after some lofty conception of the world which might frankly include the parish of Tipton and her own rule of conduct there; she was enamoured of intensity and greatness, and rash in embracing whatever seemed to her to have those aspects; likely to seek martyrdom, to make retractions, and then to incur martyrdom after all in a quarter where she had not sought it. (12) Certainly such elements in the character of a marriageable girl tended to interfere with her lot, and hinder it from being decided according to custom, by good looks, vanity, and merely canine affection. (13) With all this, she, the elder of the sisters, was not yet twenty, and they had both been educated, since they were about twelve years old and had lost their parents, on plans at once narrow and promiscuous, first in an English family and afterwards in a Swiss family at Lausanne, their bachelor uncle and guardian trying in this way to remedy the disadvantages of their orphaned condition.

Though we are told during the next few pages that she had 'large eyes' and that, when riding, 'when her eyes and cheeks glowed with mingled pleasure she looked very little like a devotee', it cannot be said that when we are called upon to see her with her sister in the act of dividing the jewellery towards the end of the chapter we are in any position to visualize her to the extent that we could visualize an actual person whom we have met for even the shortest time.

We have, it is true, been given a certain amount of information, chiefly about Dorothea's social position, family situation, and character, but the more thoroughly we consider the passage the more obvious it becomes that the provision of information is but a small part of its purpose. Since, as I have said, our ability to absorb and remember information is limited and our ability to visualize from description is very limited indeed, this is just as well. What George Eliot is most strikingly doing is establishing herself and expressing an attitude towards a subject which we are called upon to take largely on trust. Even the most clearly descriptive passages operate by asserting a kind of community of experience and reaction between the reader and the writer at least as forcefully as they define the supposed subject matter.

The main task of George Eliot (by which I mean her authorial personality in this book) is to establish her claim to tell us a story, her claim to being intelligent and sensitive and poised enough to be worth listening to. She does this partly in terms of the cogency of her comments but also—and far more importantly

—in her tone. We come to respect her judgment partly because she can draw convincing conclusions about habits of dress from the facts of social situations, but even more because her tone manifests a quality of mind which convinces us of her intelligence and flexibility of mind. She is doing this, of course, throughout the novel, but the opening is inevitably crucial and justifies detailed examination.

Sentence 1 is a straightforward declarative sentence, short, with the confidence of an apophthegm. Sentence 2, more complex, appears to amplify it, but there seems to be some discrepancy between a disparagement of 'provincial fashion' and the person of the Blessed Virgin. Retrospectively—by the time we have finished sentence 5 or 6 that is, and discovered this writer's fondness for irony—we realize that 'she could wear sleeves . . .' is not merely an observer's judgment but that Dorothea's own kind of modest vanity means that this is her own judgment as to what she could wear and still be impressive. We are likely, if we think this, to feel also that the description of her plain garments giving her 'the impressiveness of a fine quotation from the Bible,—or from one of our elder poets,—in a paragraph of today's newspaper' is not to be taken entirely at its face value; it seems rather the kind of image which those of her circle might use about her and of which she might welcome the use. This writer, one feels, might have at least a marginal awareness that some of 'our elder poets' might be decidedly unsuitable.

Sentence 3 is a short statement and has shifted from Dorothea's appearance to an opinion about her character, but with sentence 4 we revert to her appearance; the apparent jump from one subject to another and back again leaves us to deduce the connection between the two, and we recognize the implication that those who usually do the speaking about her remarkable cleverness make assumptions about its relationship to plain dress. It is perhaps not too much to say that we already sense a separation between the aspirations of Dorothea and those of her society. More important, we realize that this writer expects us to be able to make such jumps and deductions. We are being asked to enter into a partnership with the writer which is based on shrewd, ironic, worldly intelligence. The irony comes to the fore in sentences 5, 6 and 7, where the assumptions of this society and of Celia and Dorothea as members of it are made clear in terms of 'parcel-tying forefathers' and hucksters as compared with a

Puritan gentleman who retained his estate by trimming, and with the plain statement of sentence 7 that expenses which more distinctively mark their rank would take precedence over show in dress.

By this time we are prepared to take a basically disparaging view of Dorothea, to expect the strategy of the writer to be that of ironic contrast between the view of Dorothea's society, which thinks in terms of being well-bred and not a huckster's daughter, and recruits the Virgin Mary to this assumption of the social superiority of simple elegance, and the wider hints of the narrator about the self-interest of this class. But sentence 8 asserts the difference between Dorothea and her sister, indicating in the last comic clause the leadership of Dorothea, and from this point onwards the narrator directs us towards a scrutiny of Dorothea's religious views. Sentence 9 is significant. 'Dorothea knew many passages of Pascal's *Pensées* and of Jeremy Taylor by heart' is still ironic, but the second half of the sentence, where 'the light of Christianity' seems serious, and sentence 10, where the religious life has 'anxieties', indicate that the irony is being directed against attitudes more worthy than the purely snobbish. Thus the weightier judgment of sentence 11, with its straight-forward statement that Dorothea's reactions are more complex than we might have expected and that she would not shrink from martyrdom, even if not in the way she planned, obliges us to take Dorothea seriously precisely because George Eliot has already convinced us that she is not the kind of writer to be hoodwinked by mere protestations. The implied contrast in sentence 12 between Dorothea and those around her, with the sharp edge of 'canine', has been adequately prepared. This, we say, is a writer who can see her characters in relation to their society, who is not easily taken in by common conventions, who knows that a mingling of vanity, snobbery, naïvety and priggish-ness does not exclude real conviction and courage, and whom we can trust not to simplify the complicated. Drawn thus into a relation of confidence with the novelist, we are prepared to believe what she says, and the reality of Miss Brooke's existence depends less on the titbits of information which we are given than on our sense of the reliability of the person who asserts her identity and discusses her character. We do not say 'these data add up to a coherent picture of a young woman', but 'I trust this writer to tell me the truth and I accept these titbits as what she wishes for the moment to comment on in the character of a person whom I accept on her word'.

In general, credibility of fictional characters depends far less than we often think on description of character and its presentation in action and far more on our confidence in the reliability of the novelist—a reliability which is created dynamically by our response to the prose. We 'believe' the word of the novelist in the way in which we commonly 'believe' the word of the kind of person whom we describe as inspiring trust—not because he necessarily produces evidence for what he says but because his manner convinces us that his judgments will be reliable.

Thus it is that, in the creation of fictitious personages, one novelist can steal a horse while another cannot look over a hedge. We often talk as though Tolstoy, say, can create such a variety of 'living' characters because he has the gift for understanding human nature and seizing on the significant details which 'bring the man to life'. That such gifts are enormously important and that Tolstoy had them to an abundant degree needs no discussion, but they are far from the whole explanation. The main reason why Tolstoy's minor characters seem so firmly in existence is largely because he tells us that they are as they are, and his word is good enough for us. Conversely, when fictional characters do not convince us, when we find them 'thin' or 'wooden' or 'mechanical' or 'merely a bundle of attributes', this is often not because they are not shown as behaving credibly nor because they are not presented in sufficient detail, but because we have no confidence in the sensitivity, balance, intelligence, largeness of mind of the writer who asserts their existence. Our reaction to much conscientious and outwardly plausible depiction of character in second-rate novels is: 'Yes, the person to whose existence I am asked to give credence looks credible enough; but the person who is telling me this seems to be stupid (or insensitive, or self-satisfied, or monomaniacal, or uncritical, as the case may be) and I really will not take anything on his word.'

My example from *Middlemarch* of how a writer gains our assent to the existence of an asserted character is from a writer who establishes her intelligence and reliability by the detail of prose, in which shifts of tone, ironic reversals and the like play a dominant part. To some extent all writers convince us or fail to do so by the quality of their prose, the index of their minds (though the fact that Tolstoy can do this in translation shows that we are often concerned with manifestations of reliability which survive a good deal of maltreatment), but other factors contribute: the choice of shifts of viewpoint, the sequence of scenes, changes of pace, as well, of course, as overt commentary.

Nor is our sense of the writer as witness confined to novelists who function frankly as narrators. Joyce may, through Stephen Dedalus, postulate the ideal of the work from which the novelist has separated himself; James may proclaim his intention of not vouching for his characters; but the novelist never does retire to the title page. We have as strong a sense of the presence of Joyce or of James as we do of any garrulous and moralizing storyteller —indeed it is surely the experience of readers that we are usually more conscious of James than we are of Trollope.

The sense of the reliability of the witness is always crucial; it is this which allows us to enter into a relationship with him. In realistic novels, I think, there is involved in this relationship a good deal of assumption about common experience and common judgment. There are novels (as I hope to show in the next chapter) in the discussion of which the term 'realistic' is pointless, where the viewpoint has moved so far inwards into the psyche of a presented character that to say that the book is 'realistic' is simultaneously true and futile. But our common use of expressions like 'recognizable characters' is one indication of the extent to which, when we are reading Tolstoy and George Eliot, Balzac and Stendhal and Trollope, we feel assured that we live in the same kind of world as the writer. He may, like Stendhal and Tolstoy, be describing something distant in time and place from us, but we know that we could soon find our bearings in his society. Consequently such writers can bring to bear at every point in the book the power of their authority, our sense that they are good judges of the kind of world which we share with them, so that we achieve the paradox of accepting the physical reality of people about whom we may not know the height, the colour of their hair, the shape of their faces, or, indeed, anything which, in real life, we take in at first glance. Realistic novels, in short, do not affect us as being like life; they are like the experience of being told about life by someone whom we trust.

Form

The apparent contradiction between plausibility and form was described very well, as early as 1815, in Sir Walter Scott's well-known discussion of Jane Austen's *Emma* in the *Quarterly Review*:

> Now, although it may be urged that the vicissitudes of human life have occasionally led an individual through as many scenes of singular fortune as are represented in the most extravagant of these fictions [that is, the implausible novels with which he is contrasting the works of Jane Austen], still the causes and personages acting on these changes have varied with the progress of the adventurer's fortune, and do not present that combined plot, (the object of every skilful novelist,) in which all the more interesting individuals of the dramatis personae have their appropriate shares in the action and in bringing about the catastrophe. Here, even more than in its various and violent changes of fortune, rests the improbability of the novel.

It is interesting that though he goes on to praise Jane Austen for avoiding forced and implausible action, he does not suggest that the tension between lifelikeness and shape, between the demands of interest in character and of desire for form can be overcome. It is, indeed, a tension which, for several reasons, is particularly important in realistic novels. Realism demands that justice should be done—or should seem to be done—to all those elements of the accidental and the arbitrary which militate against order. Moreover, it has been during the period in which novels have been written that the large city has become a normal phenomenon and many realistic novelists have wanted to deal at large with these aggregations of disparate individuals. Clearly, the larger the cast the harder the task of organizing it.

Scott assumed that the novelist would not hesitate to choose as his principle of organization a clearly articulated plot. Virtually all novelists before the twentieth century would have agreed with him without even thinking about possible alternatives, though, of course, the degree of elaboration and the degree of obvious contrivance in the plot might have concerned them.* This dominance of plot has sometimes been considered in some way deplorable. E. M. Forster admits it ruefully; Virginia Woolf, in her celebrated essay on 'Modern Fiction', protests against the demands of plot. But it is worth pointing out that the novelist, in organizing his material in a plot, is not engaging

* See the next chapter for a discussion of the concept of realism as a developing convention.

in a specifically novelistic practice, but is exhibiting a characteristic of normal daily activity. It is in terms of sequential activities, linked by causation and selected on principles of what is relevant to this causation, that we describe to one another our own activities and those of our acquaintances. The amount of selection is, of course, enormous. Anyone who has had the experience, for example, of reading a diary after a lapse of some years will have received the shock of realizing how far (in this case retrospectively) we organize the material of our lives in our minds—normally in terms of developing human relationships or in tales of progressive self-awareness. The retrospective patterns, incidentally, would sometimes have seemed both odd and arbitrary at the time when the happenings were taking place. The value which we put upon the happenings at the time of writing sometimes seems odd and arbitrary in retrospect. There is no reason for deciding which account—the contemporary or the retrospective—is more 'real'. Our pasts are as real as our presents. We organize our recollections in terms of different values at different times; such revaluations are the basis of much of the effect of *Pride and Prejudice* and, in an extremely developed way, of *A la Recherche du Temps Perdu*.

In general, we may say that any selected period of experience includes more data than a writer can either use or wish to use. He selects from these data according to principles of their relative significance and value. Strictly, of course, we should say of the writer (as distinct from the man remembering his own life) that he invents the data which seem important and leaves the rest in the penumbra of data which he could have invented, given his conceptions of the characters represented, but which he feels to be inadequately significant.

It is interesting that, in her famous attack on the dominion of plot in 'Modern Fiction', Virginia Woolf leaves entirely out of her account the need for any kind of selection at all:

> Let us record the atoms as they fall upon the mind in the order in which they fall, let us trace the pattern, however disconnected and incoherent in appearance, which each sight or incident scores upon the consciousness. Let us not take it for granted that life exists more fully in what is commonly thought big than in what is commonly thought small.

The reason for the failure to take into account the necessity of

selection is obvious enough. Once admit that the novelist selects
—and selects according to the demands of his scale of values—
and we cannot be unaware that we are usually right to assume
that life exists more fully in what is commonly thought big, not
because novelists tied to a plot structure have said so, but because human experience in general has found it so. We also
realize that, since the novelist must select and shape, since the
very act of being aware of our own existence and perceptions
implies acts of selection from a flux of multitudinous sensations,
the choice of a plot may be as reasonable a choice as any other.*

If, as I have suggested in the first part of this chapter, the
effect of realistic novels depends very largely on our partnership
with the novelist, so that its effect is not 'like life' but like being
told about life by someone we trust, and if, as seems obvious, we
normally talk about our lives and those of others in terms of
plots, it is not surprising that the convention of plot as organizing principle has proved so general and so acceptable. It is only
if we endeavour to make novels 'like life' or if the novelist's
individual viewpoint is one which departs so far from the norm
that he does not see human life in terms of causal sequences,
that plot becomes an issue. I discuss such situations in the next
chapter, but it might be as well to say here that I imply no value
judgment in speaking of departures from the norm, but that I do
believe that such departures are rarer than some critics have
often supposed.

Literary conventions, such as the convention of plot, should
not bother us by their artificiality; art, including realistic art,
is artificial and there is clearly a very wide range of acceptable
degrees of stylizations from the highly articulated plot structure
of Hardy or Conrad to the looser organization of Tolstoy or
Charlotte Brontë. What we do demand is consistency to its
convention within each work. Our objection, for instance, to the
coincidences which, in *Middlemarch*, allow Bulstrode's secret to

---

* I hope it is needless to point out that awareness of some illogicality
in her argument here has nothing to do with comments which she may have
made elsewhere or with admiration for Virginia Woolf's novels. The essay
is very helpful in understanding the aim of her fiction; clearly the effect of,
say, *To the Lighthouse* relies upon the writer giving us the *impression* that
the atoms are being recorded as they fall. But selection according to a scale of
values is at work just as much as it is in the most plot-ridden of novels. I
discuss this passage not for any easy demonstration that Virginia Woolf's
practice does not coincide with her principles, but because the essay has
become a *locus classicus* in much subsequent discussion of modern fiction.

be revealed by Raffles is not an objection to coincidence and 'strong plot' in itself, but the inconsistency of this with the looser texture of plot which operates elsewhere in the novel. One effect, in this particular case, is the invention of a number of characters—Raffles, Rigg, to a lesser extent Featherstone—who fulfil a function within the plot but who are created at a different level of stylization from the other characters, without this stylization being a function of their distance from the centre of interest (which, since it is a feature of normal perception, would cause no problem).

We are also likely to object if the personages of the book are so subdued to a plot that they cease to give the impression of being autonomous beings. This is rarely an issue in novels which deal with a limited range of characters, and where the writer and his readers may be supposed to share major presuppositions about what aspects of human life are of importance. Jane Austen, for instance, has few doubts about what is significant and what is not; she takes it for granted that she shares these with her readers and also with her characters, which is, of course, one indication of her relationship to her society and her feelings about it. Consequently the endings of her novels are normally, in Dr Johnson's phrase, 'the end of expectation': the culminations of Emma's self-realization and of Elizabeth Bennet's change of heart are the culminations of the books in which they are the central characters. We are not likely to have felt the lack of those aspects of the characters which do not contribute towards the working out of the plot because we feel that the characters themselves would recognize this working out as their chief pre-occupation; to feel the end of the books to be arbitrary would be to feel that the characters did not regard the marriages which conclude the books as the ends towards which they had been moving.

But the aim of many major novelists is not the depiction of one clearly definable progression of a central character but an account of a complex society. This may obviously raise in an acute form the problem of how to reconcile an interest in the created characters with a desire for shapeliness. It does not necessarily do so; Conrad's *Nostromo* may be instanced as a novel in which we are concerned with a very wide range of characters but where we do not feel, as we do in *The Way We Live Now*, that this interest militates against formal order. This is because Conrad's view of human behaviour is essentially determinist; he sees freedom of choice as largely illusory and human beings as only to a limited extent autonomous beings. He can therefore organize his novel around a key symbol, the silver of the mine and the legend of the ghostly treasure-seekers of Azuera, which he announces in the first chapter and to which he reverts at various key points in the book. He is thus able to leave individual relationships in a state of irresolution or to dismiss them summarily in a few lines of Joe Mitchell's retrospective local history.

Trollope, however, like Tolstoy and the George Eliot of *Middlemarch*, has not merely a desire to deal with a wide range of characters, but also a view of society as made up of interrelated groups of people who are worthy in themselves of our interest and whom he invites us to think of as autonomous beings, free to choose between different courses of action, some of which link them with people in other groups but some of which do not. Such a view impels many writers who hold it towards what seems an inevitable structure of multiple interacting plots, each centring on one group—a business, a club, a group of neighbours, a political organization, most typically a family—with the major characters in one plot occurring as minor characters in one or more of the others. The form is a microcosm of their view of society; it allows for considerable variety and complication, but, since it rests upon a belief that society is composed of a number of stable groupings and relationships, it suggests that society is knowable and that a straightforward and logical structure best represents it. Balzac's *Comédie Humaine* is, in its entirety, an enormously extended example of this assumption and this structure.

Such novelists are faced, therefore, with the problem of effecting a compromise between a desire that their books should possess some shape and our desire to know more about the characters—including those areas of their lives which do not touch upon the experiences shared by all the characters. This manifests itself most clearly in the problems concerned with the transition between plots and with the way in which the novel comes to an end. The obvious climax of *The Way We Live Now*, for example, is the death of Melmotte; but Trollope assumes that our interest in the other characters makes us want to know what happens to them. He must go on after the obvious climax, with the risk of spoiling the shape of the novel. Similarly, the obvious climax of *Anna Karenina* is the death of Anna; but Tolstoy cannot end without pursuing Levin's life to a point at which we feel that our interest in him has been satisfied.

It is worth pointing out that this conflict is not simply between formal demands and the satisfaction of unworthy and gossipy interest in fictitious characters. It is often between two different kinds of shapeliness, for the desire to know what happens to characters is at bottom a desire that their lives should seem rounded off, complete—which usually means that they should be pursued to a point of apparent rest—to such a *rite de passage* as marriage, emigration, bankruptcy or death. This desire not to interrupt a process is observable even in non-human contexts. It is hard to tear one's attention away from the spectacle of an amoeba engulfing a diatom or a dislodged rock rolling down an uninhabited hillside. This is not because we are emotionally involved with the amoeba, nor with the rock, but because we have a sense of satisfaction in observing the completion of a process, or, more strikingly, a sense of dissatisfaction in leaving before a process is completed. The diatom once engulfed, the rock once at rest, Marie Melmotte once engaged to Fisker in New York, Lydgate once sunk in success, we are prepared to withdraw our attention. This explains, I think, why our interest in knowing what happens to characters in a novel is by no means necessarily destroyed by knowing the novel to be rubbish and by enjoying not a moment of suspended disbelief in the characters concerned. The desire to read on to the end is less of a tribute to the literary value of a book than is sometimes thought.

The most famous objection to this belief that there are inevitable problems and inevitable compromises in such a literary form comes, of course, from Henry James in his comments on 'fluid puddings' and 'loose and baggy monsters' and in his insistence that nothing makes for a leak of interest so much as a hole in the form. It is hard not to believe that he is missing the point; his own reliance upon plots which are tightly organized and not infrequently highly contrived and melodramatic may be suited to his own purpose, but that purpose is not to grapple with a vision of a society which is extensive and multifarious. Even within his own concern for small groups of people his exclusion of the accidental and his isolation of them from the concerns of the rest of society tend to diminish their social reality and with it their plausibility. More damagingly, his concern for the 'ideal of the situation' does not merely operate by causing him to exclude what does not find a place within that ideal; it is frequently manifested in the choice of characters who, themselves, are concerned with an ideal of the situation. Obviously this makes for unity of effect but it often does so at the expense of turning his characters into moral monsters, marked by gross insensitivity to those feelings of other people which do not find a place within their own ideal conceptions of their roles. Their very unselfishnesses can become monstrously self-regarding.

There is, of course, in this discussion of the structure of panoramic novels of society the danger of falling into a simple version of the 'imitative fallacy', of seeming to believe that because life is often shapeless then novels must be shapeless, that it is a positive virtue if they sprawl. Such a view lies behind the suggestion, still sometimes expressed, that fiction, especially realistic fiction, is not as amenable to rigorous critical standards as other literary forms because our interest in it is so strongly in its subject matter. Such a view rests on too limited a conception of form and perhaps on too ready an acceptance, by those who disagree with James's conclusions, of some assumptions which derive from his practice and theory. Any useful discussion of the satisfactoriness or otherwise of the forms of large novels of society must start with comparisons between like and like, and I think that a good starting point would be a comparison between the ways in which the three writers whom I have taken as typical novelists of this kind—Trollope, George Eliot and Tolstoy—deal with the compromises between conflicting demands.

George Eliot is, like Trollope, faced with the task of transferring our interest from one plot, one group of characters, to another, and she is committed, like him, to admitting those areas of her characters' lives which do not overlap. I have discussed Trollope's way of doing this in chapter 2, and have suggested that his somewhat mechanical method of stating plainly that he is now moving from one group to another may help to establish the down-to-earth ordinariness of his narration. But it is obvious that he pays a large price for this possible gain; the sense of abrupt disjunction is disturbing and there are times when, in a very elementary way, we feel that Trollope is positively amateurish. George Eliot manages her transitions a great deal less mechanically. If we consider one such transition from *Middle-*

march, moreover, we can see that more than clumsiness or neatness is involved.

The first ten chapters of the novel centre on Dorothea Brooke and her family and neighbours; thereafter, for some time, attention moves away from her to Lydgate, Rosamund Vincy and her family. The transition occurs at the end of Book I, chapter X and the beginning of chapter XI, and it is effected in a way which emphasizes the extent to which George Eliot's characters are embedded in their society. Dorothea leaves her painful reflection: 'How can I have a husband who is so much above me without knowing that he needs me less than I need him?' for the dinner-party at which the men are of a 'rather more miscellaneous' kind than usual. The men discuss Dorothea's kind of beauty; the women, who do not include Miss Vincy (for Mr Brooke is not so emancipated from social assumptions that he would wish his nieces to meet a manufacturer's daughter) discuss medicine. When the gentlemen enter the drawing-room gossip continues; talk of medicine leads to talk of the new doctor, Lydgate, and this is interspersed with reflections on Casaubon and Dorothea. We have the sense of Dorothea being an object of comment, discussion, gossip, by people who are seeing her from varying social distances. Lydgate, meeting her, reflects that she does not have the kind of beauty which he most admires and she is 'a little too earnest'. At the end of the chapter, by now well returned to her social matrix, she is temporarily dismissed from the book, but in a way which takes some of our interest with her: 'Not long after that dinner-party she had become Mrs Casaubon, and was on her way to Rome.'

When the next chapter begins: 'Lydgate, in fact was already conscious of being fascinated by a woman strikingly different from Miss Brooke . . .' there is no sense of an abrupt change, for between the close view of Dorothea's intimate feelings and a close approach to Lydgate has come the public scene in which Dorothea and Lydgate alike are seen as objects of social curiosity. In the course of moving from one plot to another George Eliot has deepened our sense of the society in which Dorothea and Lydgate exist and she has also, as we see more clearly in retrospect, implied reservations about Lydgate's values which, in the long run, are the cause of his disaster.

The shift of interest has been effected, but we are not in danger of feeling, as we often are when reading Trollope, that a closure on one kind of interest has been made and characters put in cold storage until they are next required. Our sense that both Lydgate and Dorothea exist within a society which looks at them with varying degrees of concern and interest produces an effect of simultaneity of happening rather than of exclusive sequence.

Bringing a complicated novel to an end presents even more problems than moving from one group of characters to another. Tolstoy is faced in *Anna Karenina*, as Trollope is in *The Way We Live Now*, with the problem of reconciling the bringing of the novel to a close with the desire which he has aroused in us to follow all his major characters to some point of rest. The suicide of Anna is an even more obvious dramatic conclusion than Melmotte's. But in both books there is much which is not settled by the death. It is in Tolstoy's dealing with so central a character as Vronsky that we see how different from Trollope's is his concept of a point of rest. We last see Vronsky, suffering from toothache, at the railway station on his way to the war against the Turks. Trollope, we feel, would have to tell us whether or not he was killed in battle, but Tolstoy appears to leave Vronsky at a point of suspension. Yet we are satisfied and this is due to the fact that what we are really concerned about is not whether the character is himself at rest but whether our feelings about him are. From the beginning we have seen Vronsky and Anna as living between and outside stable social groups. So many crucial scenes take place in anterooms, in carriages, as awkward meetings in public; Vronsky first meets Anna by accident at a railway station, his first declaration of love is made at a railway station, Anna throws herself under a train. This is not a matter of contrived symbolic effect; it arises perfectly naturally, as symbolic action, from the probabilities of the story. In returning at the end, after the destruction of what domesticity he has achieved, to the state of being a man under strain at a railway station, Vronsky fulfils our subconscious expectations. Our sense of the rightness of the last scene is due not merely to its psychological plausibility nor to its social comment—that men like Vronsky can only hope to find escape, from the pressures of a society which they do not question but which will not accept them as they are, in dubious warfare—but also from our sense that a pattern has been completed. Nor can we separate these factors; the social comment is involved in the pattern; the pattern is completed in terms of psychological probability.

Trollope's disposal of his characters after Melmotte's suicide is, by contrast, mechanical—a series of chapters, most of which conclude with a marriage. But this, again, is not merely a matter of clumsiness; rather is it that Trollope's conception of a point of rest is limited. Ultimately this means that, despite the devastating criticism to which society is subjected throughout the book, he can only conceive of ending his novel by the institution of a series of conventionally stable relationships. The whole movement of the book has been towards the breaking down of conventional stability; the form of the end reverses this, which is surely why *The Way We Live Now* does not seem, in retrospect, as disturbing a book as we feel it should be. There are many passages which, considered in isolation, are truly surprising—the comment on Melmotte's suicide which I have quoted, for example, or the description of the Bishop's state of mind— but they are surprising because in the long run we feel that Trollope has not found the right form to contain such perceptions. Whole sections of the book may devastate the comfortable assumptions of the implied narrator, but the form obscures this by reasserting the stable regularities. Much of what is effective in the novel comes from our relationship with the narrator, our sense that he is admitting what goes counter to his desires; but finally the form tempts us to succumb to his assumptions.

The greatest novelists, we may say, reveal most clearly the truth of the hackneyed assertion that form and content cannot be separated, and they do this precisely in those parts of their books where the tension between the claims of shapeliness and of interest in characters is most acute. It is right that, though Anna is dead, we should want to know more about Vronsky; it is right that, being interested in Dorothea, we should not want to have our attention taken away from her. What is significant in Tolstoy's way of satisfying this desire, and in George Eliot's, is that, because they think of their characters so much in terms of complex webs of relationships which help to determine their natures, our last sight of Vronsky casts light back upon his relationship with Anna and the way in which George Eliot takes Dorothea away from us reveals more clearly her existence as a social being. James's criteria are inappropriate to novels of this kind and celebrations of fiction as glorious all-embracing pictures of life which transcend shapeliness do not allow us to perceive some of the greatest triumphs.

'Of the various Kinds of Speaking or Writing, which serve Necessity or promote Pleasure, none appears so artless or easy as simple Narration; for what should make him that knows the whole Order and Progress of an Affair unable to relate it? Yet we hourly find such an endeavour to entertain or instruct us by Recitals, clouding the Facts which they intend to illustrate, and losing themselves and their Auditors in the Wilds of Digression, or the Mazes of Confusion.'

Samuel Johnson: *The Rambler*, No. 122

'You say nature is always nature, the sky is always the sky. But sit still and consider for one moment what sort of nature it was the Romans saw on the face of the earth, and what sort of heavens the medievals knew above them, and your sky will begin to crack like glass.'

D. H. Lawrence: Review of A *Second Contemporary Verse Anthology*

4

The conventions of realism: the unshared world

The convention of realism has one characteristic which marks it off from others: not only can we discuss it in comparative terms ('more realistic'), but it appears to be, and to some extent is, a progressive, developing convention. In a number of very obvious ways novels became more realistic between, say, the beginning of the eighteenth century and the end of the nineteenth. I believe that it is this sense of development within the convention, even more than the actual preponderance of realistic novels, which sometimes leads critics to speak as if the tradition of realism in English fiction is the only one.

The development can be noted in very simple ways. Fielding, for example, can individualize an eccentric like Squire Western by the way he talks, but Mrs Western, Squire Allworthy, Tom and Sophia all talk in much the same way—and that a formally rhetorical one. Jane Austen, however, takes pains to make Emma, her father, Harriet and Mr Knightley all talk differently and plausibly, and no later novelist who aimed at giving a picture of society would voluntarily be content with the earlier method. On the occasions when Henry James makes all his characters talk alike this is felt to be an issue which needs discussion, justification or reservations.

Plausibility of plot, too, can be seen to increase, along with consistency and convincingness of character. We have already noted that when, to bring Bulstrode's secret to light, George Eliot introduces into *Middlemarch* an element of strong plot, with its accompanying coincidences, we feel this as a flaw, a breach in the lifelikeness which she elsewhere maintains. We tend not merely to think of this as a regrettable weakness but as an intrusion of a more primitive device from which she has, along with other novelists, emancipated herself.

A sense that the convention is a progressive one and that it must involve all aspects of a novel seems inevitable. If, for example, we are asked (as we are) to accept at the level of plausible depictment the scene in *Felix Holt* (chapter V) in which Esther sets up elegance against honest worth, with all its detail of Felix upsetting the table and the different vocabularies of Felix, Esther and Mr Lyon, then we shall naturally rebel at a conclusion in which so many of the characters turn out to be one another's unexpected relations. We cannot switch on and off at will our recognition of verisimilitude of daily life.

Towards the end of the last century and at the beginning of this, there took place in the writing of a number of novelists two linked changes which have often been considered as logical developments of this tendency towards greater realism: the extrusion of the novelist from the novel—the removal, as it has often been put, of a personage who exists at a different level from the characters—, and the attempt to extend the individualization of characters' speech to an individualization of their processes of thought and feeling. These two developments are linked inevitably; the absence of a narrating novelist demands some other way of presenting what he has previously told us. A story-teller, as a man speaking to other men, can—as in all conversation—make what generalizations he chooses, indulge in short cuts, decide what he will foreshorten, what he will claim to understand and what he will admit to not knowing. While we have a plain teller we accept a plain tale. But these generalizations and foreshortenings are impossible if the novelist purports to tell his story through the perceptions of characters alone. He is led, therefore, to devise a manner of presenting feelings and thoughts which seems to do justice to the full density of individual experience, towards that technique which has come to be known as the 'stream of consciousness' or the 'internal monologue'.*

* A tempting alternative—the introduction of a narrator who can organize the material for the novelist and comment as the novelist feels unwilling to do—was a favourite device of both James and Conrad. But it is less of an alternative than it seems. The narrator must either be a mere mask for the novelist himself, in which case we still have within the story a person who exists at a different level from the characters, or the narrator is a character within the story, in which case the novelist is committed to as detailed a

This combination of the extrusion of the novelist and the stream of consciousness has often been hailed as a closer approximation to the direct presentation of reality. We have heard a great deal about 'immediacy', about 'involving the reader'. The matter is put briefly by W. K. Wimsatt Jr and Cleanth Brooks in *Literary Criticism: a short history* thus:

> They [Ford Madox Ford and, according to Ford, Conrad] wished to make the reader forget the writer altogether so that the story would seem to tell itself and develop with its own life. The novelist was not to 'tell the reader' about what happened but to '*render* it as action'. (p. 683)

A very clear example both of faith in an imitative, illusionist method and an assumption that this is part of a developing convention is provided in a discussion by Harry Stone of 'Dickens and the interior monologue' in *Philological Quarterly*, vol. 38, Jan 1959 (quoted in Penguin Critical Anthologies, *Charles Dickens* ed. Stephen Wall, 1970). The fact that Dickens is not, within my terms of reference, a realistic novelist is here irrelevant; the section under discussion can be taken as realistic and the critic is doing so. Stone discusses very perceptively various ways in which Dickens depicts the consciousness of his characters and ends with a commentary on the opening of *Edwin Drood*, of which he says:

> He [Dickens] was perfectly capable now (as his previous experiments demonstrate) of representing Jasper's dream-waking state with the more powerful and appropriate technique of interior monologue and its accompanying intricacies of association, discontinuity and privacy. Instead he chose to describe the images and thought processes of Jasper's scattered consciousness in clear and highly organized sentences. Technically, as a direct representation of the mind, this is a regression; but in terms of using the images and associations of a character's consciousness as an

---

rendering of his thoughts and feelings as of the others. A vast amount of discussion about the status of certain narrators, in the work of James in particular, comes from our uncertainty (and James's too, very probably) as to how far the person who is telling us the story is a narrator with authorial privileges of reliability and how far one who, like the other characters, has limitations. The governess in *The Turn of the Screw* is the most famous example of this ambiguity. One of the most obvious ways in which such ambiguities manifest themselves is related to the problem of the choice of language for rendering the perceptions of characters, which I discuss later in this chapter.

important means of unifying and illuminating a novel, *Drood* is a step forward.

Of some aspects of fiction this direct presentation had been the aim for a considerable time. Dialogue, since it is a rendering in words of what occurs in words (with linguistic elements replacing stress, intonation and other oral elements) has usually been written so that the reader may have the impression of 'hearing' the characters speak. It seemed, no doubt, a logical development to devise a manner of presenting processes of thought and feeling so that we have the impression of participating in them. Thus we come close in the 'impersonal novel' (I adopt the term from Wayne Booth) to the conception of the novel not as like the experience of hearing about life from someone we trust but as like life itself.

Much of this tendency has been summed up in what is now a critical cliché: 'Don't tell; show.' It is hard to know how far novelists and critics have really believed in so crudely illusionist a view of fiction, of the possibility of rendering experience directly without the interposition of a storyteller. The logical objections to it are so great, but we must not underrate the ability of people to talk metaphorically and then to lose their awareness that what they say is metaphorical. We should not assume that when Virginia Woolf says of James Joyce, 'If we want life itself, here surely we have it' she is actually confusing art with life, but when such comments pass into common critical parlance their essentially metaphorical nature is often forgotten. It might be thought that Dr Johnson had disposed of excessively direct ideas of how art affects us by his disposal of an earlier claim for the principle of illusion—that of the Unities:

> It is false, that any representation is mistaken for reality; that any dramatick fable in its materiality was ever credible, or for a single moment, was ever credited. . . . The truth is, that the spectators are always in their senses, and know, from the first act to the last, that the stage is only a stage, and that the players are only players.

But Wayne Booth in *The Rhetoric of Fiction* has documented the claims made for the 'impersonal novel' so thoroughly as to leave us in no doubt that both novelists and critics (novelists and critics, that is, who are worth bothering about as well as those who merely parrot current notions) have elevated one practice into a dogma and have done so by making claims for a superior realism which suggest that this is a definitive step forward to greater intensity of illusion through devices which can be shown, logically, to be superior to previous ones. At times unwary critics (and we are all unwary sometimes) have talked as if the fully developed impersonal novel is not far short of a direct, unmediated transcript of real life.

One damaging effect of such claims for the impersonal novel has been a tendency for some critics to disparage earlier novels. All conventions are the result of a balance of compromises; all contain inconsistencies. In so far as realism has been a developing convention many points on its development have been satisfactory. The danger of too progressive a view and especially of a dogmatic proclamation of the necessity for some crucial step is that this can easily lead to our refusing assent to the compromises of the past. It is perhaps necessary for novelists, occupied with the task of finding the form which best gives expression to their vision, to claim that this form is 'right' in some more absolute sense. Thus James's principle of masterly indirectness, the extrusion of the novelist as commentator, becomes for him a necessary condition of a satisfactory novel. Critics, however, should beware of general prescriptions; yet Wayne Booth demonstrates beyond any possibility of doubt that James has led many critics to dismiss the narrators of earlier novels in their entirety as devices which detract from the immediacy and authenticity of the books in which they occur, thus suggesting that George Eliot, say, was a bungler who did not understand the art of fiction.

Moreover, as I have suggested, the concept of a progressive convention may suggest that the art of fiction is moving towards a form which will not be conventional and will not involve inconsistencies. This, no doubt, is why, soon after the publication of *Ulysses*, it was felt to be an objection to Joyce's use of the stream of consciousness that the flow of sensation is not unitary but multiple. Nothing, of course, is easier than to point out 'contradictions' within conventions. One such inconsistency in the device of the stream of consciousness, which I do not remember seeing pointed out though it is very obvious, is that the flow of the thoughts and feelings of, say, Leopold Bloom, is rendered as he would experience them, but his words are set down as they would be heard by a listener. Logically, we might say, we are continually jumping backwards and forwards between the consciousness of Bloom and that of a hypothetical listener. I do not suggest that Joyce was unaware of this; doubtless he knew that such inconsistencies are inherent in writing. In Trollope, for example, we are commonly expected to take descriptions of the feelings of the characters as retrospective reflections by the narrator, but the dialogue is given as it would be heard at the moment of its occurrence. This presents no difficulty. But if ever writers or readers come to think of novels or sections of novels as what Ford Madox Ford called an 'attempt to produce in words life as it presents itself' they are bound to boggle at inconsistencies. The most useful task which the critic can set himself, however, is not to yearn towards a perfect (and impossible) non-conventional art, nor to proclaim one method as inherently superior to others; it is rather to show what attitudes are implied by one set of conventions and what by another and perhaps to speculate upon why one compromise, with its inevitable inconsistencies, was acceptable at one time and a quite different compromise at another.

If we consider some of the implications of the impersonal novel we can, I believe, understand that it is not so much a logical move towards greater realism as a redefinition of the reality with which the novel purports to deal. This becomes particularly clear if we consider not only those areas of experience to which it is especially suited, but also those areas with which it cannot deal. Such areas are inevitable, for any set of conventions makes it possible for a writer to do certain things at the cost of making it impossible for him to do others. He may accept the limitation gladly—it may, indeed, sometimes be what he is searching for. But we can sometimes see him being constrained. In particular we can often see such constraints operating in lesser (but not necessarily worthless) writers who adopt from their betters technical methods which are not totally suited to their own purposes.

Our immersion in the moment-by-moment perceptions of a character can produce great vividness and immediacy, but there are some elements of the experience of most (if not all) people which the technique can hardly convey. The most notable inadequacy is probably a lack of a just sense of what is familiar and ordinary. This results from one obvious characteristic of this technique—that what is not created as a perception of a character is felt not to exist for him. If a narrator introduces a man to us we do not feel that the whole of the man exists within that introduction.

We are prepared to be told later in the book about matters of which the man must have been aware on his appearance. We accept the impossibility of the narrator's telling us everything at once and take for granted the potential existence of information which we have not yet been given, only protesting if we feel that information is held back to achieve a contrived mystification. But if we are within a character's stream of consciousness, plunged in his mind, then what we are not told has no existence for him, for if it did have existence it would be present. Yet when a character is leading his familiar daily life he takes for granted many objects (to take the simplest example) which he does not consciously perceive but of which the reader should be aware as the background of his immediate perceptions. Not to include them is likely to befog the reader and to suggest a character less rooted in the dailiness of daily life than is probably desired. To include them within his perceptions tends to falsify his character, usually by making him more consciously ruminative about the minutiae of his surroundings than is desired. The details of daily life—of rooms, streets, food—have figured largely in the streams of consciousness of many characters in twentieth-century fiction, but they often seem too prominent, too significant, not sufficiently taken for granted, just because they are consciously registered. Even Leopold Bloom, a man whom we are meant to think of as intensely curious about the ordinary, seems on his first appearance to suffer from an excessive preoccupation with the physical detail of the ordinary. An interesting example of a writer making good use of this characteristic of the technique is *Pointed Roofs*, the first volume of Dorothy Richardson's *Pilgrimage*, where the subject is so largely the impact of new sensations (including the roofs of the title) upon her heroine. In Germany everything is new for Miriam; she registers the novelty and contrasts it naturally with what she is accustomed to. In later volumes the technique seems less inevitably apt.

What is true of familiar physical objects is, of course, equally —and often far more significantly—true of memories, associations, relationships, habits of thought, of all those matters which, taken for granted, give a dense ordinariness to our lives.

Analogous to this is the fact that if the writer, extruded from his novel, has foregone the right to give a retrospective account of the development of his characters, those parts of their behaviour which are determined by previous experience must be accounted for in terms of their recollections. Since there is only room for a limited number of recollections (unless the characters are insatiably introspective) one consequence of this is likely to be that the prominence given to those which are chosen (strictly, invented) will suggest that they have a greater specific effect than is true for most human experience. The writer will be obliged to imply that behaviour is determined, not by the accumulation of a multitude of past experiences, but by a limited number of specific experiences which a character can raise to the level of consciousness. An effect of Freudian melodrama in some of the novels of William Faulkner can, I believe, be traced to this cause.

The method of the stream of consciousness is obviously particularly well suited to the portrayal of characters who are, like Miriam in *Pointed Roofs*, undergoing strikingly new experiences. It can work very powerfully in making the reader feel that he is participating with the character in a puzzling situation where they are both finding their bearings. Even here, though, we must remember that the puzzlement of the character and the puzzlement of the reader are often not of the same kind. A clear and rather brilliant example both of the use of puzzlement and of the fact that the puzzlements are of different kinds may be seen in William Golding's *The Inheritors*, where the readers are busy coming to terms with the mind of a Neanderthaler as he is busy coming to terms with the new appearance to him of *homo sapiens*. Benjy's stream of consciousness and its effect on us in *The Sound and the Fury* is a similar case. Clearly, too, the technique is particularly satisfactory when applied to characters who are hallucinated, drunk, insane, suffering from amnesia or in some other way disorientated, for these are the states of mind in which a sense of the familiar and an awareness of the past are least present. It is no coincidence that many of the triumphs of the technique have been in the treatment of such characters and such conditions. Often, no doubt, the interest in the abnormal dictated the technical method, but I am suggesting that, regardless of what the character's state of mind is intended to be, certain qualities inherent in the technique will tend to make it seem abnormally restricted. The most obvious way of escaping from this solipsism lies in the choice of characters who are intensely reflective, self-conscious, speculative about their past and their relations with other people—characters who, in temperament, often resemble novelists. Such introspective characters have been common in fiction in this century.

The limitations of which I have spoken can be seen in operation most clearly in writers who have adopted the form of the impersonal novel somewhat against their natural bent, partly no doubt because of its deceptive appearance of logical inevitability and partly because the example of major innovating writers has great power over their lesser fellows. We can see an attempt to overcome these limitations in the tendency of a remarkable number of characters in novels of no great value to keep diaries which they re-read, write lengthy explanatory letters, or manifest unexpected talents for calling up the past in their minds, devices which perform tasks which would once have been the business of the narrating author. Nor should we assume too easily that this sense of constraint is confined to writers of no substance. A writer may find a technical method liberating in some ways but constraining in others. In *The Sound and the Fury* Faulkner uses to brilliant effect the technique of the stream of consciousness for the first three sections of the novel. In particular it enables him to present with the greatest force the contrast between the ways in which the family situation appears to three very dissimilar people and to demonstrate how far they are all imprisoned within the limitations of their own minds. But it is generally agreed that of these three sections the weakest is the second, particularly in the recollected conversation in the last four pages between Quentin (in whose mind we are placed) and his father, where Faulkner is led into typographical tricks in an endeavour to combine the sense of a dialogue simultaneously with the sense of its being a dialogue remembered:

> Just by imagining the clump it seemed to me that I could hear whispers secret surges smell the beating of hot blood under wild unsecret flesh watching against red eyelids the swine untethered in pairs rushing coupled into the sea and he we must just stay awake and see evil done for a little while its not always and it doesnt even have to be that long for a man of courage and he do you consider that courage and i yes sir dont you and he every man is the arbiter of his own virtues whether or not you consider it courageous is of more importance than the act itself than any act otherwise you could not be in earnest and i you dont believe i am serious and he i think you are too serious to give me any cause for alarm you wouldnt have felt driven to the

> expedient of telling me you have committed incest otherwise and
> i i wasnt lying i wasnt lying and he you wanted to sublimate a
> piece of natural folly into a horror and exorcize it with truth.

It seems most likely that Faulkner, a writer with a strong sense of the continuity of experience and the history of his chosen region, is here constrained by his method of presentation to introduce matter which is properly the reflective speculation of a narrator as part of an internal monologue. A discrepancy between content and form is largely responsible for the forced devices and for the ambiguity which all readers of the novel seem to have as to exactly what happened when, and for the invention of so unconvincingly sententious a ruminator as Quentin's father.

Some such tension certainly seems in other novels of Faulkner to be the likely explanation for the use which he makes of Gavin Stevens, who is given such a burden of reminiscence and speculation, without the clarity which authorial comment can possess, that his solipsistic sententiousness casts a blight of boredom and implausibility over most of the scenes in which he occurs. Here, however, I am speculating. I cannot be sure that I am not inverting cause and effect. It may be that Faulkner was fascinated by Gavin Stevens and the technical method followed inevitably. Conversely, there is room for argument about the reasons often given for some of the effects achieved by James. It is often said that his belief in the indirect method led him to introduce characters who function as observing narrators and that, since these observers cannot be uninvolved in what they observe, their feelings move towards the centre of the stage. This inevitably leads to ambiguities and to a concentration on the observers' interpretations and motives. It may be, on the other hand, that James's (not necessarily conscious) fascination by the ambiguities of feeling of the man whose chief interest is the observation of other people leads him to his method, which he then rationalizes as a technical demand which is morally and emotionally neutral.

Fortunately we do not have to decide precisely why writers choose the techniques they do and how conscious they are of their reasons, nor how right we may be if we choose to speculate about their motives. We may feel convinced that some writers are led by reigning ideas about fiction to choose techniques which do not serve their purpose and that others, as my example from Faulkner suggests, sometimes have to suffer from limitations as the price of being liberated in other ways. But we can hardly doubt that the restriction of some kinds of subject matter and the enlargement of others which is implied by the impersonal novel corresponds to a change in attitude towards their subject matter as a whole on the part of those major writers who develop this form or adopt it. Joyce and Proust, Virginia Woolf and the Chekhov of some of the short stories had to innovate because older forms would not express what they wanted to say. My emphasis upon what the impersonal novel will not allow the novelist to do is not intended to suggest that it is a particularly restrictive form, but to make clear some of the important elements in a change of vision and to contrast this with what is implied by previous fictional techniques.

The form chosen by such nineteenth-century writers as Trollope, George Eliot, Thackeray, Tolstoy, Stendhal, implies, as I have said in the previous chapter, that society is composed of a number of stable groupings and relationships which are comprehensible, potentially knowable to the informed imagination of any of the more intelligent and socially favoured characters and to both the narrator and his readers, who are thought of as sharing a large world of assumptions and experiences. (I do not, of course, mean that they are necessarily right in these assumptions; they sometimes seem, in retrospect, grossly to have misunderstood what was happening in their society.) The writer may sometimes play off the limitations of his authorial narrating *persona* against the greater perceptiveness and intelligence of his readers, as Trollope does in *The Way We Live Now*, but they are men of the same world; when the narrator tells us about the behaviour of men in society we respond as we do because we are assumed to have basically the same kind of experience. One effect of this technical method, which may seem an inevitable limitation of the convention, is that the book may be less disturbing, altogether more cosy and reassuring, than its contents suggest. The mere fact that a narrator can talk to us throughout and go on talking at the end may suggest more stability and more continuity than the writer desires. In *A Passage to India* Forster has Fielding say: 'I used to feel death selected people, it is a notion one gets from novels, because some of the characters are usually left talking at the end.' The continuing presence of a narrator may have a similar effect; as I have suggested, this seems true of *The Way We Live Now*.

The impersonal novel, by contrast, makes possible—and indeed enforces—a view of the world in which a widely ranging social view can hardly ever appear, in which the familiar and the ordinary, that which is taken for granted, play a small part and, indeed, often seem to be denied existence. It tends to suggest a simple, often rather mechanical, view of psychological causation, well suited to a view of human nature which (as in a simplified form of Freudian psychoanalysis) seeks for single causes, and thus emphasizes the fragmentary rather than the continuous nature of experience. It implies, too, that the stability of outlook of most nineteenth-century novelists, and even more the sense of comprehensibility, of there being a great deal which can be taken for granted, has disappeared. Essentially it tends towards the assumption that each character inhabits his own private world and also that nothing can be assumed as shared between the writer and the reader. An extreme form of this last possibility was expressed as a joke very early. Sterne begins chapter XVII of volume II of *Tristram Shandy*:

> —But, before the Corporal begins, I must first give you a description of his attitude;—otherwise he will naturally stand represented by your imagination in an uneasy posture—stiff—perpendicular—dividing the weight of his body equally upon both legs;—his eye fixed, as if on duty;—his look determined, clenching the sermon in his left hand, like his firelock.—In a word, you would be apt to paint Trim as if he was standing in his platoon, ready for action. His attitude was as unlike this as you can conceive.
>
> He stood before them with his body swayed and bent forwards, just so far as to make an angle of eighty-five degrees and a half upon the plane of the horizon . . .

But, though *Tristram Shandy* is all within the rambling mind of Tristram himself, and though Sterne does give a sidelong glance at many of the basic assumptions of realism, this is a joke, and it is a joke at the expense of Tristram/Sterne which takes its point largely from the fact that we feel convinced that the reader would be contented with the statement: 'He stood in the middle of the room.'

For writers like Virginia Woolf and Proust and Alain Robbe-Grillet the sense that there is not a world of experience and assumptions which is shared by the writer and the reader, as well as by the characters, is no joke. Nothing can be accepted as existing until it has been created within the book and, since this creation always lies within the mind of a character, what can be created has certain characteristics—discontinuity, the absence of a sense of the familiar, an emphasis on the privacy of experience—which increases our sense of isolation and precariousness. The writer cannot avoid, even if he would, giving his reader the feeling that much of the experience of reading the novel is one of uncertainty, of finding his bearings, of not being able entirely to bring together in a coherent view the fragments of experience with which he is presented. Here, obviously, we no longer have the sense of a novel as the experience of being told about life by someone whom we trust; what is presented is the rendering of an often fragmentary and not fully understood experience which is all that the novelist will commit himself to. At this point the term 'realism', though it may be logically justifiable, is useless. The rendering of the inner experience of a character is, in one sense, a closer approximation to realism than a more distant commentary on that character; but if we consider, in particular, the dramatization of a state of mind which is highly eccentric, deluded or insane, we can say of it simultaneously that it is intensely lifelike and totally fantastic. When, for example, we are in the mind of the Consul in Malcolm Lowry's *Under the Volcano* we feel both a sense of conviction of its credibility and doubt of its reliability. When we are plunged into the consciousness of the observer in Nathalie Sarraute's *Portrait d'un Inconnu* we combine a strong sense of his identity with great uncertainty as to whether his perceptions have any relationship to any other reality. The more 'realistic' the novelist makes the portrayal of such a state of mind the less use the word 'realistic' becomes.

Clearly the effect of much modern fiction is that of a forceful presentation of a sense of meaninglessness and insecurity, of a doubt about the status of a word like 'reality'. It is at this point in discussion, endeavouring to explain why the change has come about, that commentators tend to grow metaphysical and to talk about the meaninglessness of modern life and the concept of the modern world as a panorama of futility. For some writers, for Beckett for example, this may be appropriate. But such comments often purport to be a diagnosis of a general state which all—or almost all—significant writers are reflecting; here, I believe, we are often in the presence of cant behind which, it is as well to remember, lie political and theological assumptions—often unavowed—of a highly dogmatic and assured kind. What we are actually justified in finding in many novels is frequently much more modest: a sense of the extreme complexity and diversification of modern society, a feeling that social assumptions and experience are so varied that individual experience alone is reliable. Jane Austen, without being either stupid or insensitive, could take the experience and the standards of her immediate environment as a norm. Various social and technological changes, not least the vastly increased speed of communications, both physical travel and the dissemination of information, have so changed our ways of looking at society that a portrayal of it in terms of two or three families in a village, whose reflections are confined to what immediately surrounds them, would now only be possible to a writer who was either stupid or grossly insensitive. A refusal to present private experience within the context of society and a doubt about how much the writer shares with his readers becomes inevitable, whether we attribute it to justified modesty or call it a failure of nerve. But if we consider one characteristic of the impersonal novel about which I have not yet spoken, I believe that we can see that this form involves a dilemma whose resolution compounds the feeling of privacy and insecurity to an extent which the writers may not always desire, but which they cannot avoid.

I have spoken of writers as being willing to commit themselves only to the rendering of individual experience, often fragmented and unrelated to any wider experience, and of their not feeling able to assume shared assumptions between the writer and the reader. But this is to speak metaphorically of the effect produced by (sometimes, as I have suggested, imposed by) the convention of the impersonal novel. In fact, the writer cannot but claim both superior knowledge to his characters and shared experience with his readers. Virginia Woolf may eschew general comments which will relate the perceptions of Lily Briscoe, say, to general assumptions; Nathalie Sarraute may refuse to commit herself as to how much of what her central character claims is actually illusory; Joyce may, in the last section of *Ulysses*, claim simply to let Molly Bloom's recollections unroll. But they are, of course, making choices about what will be presented, just as much as the most garrulous narrator, and the reader, even as he responds to the impression of the direct presentation of experience and the absence of a teller of the tale, is acutely aware of the presence of the novelist. Above all, the writer uses language, a public referential system, to assert the absence of shared experience.* The writer can never withdraw from his novel; he always implies judgments; every sentence which he writes is an appeal to a shared experience.

Paradoxically, the author of the impersonal novel is thrust more into the centre of the stage than was the authorial narrator of the nineteenth-century social novel. One of the main causes for this can be seen when we consider the two possible solutions to his problem of the choice of language which Henry James discusses in his Preface to *What Maisie Knew*. Having decided that: 'The one presented register of the whole complexity would be the play of the child's confused and obscure notation of it', James is faced with a decision as to what language to use for this presentation, and decides against a restriction to Maisie's own terms. 'Small children', he says, 'have many more perceptions than they have terms to translate them; their vision is at any moment much richer, their apprehension even constantly stronger, than their prompt, their at all producible, vocabulary.' Yet every reader must have been aware that, despite the dazzling effects which James produces with his combination of the child's point of view and an adult vocabulary, nevertheless there are moments when the vocabulary and syntax suggest awarenesses in Maisie in which we cannot believe; at these points we are almost embarrassingly conscious of James. The alternative— *What Maisie Knew* in the language of childhood—would, of course, produce different but no less difficult problems of response.

When the novelist's centre of consciousness is adult the problem seems more acute; we are less prepared to accept a discrepancy between perceptions and language. If the writer opts for appropriate language he will be led, unless his centre of consciousness is a notably articulate personage who is hardly to be distinguished from himself, into sustained essays in ventriloquism which never lose the effect of parody or the *tour de force*.

* I use the word 'public' in the sense that the English language, say, is the public possession of the English people. But there is room for a great deal of discussion of what sections of that people are appealed to. The language may be chosen, deliberately or not, so as to appeal to particular groups. Of Virginia Woolf, for example, it may sometimes be said that she asserts the privacy of experience in a language which, by its overtones and associations, implies the values of a particular social class.

Both the last section of *Ulysses* and the opening section of *The Sound and the Fury*, superb though they are and necessary parts of the novels, never allow us to forget the brilliance of their creators. Because they offer an illusion they never allow us to overcome our sense of the novelists as dazzling illusionists. We cannot read them without remembering their authors to a far greater extent than we remember, as we read *The Way We Live Now*, that its author is Trollope. We cannot respond to the words only as if they were Molly's or Benjy's; we know that they are Joyce's and Faulkner's. This is akin to the point made by Jorge Luis Borges in his entertaining *ficcion*, 'Pierre Menard, Author of Don Quixote'. Menard's lifework is to write *Don Quixote*, a creation of his own which will coincide, word for word, with that of Cervantes. Borges compares the effect of passages by Cervantes and identical passages from Menard's re-creation; though the words are the same, the effect is quite different:

> . . . the fragmentary *Don Quixote* of Menard is more subtle than that of Cervantes. The latter indulges in a rather coarse opposition between tales of knighthood and the meager, provincial reality of his country; Menard chooses as 'reality' the land of Carmen during the century of Lepanto and Lope. What Hispanophile would not have advised Maurice Barrès or Dr Rodríguez Larreta to make such a choice! Menard, as if it were the most natural thing in the world, eludes them. In his work there are neither bands of gypsies, conquistadores, mystics, Philip the Seconds, nor autos-da-fe. He disregards or proscribes local color. This disdain condemns *Salammbô* without appeal. (J. L. Borges: 'Pierre Menard, Author of Don Quixote', translated by Anthony Bonner, from *Ficciones*, ed. Anthony Kerrigan, 1962.)

If, on the other hand, the writer opts for the rendering of the character's perceptions in the language of the writer, he is faced (unless his character is to all intents and purposes himself) by the risk of a discrepancy between the effect upon us of what the character says and does and what are presented as his perceptions. The blurring which often occurs in the novels of Virginia Woolf between the thoughts and feelings of the characters and those of the novelist and the consequent ambiguity and uncertainty of judgment have often been commented on. The novels of Elizabeth Bowen suffer similarly: the perceptions of some of her characters seem finer, more sensitive, more sophisticated than their words and deeds. Puzzling over this, we find that we are speculating about the writer.

Whichever solution the writer chooses to the problem of the choice of language, in fact, we are made acutely aware of his presence. But we are not aware of him as we are aware of George Eliot or Tolstoy or Trollope—as someone whom we trust, telling us about life in terms which we share with him. We are aware of him in terms of ventriloquistic illusion, or of autobiography, or of ambiguities and discrepancies. We are likely to end up admiring a performance and speculating about the performer and his motives, or wondering just how autobiographically accurate the book is meant to be, or reconstructing the personality of the writer from the discrepancies which thrust themselves on us. The effect is very often that of being presented with an account of experiences by someone whom we do not know whether to trust or not, or, in some of the more extreme cases of discrepancy, by someone whom we certainly do not trust.

The result, in short, of the novelist's claimed withdrawal from his novel—a withdrawal which, it has often been asserted, permits a more direct presentation of the world without the interposition of a narrator—is often to oblige us to read the work in an extremely sophisticated way as an objective correlative for a vision which may leave us in grave doubts as to its trustworthiness. The more the novelist 'withdraws' from his novel the more we are aware of it as his construct. We search for the writer behind the construct and read the novel as a metaphor for its author.

5

The logical prison:
Little Dorrit

Dickens begins *Little Dorrit* with a chapter which proves not to be the beginning of the action of the story; it has no relationship to the succeeding chapter except identity of location, and it presents characters who do not reappear for ten chapters and have no significant connection with the main centres of interest in the novel until much later still. This opening is clearly part of the plan which Dickens noted as central to his conception of the book—though its importance may have decreased in the writing of it—and which is summed up by Miss Wade in chapter II: 'In our course through life we shall meet the people who are coming to meet *us*, from many strange places and by many strange roads.' Its more immediate effect upon the reader, however, is to accentuate the degree to which the opening establishes the tone of the book and indicates the kind of attention which it demands. The first few pages of most novels give us unambiguous instructions as to how to read them; we are rarely in doubt for long as to the kind of response demanded of us. When this is not so, the discrepancy between expectation and fulfilment becomes an important element in the effect of the book. The first two chapters of *Wuthering Heights*, for example, lead us to expect a very different book from what follows, but we come to realize that the conflict represents in formal terms the main theme of the novel—the clash between two irreconcilable modes of feeling. Such discrepancies are, however, rare; fulfilment of our aroused expectations is far more usual.

The opening pages of *Little Dorrit* establish very quickly indeed a characteristic tone, a marked way of inviting us to think and feel, and the fact that the first chapter stands as an apparent whole, seemingly unrelated to what follows, encourages us to give it the kind of interpretative attention appropriate to self-contained utterances. Unable to relate what happens to plot or to the development of relationships, we scrutinize the chapter for meaning rather as we would a short story.

The characteristics which dominate the prose are clear. Repetition is one of the most striking. Dickens is particularly fond of descriptions which make their effect (either of vividness or monotony) by the steady hammering of a key word:

> Everything in Marseilles, and about Marseilles, had stared at the fervid sky, and been stared at in return, until a staring habit had become universal there. Strangers were stared out of countenance by staring white houses, staring white walls, staring white streets, staring tracts of arid road, staring hills from which verdure was burnt away.

The key word is repeated, though with less obvious iteration, for the first few paragraphs, until we come to the next piling up of repetitions in the description of the prison:

> The imprisoned air, the imprisoned light, the imprisoned damps, the imprisoned men, were all deteriorated by confinement.

and of one of the prisoners, Cavalletto:

> A sunburnt, quick, lithe, little man, though rather thick-set. Earrings in his brown ears, white teeth lighting up his grotesque brown face, intensely black hair clustering about his brown throat, a ragged red shirt open at his brown breast.

Dickens is fond, too, of similitudes expressed with great precision of imagery, pointed by an insistence on parallels and by a repeated rhythm:

> As the captive men were faded and haggard, so the iron was rusty, the stone was slimy, the wood was rotten, the air was faint, the light was dim. Like a well, like a vault, like a tomb, the prison had no knowledge of the brightness outside . . .

His predilection for parallels is only equalled by one for extreme contrasts; the staring light outside and the darkness inside the prison is the most striking of these, but we also find (in relation, as we later realize, to the image of the sea as the final cleansing destiny of all those rivers which can stand for the river of life):

> There was no wind to make a ripple on the foul water within the harbour, or on the beautiful sea without. The line of

demarcation between the two colours, black and blue, showed the point which the pure sea would not pass; but it lay as quiet as the abominable pool, with which it never mixed.

Objects, in short, are rarely of neutral significance; they tend to take their place either as part of a system of similitudes or an equally clear and striking system of contrasts. The imagery in which they are presented, moreover, is frequently animistic, breaking down the distinction of vitality between things and men. Strangers are stared out of countenance by staring objects; the imprisoned air is like the imprisoned men in being deteriorated; the atmosphere is 'as if the air itself were panting', the stare 'blinks' at the prison; the vines 'wink a little'; in the final sentence of the chapter the sea 'scarcely whispered of the time when it shall give up its dead'.

The first chapter, in short, prepares us for a view of the world in terms of violent contrasts, striking parallels, repetitions—not only, as here, of words, but also of ideas, concepts, situations. We are prepared, too, for a world in which things will have nearly as much life as people—indeed, for one in which some things will have more life than some people. Above all, we are prepared for the steady hammering of a key word or a key image.

As the book goes on, we realize—as very many critics have pointed out—that the first chapter is a microcosm of the whole.* Both the guilty and the more-or-less innocent are in the same prison; one prisoner lords it over another; class distinctions are no less effective inside the walls; the great ones of the world, as Rigaud says, are not greatly different from criminals; the innocent child appears like an angel in prison. But even if we did not know that these themes would be taken up, I think that the apparently self-contained nature of the first chapter would predispose us to take it as a general or typical statement.

There is, of course, a link between the first chapter and what follows, though it is not a link of narrative or plot. It is precisely the kind of link which the first chapter has prepared us to perceive. Mr Meagles, as yet unnamed, complains of being shut up

* So much has been written about *Little Dorrit* that it is impossible either to avoid other people's comments or to acknowledge them all. I therefore acknowledge my large and obvious debt to many other students of Dickens. My purpose in this chapter is less to provide a critical assessment of the book than to define—often by implicit contrast with *The Way We Live Now*—the *kind* of novel which it is and the *kind* of judgments about it to which we are led.

in quarantine and likens himself to 'a sane man shut up in a madhouse' and speaks of 'we jail birds'. Clennam, describing his life to Meagles, then takes up the theme; he has been, he says:

> Trained by main force; broken, not bent; heavily ironed with an object on which I was never consulted and which was never mine; shipped away to the other end of the world before I was of age, and exiled there until my father's death there, a year ago; always grinding in a mill I always hated.

No sooner are they released from the quarantine prison than Mr Meagles is involved in an argument with Miss Wade as to whether a prisoner ever relents towards his prison; she denies it and withdraws to look at the view with 'the reflection of the water, as it made a silver quivering on the bars of the lattice'.

The third chapter shows us Arthur Clennam in London, remembering his childhood when, 'like a military deserter, he was marched to chapel by a picquet of teachers three times a day, morally handcuffed to another boy' and when he saw his mother behind her bible, 'with one dinted ornament on the cover like the drag of a chain'. The imagery of imprisonment recurs as he looks at the London to which he has returned: 'He sat in the same place as the day died, looking at the dull houses opposite, and thinking, if the disembodied spirits of former inhabitants were ever conscious of them, how they must pity themselves for their old places of imprisonment.' He goes to see his mother, passing the closet in which as a child he was sometimes shut up, and finds her glorying in her self-imposed imprisonment.

Repetition, the seizing of resemblances, the recurrence of key themes, invited by the first chapter, are quickly seen as central to the novel. We do not enter on a series of relationships or the exploration of emotional or psychological states or problems, we do not have anything even remotely approaching a plot or even a connected narrative until after we have been obliged to see that a fruitful reading of the book is likely to be in terms of its key symbols and, pre-eminently, that of imprisonment. The two characters of the first chapter do not reappear until chapter XI; Cavalletto re-enters the story in chapter XIII, but Rigaud-Blandois is not seen again until chapter XXIX; Miss Wade is not mentioned after the second chapter until chapter XVI and after that she drops from sight until chapter XXVII; the Meagleses are not seen again until chapter X. But even before chapter VI, when we enter the Marshalsea, the prison around which so much of the action of the book is to centre and into which, in one role or another, all the main characters penetrate, we realize that virtually every character and every incident is centred on one form or another of imprisonment. It is also clear to us that the psychological prisons of Mrs Clennam and her son are as effective as the physical prison of Rigaud and Cavalletto. It is clear, too, that the idea of imprisonment is extended—most strikingly at the beginning of chapter III—to take in a whole society.

It used to be held against Dickens that he is unable to explore human character through a sustained presentation of feeling and behaviour, so that his characters are all caricatures, 'flat' stereotypes. This is not by any means entirely true. Leaving on one side the observation that the world is full of people every bit as grotesque to the observer as Mr Pancks, say, or Mr F.'s aunt, we must surely admit that 'The History of a Self Tormentor' is a brilliant study of paranoia (it alone would be enough to suggest why Dostoevsky proclaimed Dickens as his master) and that the decline of Mr Dorrit is pursued steadily through scene after scene, like the chapter 'The Father of the Marshalsea in two or three Relations', where we see him progressing from emotional blackmail through self-reproach and maudlin self-pity to a pride in his degradation. But Dickens certainly does not normally develop his subject by the extended study of the relationships of realistically plausible characters. He does it in terms of melo-drama, sudden jumps, grotesques, dazzling concentration on significant objects. His effects can, of course, be self-indulgently local in the impression which they give, but usually in *Little Dorrit* they appear as manifestations of a highly unified vision of society, and the characters are recognized as basic human types forced into their often narrow moulds by the pressures of this society.

The plot—in so far as it can be said to exist—is not merely implausible; it is surely deliberately perfunctory. The relation-ships between the Clennams and the Dorrits and the function of Flintwinch's twin brother are of such complexity and are pre-sented with such offhand abandon that it is unlikely than one reader in ten could give an accurate account of them a week after finishing the book. There is a similar perfunctoriness about the Dorrit inheritance—'Her father was heir-at-law to a great estate that had long lain unknown of, unclaimed, and accumulat-ing' is all we are told. The effect of the plot is summed up in the description of 'the secrets of the river, as it rolled its turbid tide between two frowning wildernesses of secrets, extending, thick and dense, for many miles, and warding off the free air and the free country swept by winds and wings of birds' (The Oxford Illustrated Dickens, *Little Dorrit*, p. 542). It gives us, that is, a sense of multitudinous connections, mostly undesired, which make it impossible for anyone in the society to dissociate himself from anyone else. It is this, for example, which gives an emotional justification to Arthur Clennam's suspicions at the beginning of the book that there is some connection between his mother and Little Dorrit, between her self-imposed imprisonment and the actual imprisonment in the Marshalsea of Mr Dorrit. Such a sense of the impossibility of dissociating oneself even from those who seem most foreign is one of Dickens's most constant themes in his later novels; it is, for example, the purpose of the fantastic coincidences of *Great Expectations*. These coincidences do not serve to extricate Dickens from tight corners in the plotting, but to make a statement about society. Plot here is not a structural device so much as an intermittently applied metaphor. Unity and structure come from the key symbols.

Of these the idea of the inexorable approach of travellers to a predestined meeting place, though it is specifically mentioned a number of times near the beginning and though it is enacted in the structure, with its originally widely separated personages gradually coming together, seems nevertheless to have been progressively abandoned in the writing of the book. It has, however, one effect which is not negligible. It gives a particular point to the loose sequence of happenings which is normal with Dickens and which inevitably involves him in frequent jumps from one set of characters to another. We have seen how the maintenance of interest in the panoramic realistic novel of society confronts the writer with this structural problem; this is always far less acute in Dickens because the nature of our interest in the characters is so different; we see them less as autonomous beings and more as manifestations of a central theme. Here, in particular, the explicit theme of the converging travellers gives a sense of necessity to such sudden leaps as that from chapter X, in the Circumlocution Office, to XI—Rigaud-Blandois and Cavalletto at Chalons—and back to XII—'Bleeding Heart Yard'.

The third key symbol, of far less importance than those of

prison and of travellers converging, is that of the river which, starting clear and fresh near its source, runs as a 'deadly sewer' through London, and finally reaches the sea and, in death, renewed cleanliness. Dickens can make good use of the dirty Thames as an image of corruption, but its association at Twickenham with Pet and the 'flowing road of time' shows him at his most ineffectively hackneyed.

In saying that the key symbol of prison is the most important I do not merely mean that it recurs more often but that it carries far more of the meaning of the book. The sense of momentum, the excitement of discovery, come from the manner in which Dickens uses it to make coherent sense of the society of which he is writing.

The Circumlocution Office ties up the whole country in red tape so that, we are told, those who become involved with it 'never reappeared in the light of day', and those with business there are referred to as 'convicts who were under sentence to be broken alive on that wheel'. It is typical that young Ferdinand Barnacle should expect that the Circumlocution Office is responsible for Arthur Clennam's imprisonment in the Marshalsea. The Office bears the responsibility, too, for the economic imprisonment of Bleeding Heart Yard and Dickens comments that 'Britannia herself might come to look for lodgings in Bleeding Heart Yard, some ugly day or other, if she over-did the Circumlocution Office' (p. 123).

The power of finance is most directly represented by Mr Merdle, who ruins investors so that they end in the Marshalsea. But in Mr Merdle we see the ambivalence of such power, for he is the prisoner of his own situation, slinking about his house, 'with his hands crossed under his uneasy coat-cuffs, clasping his wrists as if he were taking himself into custody' (p. 394), in awe of his butler who seems more to resemble a gaoler. In this he is merely suffering more acutely from the restrictions which apply even to the Barnacles, who are obliged by their sense of what is fitting to occupy 'fearful little coops', one of which is described at length in the chapter 'Containing the Whole Science of Government', with its 'close back parlour' and 'low blinding back wall three feet off'.

But the most developed study of self-imprisonment is that of Mrs Clennam. Our first meeting with her comes as the culmination of that description of London which begins chapter III, but we have already heard her essence described by Clennam to Mr Meagles:

> I am the only child of parents who weighed, measured, and priced everything; for whom what could not be weighed, measured, and priced, had no existence. Strict people as the phrase is, professors of a stern religion, their very religion was a gloomy sacrifice of tastes and sympathies that were never their own, offered up as a part of a bargain for the security of their possessions. (pp. 20–1)

Her justification for that mixture of commercial tight-fistedness and vengeful puritanism is that she has chosen to incarcerate herself. She appeals to Arthur to see her 'in prison and in bonds'. Flintwinch, her ally, may keep his wife shut up for love of money and power, but Mrs Clennam is convinced that to imprison herself and others is a religious duty.

It is in relation to Mrs Clennam's religion that we see the relevance to the central theme of the novel of the self-imprisoned Miss Wade and Tattycoram. As a study in paranoia and (in a veiled manner) of a Lesbian affection, the sections of the book which deal with Miss Wade are among the best, but to grasp their full force we must see that they are related to Mrs Clennam's desire that those who have transgressed the sexual code shall be punished by the removal of love and that the offspring of their sin shall live a life of what, in relation to her son, she calls 'practical contrition for the sins that were heavy on his head before his entrance into this condemned world' (p. 777). Tattycoram herself says: 'I used to think, when I got into that state, that people were all against me because of my first beginning' (p. 811). Miss Wade, in her settled hatred of the world, and Tattycoram in her rages are a tribute to the widespread power of Mrs Clennam's beliefs.

From the Marshalsea or the prison at Marseilles there may be release, but for one who, in the words describing Tip, 'take the prison walls with him' there is little hope. Nowhere is this more closely worked out than in the life of Mr Dorrit. The prophetic words of the turnkey when he first enters the Marshalsea are 'Out? . . . he'll never get out' and by the time the action of the book begins he is subdued to his imprisonment to the point at which, like Mrs Clennam, he glories in it and can bestow 'his life of degradation as a sort of portion' on Little Dorrit. Logically enough, therefore, we first see him after his release—which his daughter believes will enable her to see him 'with the dark cloud cleared away'—in the prison-like Hospice of the Great St Bernard, where the guests retire to sleep in their cells. He employs Mrs General to act as a gaoler to keep his daughters within the proprieties which his weak pride and obsession with his past imprisonment make so important, and conducts them on a grand tour where their life seems to Little Dorrit like 'a superior sort of Marshalsea'. His hallucinated reversion to the Marshalsea at his last dinner party is merely the logical confirmation that morally he has never left it.

The unifying power, the sense of energy in the book, comes from the manner in which these various kinds of imprisonment work together, the powers of money, administration, puritanism, conventionality, snobbery, fear, combining to drive so many of the characters into a state in which they assent to their imprisonment, glory in it, and imprison others. In this world love, spontaneity and vitality are suppressed—a point made, at very different levels of seriousness, by Mrs Clennam's paralysis and Mrs General's rejection of 'tumbled over the subject' in favour of 'inadvertently lighted upon' or 'accidentally referred to'.

The novel might, given so repetitive a theme and so tightly organized a symbolic structure, be unduly schematic were it not for the impression which Dickens gives of boundless inventiveness—not only that ability to create the seemingly unending series of characters upon which his fame has always so largely rested, but also an equally striking verbal creativity. Much of what is funny in the book comes from Dickens's metaphorical wit, and it must be said here (lest so obvious a point might go by default) that Dickens's humour remains funny. He is not a writer to whose humour only lip service is paid. We laugh, and we are laughing as often as not at such a mingling of satire and verbal conceit as the description of Mr Gowan's father who 'had died at his post with his drawn salary in his hand, nobly defending it to the last extremity'. The inventiveness often appears in such bravura lists as: 'The whole business of the human race between London and Dover, being spoliation, Mr Dorrit was waylaid at Dartford, pillaged at Gravesend, rifled at Rochester, fleeced at Sittingbourne, and sacked at Canterbury' (p. 634). It is vital in a novel whose thematic principle is one of repetition to the verge of monotony that we should feel that the writer can invent endlessly and can always surprise us with a turn of phrase.

Different elements in the story are presented in very different manners. The Circumlocution Office and that part of the novel which revolves round Mr Merdle are presented in a mode of allegorical farce, the characters tending to have either allegorical names or to be unindividualized representatives of types, such as 'Bar' and 'Bishop', and Dickens makes his effects here by a mixture of gross exaggeration ('several sacks of official memoranda, and a family-vault full of ungrammatical correspondence') and the use of the jargon of officialdom and the professions ('Surely the goods of this world, it occurred in an accidental way to Bishop to remark, could scarcely be directed into happier channels than when they accumulated under the magic touch of the wise and sagacious, who, while they knew the just value of riches . . .'). Mrs Clennam's household, appropriately, is shown in alternations between detailed description of material objects and nightmare fantasy. Miss Wade and Tattycoram are treated by psychological analysis of a relatively naturalistic kind. There are not, of course, sharp lines of division between the different techniques and we find multitudinous gradations between the world of allegory, farce, nightmare, local realism, satire and melodrama; but each group tends to have a central style in which it is most at home. Individuals, too, tend to have not only their own typifying verbal characteristics but very often to be presented by a characteristic and specific technique. Barnacle Junior, for example, is projected by way of his eye-glass:

> He had a superior eye-glass dangling round his neck, but unfortunately had such flat orbits to his eyes, and such limp little eyelids, that it wouldn't stick in when he put it up, but kept tumbling out against his waistcoat buttons with a click that discomposed him very much.
>
> 'Oh, I say. Look here! My father's not in the way, and won't be in the way today,' said Barnacle Junior. 'Is this anything that I can do?'
>
> (Click! Eye-glass down. Barnacle Junior quite frightened and feeling all round himself, but not able to find it.)
>
> 'You are very good,' said Arthur Clennam. 'I wish however to see Mr Barnacle.'
>
> 'But I say. Look here! You haven't got any appointment, you know,' said Barnacle Junior.

(By this time he had found the eye-glass, and put it up again.)

'No,' said Arthur Clennam. 'That is what I wish to have.'

'But I say. Look here! Is this public business?' asked Barnacle Junior.

(Click! Eye-glass down again. Barnacle Junior in that state of search after it, that Mr Clennam felt it useless to reply at present.) (p. 108)

Mr Barnacle Senior appears a few pages later in terms of his clothes:

> He wound and wound folds of white cravat round his neck, as he wound and wound folds of tape and paper round the neck of the country. His wristbands and collar were oppressive, his voice and manner were oppressive. He had a large watch-chain and bunch of seals, a coat buttoned up to inconvenience, a waist-coat buttoned up to inconvenience, an unwrinkled pair of trousers, a stiff pair of boots. (p. 111)

He has no face. The prose which describes Mr Dorrit and his actions takes its tone from his own speech and is a parody of the orotund and patronizing politeness of a ruling class. Mrs General is propriety of utterance. Flora Finching exists entirely in free association within the imagery of sentimental poetry.

Throughout the book Dickens's intensely metaphorical prose breaks down the distinction between people and objects. At times this seems little more than an effective and often comic trick:

> Mr Casby lived in a street in the Gray's Inn Road, which had set off from that thoroughfare with the intention of running at one heat down into the valley, and up again to the top of Pentonville Hill; but which had run itself out of breath in twenty yards, and had stood still ever since. (p. 144)

More often, though, it gives a sense of oppressive power to things which influence and sometimes even dominate people—like the 'maimed table' and 'crippled wardrobe' of Mrs Clennam's house. Conversely, people become things. Pancks as a tug is the most obvious example, but we may instance also Mrs Merdle—'the bosom' ('It was not a bosom to repose upon, but it was a capital bosom to hang jewels upon')—and Lord Lancaster Stiltstalking: 'This noble Refrigerator had iced several European courts in his time. . . . He shaded the dinner, cooled the wines, chilled the gravy, and blighted the vegetables' (p. 313).

The opening of chapter xv of the first Book shows most clearly this abolition of the distinction between the animate and the inanimate:

> The debilitated old house in the city, wrapped in its mantle of soot, and leaning heavily on the crutches that had partaken of its decay and worn out with it, never knew a healthy or a cheerful interval, let what would betide. If the sun ever touched it, it was but with a ray, and that was gone in half an hour; if the moonlight ever fell upon it, it was only to put a few patches on its doleful cloak, and make it look more wretched. The stars, to be sure, coldly watched it when the nights and the smoke were clear enough; and all bad weather stood by it with a rare fidelity. You should alike find rain, hail, frost, and thaw lingering in that dismal enclosure, when they had vanished from other places; and as to snow, you should see it there for weeks, long after it had changed from yellow to black, slowly weeping away its grimy life. The place had no other adherents. As to street noises, the rumbling of wheels in the lane merely rushed in at the gateway in going past, and rushed out again: making the listening Mistress Affery feel as if she were deaf, and recovered the sense of hearing by instantaneous flashes. So with whistling, singing, talking, laughing, and all pleasant human sounds. They leaped the gap in a moment, and went upon their way.
> The varying light of fire and candle in Mrs Clennam's room made the greatest change that ever broke the dead monotony of the spot. In her two long narrow windows, the fire shone sullenly all day, and sullenly all night. On rare occasions, it flashed up passionately, as she did; but for the most part it was suppressed like her, and preyed upon itself evenly and slowly. (p. 178)

It would be hard to say of those last sentences whether we feel that Mrs Clennam metaphorically describes the fire (as is nominally the case) or whether the fire expresses Mrs Clennam's spirit —with the two windows, one might not altogether fancifully add, suggesting her eyes.

Such imagery contributes powerfully to the effect of a novel which is concerned with the oppressive power of things and places—money, for example, and a London which embodies commercial ruthlessness and ugly puritanism—and with the dehumanization of people. More generally, we can recognize in it an extreme example of Dickens's way of creating a world which, though related to that of ordinary observation—at times very closely related to it—is not identical with it. Trollope's method, as we have seen, is to tell his story through a narrator who embodies the ordinariness of the generally accepted and who refers to a world of facts and people and assumptions which are taken as a commonly agreed possession between himself and the readers. Dickens, on the contrary, is creating a world which is not a shared possession. He deploys a variety of techniques, a profusion of inventiveness and a startling metaphorical power to convince us that a parable with a tight thematic structure is nevertheless not the wanton imposition of a narrow and arbitrary vision.

That vision is, of course, variously convincing in various parts of the book; if we look at the weaknesses we can see how far our acceptance of his world depends upon the metaphorical life of the prose. It is generally agreed that Little Dorrit herself is probably the greatest weakness in the book. Her function within the pattern is, theoretically, clear. It is stated in the first chapter in terms of her prototype, the gaoler's little daughter. The manner of its stating is significant; the prose which, so far, has been lively, inventive, specific, descends to unoriginal insipidity: 'The fair little face, touched with divine compassion, as it peeped shrinkingly through the grate, was like an angel's in the prison.' The case is the same with Little Dorrit herself. Our dissatisfaction is provoked, not by any rejection of her theoretical role—the proof that only self-sacrificing love can survive untainted in prison and bring comfort to the imprisoned—nor mainly by any sense that her behaviour is psychologically implausible, but by the banality of the rhetoric in which she is presented. She is described thus in the chapter 'The Child of the Marshalsea' in which we are first told of her:

> What her pitiful look saw, at that early time, in her father, in her sister, in her brother, in the jail; how much, or how little of the wretched truth it pleased God to make visible to her; lies hidden with many mysteries. It is enough that she was inspired to be something which was not what the rest were, and to be that something, different and laborious, for the sake of the rest. Inspired? Yes. Shall we speak of the inspiration of a poet or a priest, and not of the heart impelled by love and self-devotion to the lowliest work in the lowliest way of life! (p. 71)

The rhetorical device of winning victory over an opponent who only exists to be defeated ('Inspired? Yes.') is unconvincing enough, but it is less damaging than the flatness, the lack of concreteness, the utter absence of Dickens's normally abundant invention in 'she was inspired to be something which was not what the rest were. . . .'

The more crucial her role the more obvious such lapses are. When she is oppressed by Fanny and Mrs General in Switzerland her position as victim and, by implication, judge of pretentious falsity is shown in a manner which, if not brilliant in the way in which the treatment of Mrs Clennam or Miss Wade or the Barnacles is brilliant, is at least tolerably lively. But this is a part of the book where her role is a minor one; when she has to carry any weight within the main theme of the novel the prose deteriorates. Her great moment towards the end of the novel occurs when she resumes her position as comforter in the Marshalsea, though this time to Arthur Clennam and not to her father. The prose here is sub-biblical, the imagery of perfect triteness, the rhythm, with its cumulative rising repetitions and its delayed climax, a gross incitement to tears:

> He roused himself, and cried out. And then he saw, in the loving, pitying, sorrowing, dear face, as in a mirror, how changed he was; and she came towards him; and with her hands laid on his breast to keep him in his chair, and with her knees upon the floor at his feet, and with her lips raised up to kiss him, and with her tears dropping on him as the rain from Heaven had dropped upon the flowers, Little Dorrit, a living presence, called him by his name. (p. 756)

At this stage in the book, too, the mawkishness and the lack of convincing vigour infect her surroundings. It is hard to believe that the writer who created the description of the Clennam house which I quoted a few pages back also wrote of Little Dorrit's gift to Clennam: 'Beside the tea-cup on his table he saw, then, a blooming nosegay: a wonderful handful of the choicest and most lovely flowers' (p. 755). Clennam, indeed, sounds at times like her father in one of his more maudlin moods. As, of course, he well might, since this is the role which he is taking over. William Dorrit, physically imprisoned in the Marshalsea for debt, comes to accept his imprisonment and to glory in it. Arthur Clennam, psychologically imprisoned by his upbringing, upright, self-sacrificing, but emotionally frozen, accepts his unwise speculations as an outward form of the guilt which has been bred into him and accepts almost enthusiastically his imprisonment in the Marshalsea. Mr Dorrit acquires his emotional bondage as a result of his physical incarceration. Clennam enters the Marshalsea almost as an outward sign of his inner bondage. And he chooses the Marshalsea rather than the more distinguished King's Bench because it is associated in his mind with the ministrations of Little Dorrit.

It seems reasonably certain that Dickens's conscious intentions in the latter part of the novel are not entirely in accordance with the effect which the book actually has upon us. This is obviously due in part to his inability to create the redeeming person of Little Dorrit with the necessary strength, but also to his frustrating the logic of his symbolic scheme in the interests of an ending which rewards virtue and punishes vice. The overt meaning may be briefly described thus: Arthur Clennam, ruined in the Merdle crash, feels guilty at having speculated and lost the money of his partner, Daniel Doyce. Imprisoned in the Marshalsea, his naturally melancholy disposition causes him to fall into a decline. Little Dorrit appears and offers him her love and, therefore, her money. But he will not, as a scrupulous man, accept her money, nor, therefore, her person. From this impasse he is saved by the discovery that she has lost all her money in the smash and by the reappearance of Doyce, who has prospered in a foreign country which is not under the sway of the Circumlocution Office. His debts paid, his partnership re-established, he marries Little Dorrit and together they leave the Marshalsea.

To this one must say that what we are obviously intended to applaud is in places moral and emotional lunacy. Let us consider the scene in which he refuses Little Dorrit:

'. . . If, in the by-gone days when this was your home and when this was your dress, I had understood myself (I speak only of myself) better, and had read the secrets of my own breast more distinctly; if, through my reserve and self-mistrust, I had discerned a light that I see brightly now when it has passed far away, and my weak footsteps can never overtake it; if I had then known, and told you that I loved and honoured you, not as the poor child I used to call you, but as a woman whose true hand would raise me high above myself, and make me a far happier and better man; if I had so used the opportunity there is no recalling—as I wish I had, O I wish I had!—and if something had kept us apart then, when I was moderately thriving,

and when you were poor; I might have met your noble offer of
your fortune, dearest girl, with other words than these, and
still have blushed to touch it. But, as it is, I must never touch it,
never!'

She besought him, more pathetically and earnestly, with her
little supplicatory hand, than she could have done in any words.

'I am disgraced enough, my Little Dorrit. I must not descend
so low as that, and carry you—so dear, so generous, so good—
down with me. GOD bless you, GOD reward you! It is past.'

He took her in his arms, as if she had been his daughter.
(p. 760)

We are surely meant to applaud this as the antithesis of that
greed for money which obsesses so many of the other characters.
But in fact it is a proclamation that the power of money—the
fear of seeming mercenary in the world's eyes (for Little Dorrit
would not believe him mercenary)—is so great in his mind that
to it he will sacrifice, not only his love, but hers. It reminds us of
Mr Dorrit's bestowing of his imprisonment and degradation as a
portion on his daughter. Clennam can only accept Little Dorrit's
love when she, too, is ruined and when she can proclaim her
satisfaction at the virtual re-establishment of her life in the
Marshalsea with her father:

'Never to part, my dearest Arthur; never any more until the
last! I never was rich before, I never was proud before, I never
was happy before, I am rich in being taken by you, I am proud
in having been resigned by you, I am happy in being with you
in this prison, as I should be happy in coming back to it with
you, if it should be the will of GOD, and comforting and serving
you with all my love and truth. I am yours anywhere, everywhere! I love you dearly! I would rather pass my life here with
you, and go out daily, working for our bread, than I would have
the greatest fortune that ever was told, and be the greatest lady
that ever was honoured. O, if poor papa may only know how
blest at last my heart is, in this room where he suffered for so
many years!' (pp. 817–18)

From this grim fulfilment of the logic of the book, with Arthur
Clennam glorying in his imprisonment as his mother and Mr
Dorrit have gloried in theirs, and little Dorrit confined within
her role as the angel in the prison, they are released by Daniel
Doyce.

In terms of quasi-historical plausibility we might be prepared to accept this timely reappearance of Doyce with an offer of money and the continuation of a useful job: invention, smothered at home by the Circumlocution Office, finds its rewards abroad. But the world which Dickens has created in the novel has a shape and a logic which demands a conclusion in its own terms and not merely in those of factual plausibility. The world presented is that of society, England, a prison of many cells; 'abroad', as we have seen it throughout the novel, is virtually an extension of the Marshalsea; the whole of the Dorrits' travels have been shown as an inability to escape from the pressures of life in England. Doyce's successful industry in a foreign country as a solution of the problems of those caught in English imprisonment is a solution in terms outside those of the novel.

Clennam and Little Dorrit choose to be married from the Marshalsea, but before they leave Arthur, at Little Dorrit's request, burns unread the paper which tells the secret of his birth, the story of sexual passion between his father and a protégée of Frederick Dorrit. This is ostensibly done to save Mrs Clennam from shame and Arthur from suffering; but for an Arthur who, after his rejection of love for Little Dorrit, takes her in his arms 'as if she had been his daughter' this burning of the truth of sexual passion seems appropriate.

Not, of course, that we could imagine Little Dorrit responding to any manifestation of sexual passion. Dickens has fixed her too thoroughly as Little Dorrit, as perpetual mixture of daughter and little mother. When, for example, Clennam calls her 'Amy' she insists on being called by her accustomed name—'Never any other name' (p. 822). It is easy enough to say that this is a general inability in Dickens, that he can never in his novels conceive of powerful sexual feelings as other than destructive. But the inability is more damaging here than in most of his other works, because the logic of the issues demands such feelings. The whole of Clennam's self-imprisonment, his sense that 'Will, purpose, hope? All those lights were extinguished before I could sound the words' (p. 20), the paralysis of feeling which is re-doubled when he enters the Marshalsea, all come from his up-bringing by his mother as a child of sin. She has proclaimed that her aim is 'to bring him up in fear and trembling, and in a life of practical contrition for the sins that were heavy on his head before his entrance into this condemned world' (p. 777). She has succeeded; his upbringing has left him emotionally impotent.

If Little Dorrit is to re-enact her role as protecting daughter to an imprisoned Arthur, her virtual sexlessness is appropriate. But if she is to save him from his miserable sense of guilt, if he is to leave the Marshalsea and the state of inertia which belongs there, then she could only do so by the power of a love akin to that whose suppression and punishment has cast a blight over his life.*

The weaknesses of *Little Dorrit* are ones to which, in themselves, we are likely to be especially intolerant, but for which we are nevertheless probably rather ready to forgive Dickens. They are weaknesses which we tend to find unsurprising in English novels of this period, and we feel them to be for a novelist who, like Dickens, is working so close to a popular tradition almost unavoidable. The gentlemanly refusal of proffered money from a woman, the burning of an unread letter, the sexless little mother —all these are stock features. Dickens's attempt to frustrate the grim logic of his symbolic pattern damages the last few chapters; in retrospect we tend to think of them as local weaknesses, the price we have to pay for a novel which is both an assured performance by a great popular writer and a coherent and complex metaphor for his society.

* In Chapter 7 I discuss further the interpretation of the last chapters and various problems concerned with such interpretations.

' "Superintendent," said K., "you interpret the letter so well that nothing remains of it but a signature on a blank sheet of paper. Don't you see that in doing this you depreciate Klamm's name, which you pretend to respect?" '

Franz Kafka: *The Castle*, translated by Willa and Edwin Muir

6

Interpretation and over-interpretation

For novels like *The Way We Live Now* we have a useful and generally accepted descriptive term—realistic. For a novel like *Little Dorrit* we have not. There is no especial virtue in amplitude of critical terminology, yet such a term would be convenient, for a considerable number of English novels and a higher proportion of American ones belong recognizably to this genre. The chief distinguishing feature of such books is that they are organized around systems of key metaphors or symbols or images, which direct our attention within a fictional world inhabited by characters presented with varying degrees of stylization and not usually with much concern for realistic psychological detail. These characters are often described as being 'larger than life'—by which is meant that they are summations of simplified, often basic, human traits unblurred by the minutiae of daily life and all its accidents. The settings and the landscapes of these stories are usually created as contributory parts of the themes, and the effect of this is often to seem to break down the barrier between the animate and the inanimate. These novels, therefore, usually yield up reserves of meaning when we consider them in terms of symbol, metaphor, imagery. Besides the novels of Dickens, obvious examples are *Wuthering Heights* and *Moby Dick*. In practice one of the most distinctive characteristics which they present when we discuss them is that they cry out for interpretation. They are the novels about which much criticism—especially in America—now accumulates, and I think it would be fairly generally agreed that they have attracted a good deal of over-interpretation and perverse interpretation.

If, as Northrop Frye wishes, we could resurrect the term

'romance' it would be a suitable one to describe them, but it seems too late to strip it of its associations of triviality and radical untruthfulness to human experience. 'Metaphorical novel' would do very well were it not that all novels are in a very real sense metaphorical and the fact is too important to risk confusion. I shall follow the practice of calling them, for want of a better term and though I do not much like it, 'symbolic novels', a name which they are often given and which seems appropriate because it points to what I have described as their central characteristic—that, throughout them, used not locally but as a structural principle, there are objects or actions or relationships which stand for something more than their plain or surface meaning.

Symbolism is, of course, an inevitable and inherent part of all novels. All novels tend to be taken as specific embodiments of general truths. The most unsophisticated reader's comment, 'But life isn't like that', cannot be controverted by finding a parallel from real life to the particular concatenation of farfetched circumstances about which he is complaining; he is demanding—and quite rightly demanding—what in the terminology of another age Johnson called 'just representations of general nature'; he can only be reconciled to the book by being shown that, eccentric though these happenings may be, yet they embody a truth of some general validity, that they are an acceptable metaphor for life. Within realistic novels those happenings, say, which are illustrative of the general tenor of the work are also in their way symbolic, but, being merely a description of the way in which detail operates upon the mind, this normally can go without saying. To point out that the jewels which Dorothea discusses with Celia in the first chapter of *Middlemarch* are symbols of the temptations of the world which she rejects and makes a virtue of rejecting and which yet tempt her is to make a statement which is perfectly true and perfectly useless; its only effect is to suggest that one's sole acquaintance with either jewellery or young women has been obtained from nineteenth-century fiction.

Realistic novels normally require for their effect some sense of the accidental, and details function to support the impression of the reality of a scene or a happening or a person. When, in the first chapter of *The Way We Live Now*, Mr Booker is described as 'a bald-headed old man of sixty, with a large family of daughters, one of whom was a widow dependent on him with two little children', we need to feel that the answer to the question 'Why was he bald-headed?' is simply 'Because he had lost his hair', and that the *Literary Chronicle* might have been edited by a man with a luxuriant crop. The detail is, of course, chosen by the writer because it appears significant; in this case it is significant of the kind of person whom we are likely to be prepared to believe will find himself filling the editorial chair; it is not significant as part of an overriding scheme of significances. Similarly when, in *Pride and Prejudice*, Jane Bennet catches cold as a result of riding to visit the Bingleys we feel that, within the terms of early nineteenth-century medicine, this is the sort of accident which might well occur and which is thus a convenient and acceptable device in the plot. To hypothesize that it is significant because the 'Bennet world' 'catches cold' when it goes to the 'Bingley world' would not merely be foolish; it would be destructive of the effect of the book.

I am not suggesting that it is never useful to talk about symbolism in a discussion of realistic novels; clearly there are occasions when we can, by invoking symbolism, point to an impression of unity or to an implied judgment of value. But to rush into explanations of why something is as it is and not otherwise in terms of symbolic plan is to risk destroying a vital element in our response. There is, for example, a very striking scene near the beginning of *Anna Karenina* which clearly belongs within that series of recurring happenings which have the effect of a symbol, and which I have mentioned in chapter 3. But it is essential that the scene should first affect us as a natural, accidental, psychologically convincing happening with no suspicion of authorial planning. In Part I, chapter XXI, Anna, staying with the Oblonskys, leaves the drawing-room to go to her bedroom to fetch a photograph of her son. As she mounts the staircase Vronsky is shown into the house; she looks down from the landing and they see one another with feelings of uneasiness which are, to both of them at the time, inexplicable. They have previously met at the railway station; Vronsky is first to declare his love at a railway station; Anna is to die at a railway station and Vronsky is last to be seen walking up and down a station platform. Many of the most crucial scenes in which either of them is concerned are to take place in trains, carriages, streets. The scene on the staircase is effective in part because it belongs with this emphasis on the unrooted, travelling quality of the passion of Anna and Vronsky, the fact that their love cannot be expressed in the rooms where people in society are safe. Anna is caught by her uneasiness on a staircase between the safety of the family drawing-room and the safety of the bedroom where she has the photograph of her son. To point to this, to say that this meeting place, like so many others in the novel, is of symbolic significance, is usefully to indicate a unity of effect in the novel which enforces a judgment. But we must start with a recognition of the unforced plausibility of the scene. We must feel that it is natural at this moment that Anna, away from home, would want to show the photograph of her son. We must be aware of the density of effect which comes in part, for example, from the fact that Oblonsky's explanation that Vronsky had called about 'a dinner they were giving next day to a celebrity who was visiting Moscow' is a euphemistic account of the proposed supper for the opera singer, with all the implications which this has for Oblonsky's reconciliation with his wife and Vronsky's habitual way of life and the change which is to come over it. If we start by looking at the scene as part of a sustained symbol we are likely, especially in the present state of criticism, to short-circuit these necessary complex responses and replace them by something much simpler and much more apparently contrived.

But the manner in which symbols function in symbolic novels is very different. If we do not read *Little Dorrit* in terms of its central symbols we are likely to miss the point of the book and we shall probably end up complaining that it is a shapeless novel. If we fail to observe that Melville's Captain Ahab is a nineteenth-century Faust and the hunt for the White Whale a bodying forth of Faust's self-destructive quest, our loss will be more than a minor and local weakness. If we do not recognize that Wuthering Heights and Thrushcross Grange represent two incompatible worlds of value, each elucidated by the imagery in which it is described, we shall never understand what it is that gives such convincing force to Emily Brontë's story. If the structural principle of a novel is symbolic, then it is upon the symbols that —largely though not exclusively—we must focus our attention.

Two problems arise for the reader of symbolic novels—that of knowing how to determine between two or more possible and incompatible interpretations (about which I speak in the next chapter) and that of knowing how far to go in scrutinizing detail for symbolic meaning. Of these the latter is—certainly at the moment, in the present state of criticism—the more important.

If all the main actions and scenes of a book are to be read in a symbolic light, then we will tend to scrutinize the details of those actions and scenes by the same illumination. When, at her first appearance in chapter II of *Little Dorrit*, Miss Wade is described as 'Seeming to watch the reflection of the water, as it made a silver quivering on the bars of the lattice' (p. 23: all page references are to the Oxford Illustrated Dickens), it does not seem accidental that she is looking out between bars. Is it significant that she is looking out at the sea which is the final, cleansing destiny of those polluted rivers which stand, in various places in the book, for the river of life? Is it in any way significant that the quivering is 'silver'—in a novel which is so much concerned with the power of money and in a chapter which opens with Mr Meagles, to whom she has just been speaking, rattling his money in his pocket? And so on. Presumably we have to decide at what point to stop scrutinizing detail for symbolic significance.

To speak in terms of deciding makes the matter sound very conscious and very systematic, and no doubt we very often read correctly without being aware that we have made any decisions, so that it appears as if each book dictates its own terms and that only those who suffer from perverse ingenuity or blunt in-sensitivity go astray. But this is to underrate the extent to which literary response is to some extent a learned response. We all move towards the happy state of naturally reading aright by thinking about our responses; discussion with other readers sometimes makes us change our minds. A proper response to the direction of a novel is the result of weighing, in relation to this book and to other books, arguments which could be sustained rationally. Our decisions may not always be conscious but we must try to bring them into consciousness if we are to convey them to others, including those others with whom we disagree.

There is another possible objection to my suggestion that we have to decide where to draw a line. It is that we do not need to decide because a symbolic effect may be possible but not neces-sary, that a reader who takes naturally to a symbolic reading will perceive resonances which may deepen the effect of a pas-sage for him, while another reader will take description at its face value and might be put out by suggestions of anything else. Such an objector would point out that even the most tenuous symbolic significances, so long as they do not clash with other elements in a work, will not change its meaning for the reader; to be aware of them is thus, so to say, a bonus for certain kinds of reader. In my example from the description of Miss Wade's looking out of the window he might say that we are not going against the general meaning of the book if we interpret it by saying that for Miss Wade even the contemplation of the ultimate end of the stream of life is touched by the concept of money, since she is in the room with Mr Meagles and is later to be concerned with the conflict between freedom and the power of property. But the effect of a novel is not simply the 'meaning' in this limited sense; the reader who is attentive to every verbal echo is reading a very different *kind* of book from one who takes the reflection of the water as merely a description of a plausible scene. He is likely, for example, to have less of a sense of the characters as autonomous beings in a world where accident plays its part. Moreover the whole suggestion of freedom of consumer choice seems to me to be illogical. Of course there will be differences of response, but presumably we believe that there is a proper reading for that potentially perfect reader who is as necessary a character as the law's reasonable man. To put the matter in terms of this passage: would we point out the possible significance of 'silver' to someone who has not noticed it? If not, would we point out the significance of the ultimate end of the river of life? If not, would we point out the significance of the bars? If not, would we mention the overriding symbol of prison to someone who has been blind to it? Unless we make a practice of never commenting on novels at all, we would be bound to reach a point at which—whatever theoretical case for freedom of interpretation we might argue—we would draw a line and would be faced by the need to justify it.

The chief current aberration of criticism of symbolic novels (and sometimes of other novels, too) seems to me to be a belief that no line needs to be drawn, that it is useful to pursue symbolic significance, verbal echoes, patterns of imagery to an unlimited extent. Interpretation of this kind is very easy, largely because it normally takes place within a framework of relevance so loose as to make it very hard to confute an interpretation by arguments about whether or not a passage will bear a certain symbolic meaning. We are therefore all familiar with masterpieces of ingenuity which set a great space between the interpreter and the common reader (or, let us say, the uncommon reader of earlier generations) and fill the space with significances relentlessly extracted from a selection of the minutest details. Against this we often make appeals to common sense and literary tact. Unfortunately one man's common sense and tact is another man's timidity and obtuseness. We need to argue rationally with a tendency to over-interpretation, not least because, if we consider the reasons for it, we see that it is unlikely to diminish and that the reasons for it have wider implications concerning the kinds of attention which we ought to give to novels.

One obvious cause, which need not detain us long, can be summed up as the urge or need to publish. There are at the moment a very large number of professional teachers in the British Isles, the Commonwealth and, particularly, the United States. They are all encouraged—some are virtually compelled—to publish books and articles. The supply of novels worth serious discussion has nothing like kept pace with the supply of critics. Thus there is intense critical activity upon a limited number of writers, mass descents of interpreters, in particular, on those writers who seem to give most scope for interpretation. If one reads through the extant criticism of any work by Conrad, Melville, or Faulkner, say, it is hard not to feel that many of the critics are driven by the pressure of competition to achieve some originality by placing more and more weight on smaller and smaller bearing surfaces. This tendency is not likely to be reversed, and may well get worse. But some of the other possible reasons—those concerned rather with critical than with market forces—are related to critical attitudes which are discussable and thus changeable.

The critic of novels, unlike the critic of poetry, can never forget that the vast majority of novels are ephemeral and thus neither demand nor repay close attention. Most people form their reading habits largely in terms of that ephemeral mass of writing. He has probably done so himself. He is very likely still to read such works for one reason or another, at one time or another. There are those who, recovering from illness or childbirth, sitting in a deckchair in the garden amid children, lying in bed with failing concentration, either eschew fiction or confine themselves to Dostoevsky, James, Beckett, Mann. But most of us do not, and one of the effects of this situation is that we emphasize and re-emphasize the necessity for close attention to those works which deserve it. We cultivate a kind of slow brood-ing over them, paying particular attention to those aspects of them which are absent in the ephemeral. We add to this a wholly desirable emphasis on the essential unity of a work of art not only as against the habit of reading ephemeral works 'to find out what happens next' but also against the criticism of novels—now fortunately out of date—which discussed plot, characters and style separately. Critics who were opposing this kind of criticism often found the unity which they were seeking in patterns of imagery and structures of symbols. While this divisive criticism was common the emphasis was salutary, but critical habits may outlive the situation which provoked them. This one was reinforced by the need, earlier in the century, to fight for the acceptance of novels which did not appear to tell a story, nor to put the main focus of interest upon the study of character in the traditional way. Here again the principle of unity was often seen in the symbolic structure and it was felt, naturally enough, that its importance was in no danger of being over-emphasized. But it seems now that this often led critics to overlook the degree to which a novel is a series of experiences of varying kinds and of varying intensities and the extent to which useful statements about its essential unity should take this into account.

We have probably been hindered from developing an adequate conception of this—an adequate conception of narrative—because the great successes of modern criticism have tended to be in the close reading of relatively short works—those works, in fact, where we give virtually the same kind of attention to all parts of the work and where the relationship between the 'spatial' and the 'temporal' aspects of our reading causes little bother. One consequence of this, as has been pointed out, has been a decrease in our ability to read really lengthy poems. The case is the same with novels. Our ability to read closely, to elucidate patterns of imagery and to seize on symbolic overtones, has not been accompanied by any comparable concern for an understanding of narrative in terms of variation of pace, of tone, of demanded attention. It is in a consideration of such matters as these, I believe, that we shall find help in determining criteria for deciding when we are in danger of over-interpreting symbolic works.

I therefore propose to set out, somewhat schematically and for exemplary purposes, some possible interpretations of a number of passages from *Little Dorrit*—those concerned with the Iron Bridge, where Arthur Clennam and Little Dorrit go to talk in quiet in Book I, chapter IX, where they meet by accident in chapter XXII, and which they come to associate with one another —and to suggest some principles by which we may judge their validity. I arrange these interpretations in an ascending order of specificity, which is also an ascending order of ingenuity and, I think, a probably descending order of general acceptability. But, in a novel which is organized around a number of key symbols and in which detail so often takes on meaning from its relation to the symbolic scheme, none of them is, I think, obviously perverse. If we are to judge any of them as unacceptable it will be in some other terms than that, regarded in isolation, they are inconsistent with the main themes of the novel.

(1) The Iron Bridge is a perfectly natural meeting place; when Clennam first proposes walking over it, he says that it is 'an escape from the noise of the streets' (p. 95); it is 'as quiet after the roaring streets, as though it had been open country' (p. 96). The view from it is described several times with emphasis on the same particulars—'the piles of city roofs and chimneys among which the smoke was rolling heavily, and . . . the wilderness of masts on the river, and the wilderness of steeples on the shore . . .' (p. 99).

We are invited to see it as having an associative value for both Little Dorrit and Arthur Clennam; they choose it in preference to other crossings of the river or other places to walk, despite having to pay to cross it. Are we not justified in observing that, bearing as it does this symbolic sense, it is, though the best meeting place available, nevertheless still an iron bridge across a dirty river with a gloomy view, so that the details of description emphasize the pathos of Little Dorrit and of her love for Clennam?

(2) But we can be more specific, if we choose; we can extract more meaning from the details. The river which is spanned by the bridge is used by Dickens in a number of passages in the book as an emblem of human life, starting fresh and clean, growing polluted, ending at the sea. At London it is described as a foul sewer, rolling 'its turbid tide between two frowning wildernesses of secrets' (p. 542). The couple, then, we may say, can only find privacy on an iron bridge (conceivably calling up

associations of coldness, hardness, man-madeness) above an image of the corruption of human life, half way between two lots of secrets.

(3) We can press the point farther, relating the details of description to passages elsewhere in the book which may be thought to bear on them. The wildernesses of masts and steeples hark back to Clennam's view of London on his return from abroad. There, in chapter III, the 'church bells, of all degrees of dissonance, sharp and flat, cracked and clear, fast and slow' form part of the horror of London and contribute to the sense of the oppressions of religion, the prison-like puritanism of his upbringing. May we not say, therefore, that the steeples from which the bells ring are peculiarly in place here and that they are rightly linked with the masts which remind us of commerce, and commerce, in particular, which involves exile, like his, from one's native land?

Their sense of escape, then, is ironically fallacious. Little Dorrit deceives herself when she daydreams of Arthur loving her, because their meeting place, the bridge which she especially associates with him, is inherently connected by trains of imagery with everything which makes it impossible for him to feel love, with oppressive religion, with a sense of the corruption of life, of youth destroyed in exile, with the symbol of London, the great prison.

(4) Finally, we can bear down even more heavily on a specific verbal echo. When Clennam and Little Dorrit first walk there in search of quiet: 'Thus they emerged upon the Iron Bridge, which was as quiet after the roaring streets, as though it had been open country' (p. 96). In the much-admired last sentence of the novel there is an echo of this and we might claim that it indicates where escape, impossible upon the bridge, is truly to be found: 'They went quietly down into the roaring streets, inseparable and blessed; and as they passed along in sunshine and shade, the noisy and the eager, and the arrogant and the froward and the vain, fretted, and chafed, and made their usual uproar.' We might say that the sentence looks back to the emphatic contrast of the first chapter—'Sun and Shadow'—between sunshine and shade, the dazzling and oppressive sunshine of the world outside the Marseilles prison and the gloomy shadow within. Now, in all senses free at last, Clennam and Little Dorrit can move 'in sunshine and shade'. Similarly, it looks back to the description of

the Iron Bridge, the meeting place where love was hopeless, and the repetition of the phrase 'roaring streets' tells us that they have found freedom because they have not sought to escape from the streets but have gone down into them.

Have I, at some point in this chain of speculations become too ingenious? Have I, in the common phrase, begun to 'read things into' the book? How can this be decided? It is important to reiterate that none of the interpretations is wantonly perverse; each, considered on its own, is consonant with our other feelings about the book. We are not here concerned with re-interpretation, with any attempt to effect a radical reorientation of our responses, but only with the possibility of over-interpretation. If we decide that any of the interpretations is too ingenious it cannot be by considering it in isolation and controverting it logically.

It is equally important in our search for criteria to realize that not all the problems of what we should scrutinize for symbolic significance and what we should accept simply as given detail come from the perversities of over-industrious critics. The writer, too, may not be faithful to his inspiration. It is presumably Dickens's intention that Mr Merdle's name should suggest 'merde'; yet most readers will surely decide, if they notice the bilingual pun and its symbolic reference, that it is as inert a piece of ingenuity as any critic's speculations. Again, it seems most likely that the jingle Marseilles/Marshalsea (more obvious in the anglicized pronunciation of Marseilles which was probably that of Dickens and the majority of his readers) is either intentional or that the choice of Marseilles rather than any other staging port on the Mediterranean littoral was determined, albeit not consciously, because of a similarity of sound which underlies the similarities of incarceration in both places (Rigaud lords it as a gentleman over Cavaletto just as Mr Dorrit lords it over the Collegians, the gaoler's daughter is a proto-Little Dorrit, etc.). Here, too, I think that most readers exclude the pun from their responses to the book on the grounds—if they think about the reasons—that though indubitably 'there' it does not contribute to the kind of significance which the book as a whole creates. It is tempting—to take an example from another writer—to believe that James Joyce's comment, late in life, that perhaps he had over-elaborated Ulysses was a recognition that the inclusion in various sections of that novel of systematized references to colours, precious stones, organs of the body and so forth was a form of symbolic reference either inert or, if perceived, actually hostile to the main effect of his work.

I think that the existence of significances of this kind which are deliberate or which we feel sure were part of the pattern within the writer's mind, but which we nevertheless succeed in excluding from our own responses (or wish we had never noticed because we cannot succeed in excluding them), provides us with an indication of the right kind of criterion to apply to our problem of how closely to scrutinize. The question is not, as it is commonly phrased, 'Is the effect there or are we reading it into the book?' but rather: 'Does this effect function valuably within the book or does it, if admitted, harmfully modify our responses to the whole? Can we only pay this kind of attention at the expense of others?' There will remain wide scope for disagreement between individual readers, but it will be disagreement which admits of discussion only in literary terms rather than, as so often, in terms more appropriate to cryptograms and puzzles. Above all, it will force us to take into account the variety of ways in which we react to a novel, to speak of our reactions to characters and to the flow of narration, for example, in relation to the perception of possibly symbolic detail.

Two basic features of all novels—features shared by realistic novels and by symbolic ones—indicate the kind of literary terms within which the problem needs to be discussed. They are features so basic as to appear almost tautologous: novels are about people in whom we take some kind of interest as persons, and novels are of some length.

It is, of course, true that the kind of interest we take in characters varies from one novel to another. In as thoroughly realistic a novel as *Anna Karenina*, say, we have a striking impression of the people as autonomous beings living in a contingent world. Novels in which a symbolic scheme plays a large part seem by contrast almost inevitably to present a determinist view of human affairs. This is particularly true of those, like *Little Dorrit*, in which the guiding symbols are announced in unambiguous terms at the beginning. Much of the reader's satisfaction comes from observing how far the characters and their actions are subject to the key symbols which the writer has established— how far, that is, the symbolic pattern provides not merely a formal unity but also a convincing emotional and moral one. It is this, for example, which contributes so greatly to the force of the scene in which Mr Dorrit, dying, shows that he has never truly been freed from the Marshalsea. But, though appearing to possess far less free will than the characters in realistic novels, it is essential that those whom we encounter in symbolic ones should not seem to be entirely fettered within a world which, down to its tiniest detail, functions as the expression of a scheme of prearranged data. We need to feel some freedom of choice even in so thoroughgoing a denial of freedom as the scene in Kafka's *The Castle* in which K. hopes to waylay Klamm (a scene which, incidentally, sums up the situation of the tramps in *Waiting for Godot* and indeed may have suggested it): ' "You'll miss him in any case, whether you go or stay," said the gentleman, expressing himself bluntly, but showing an unexpected consideration for K.'s line of thought. "Then I would rather wait for him and miss him," said K. defiantly.' If all sense of a character's possible freedom vanishes, then our sense of him as a moral agent whose plight concerns us will evaporate too.

More important, however—and much less generally considered—are the consequences of the relatively great length of novels. These consequences manifest themselves in two ways which concern us here: in the question of whether a certain kind of attention to part of a novel causes us to lose our sense of the whole, and the other question of how far different parts of a book demand different kinds of attention.

We sometimes speak as if the perfect reader is a man of unlimited sensitivity and receptivity, able to scrutinize the smallest detail without ever losing the sense of the whole. I do not believe that he exists; I believe rather in critics with unlimited time. I believe, that is, that serial activity is often mistaken for simultaneous activity. We often speak as if the first, relatively simple reading of a novel is replaced, on a second reading, by a more complex one and that, in its turn, by a more complex one still, but that, throughout, the initial impact of the book remains in its essentials. It seems more likely that certain *necessary* simple reactions cannot coexist with some more sophisticated ones and are replaced by them.* There can come a moment, for example,

---

* One unavoidable manifestation of this is our inability to be surprised by the happenings in books which we know well. The first time we read Forster's *The Longest Journey*, Gerald's death is a shock. Later, we know before we start that he is going to be broken up in the football match. There is very little that we can do about this; but nobody ever seems to mention it, presumably because they think it is so obvious. Unfortunately, in a critical

in which we not only feel that Arthur Clennam and Little Dorrit could not choose to meet save on a symbolically significant bridge, but when our minds are so actively engaged in speculations about the farther reaches of this symbolism that we lose all sense of them as two people meeting there at a certain point in the development of their relationship.

When we consider how far different parts of a novel demand different kinds of attention we become particularly aware of the influence upon us of the kind of criticism which has been most fruitful in the discussion of poetry. A short poem appears to be emancipated from time, to exist in our perception in a single moment as a single experience, so that we apply the same degree of attention to all parts of it—indeed, we do not think of it as having parts; it is a whole. Some novels, especially symbolic ones, certainly demand to a greater extent than others this kind of untemporal reading; the symbolic structure may only reveal itself fully in retrospect. But a work of the length of a novel—and the same is true of a long poem—must have as part of its effect the experience of the passage of time, not merely within the story, but in the process of reading. It is a series of experiences whose succession is a part of their meaning. Some of these experiences will be of greater intensity, even of greater specific memorability, than others. The variations of intensity which manifest themselves as variations of reading speed and in the nature of our attention are an integral part of the effect. A reading, or—as it usually is—a critical argument about the meaning, of a novel which flattens out these variations of tension gains certain kinds of apparent significance at the expense of losing other and often more important ones.

Let us apply these criteria to the four possible interpretations of the significance of the Iron Bridge.

The reader who does not perceive meaning (1)—that the best meeting place which they can find is nevertheless gloomy and ominous—is surely reading too superficially, for he is totally failing to relate the actual meetings to the rest of the book. The dirt of the river and the oppressive horror of the city are described

age when everything is talked about at such length, what is not mentioned is likely to be ignored. In the case of Gerald's death, I think that we can carry the initial shock in our minds and take it into account, but often later readings must weaken some initial reactions or knock them out altogether. I think, for example, that my inability, in reading 'Heart of Darkness', to wonder what Marlow is going to find when he reaches Kurtz is a pity.

so frequently and so forcefully that only a very episodic attention could account for forgetting them. Moreover, on their first meeting there, Clennam reflects on the pathos of Little Dorrit's seeing the Marshalsea coffee house as a majestic hotel. It is a simple train of thought which leads to the reflection that the open-air meeting place, which seems like freedom after the prison, is far from ideal.

From the beginning, moreover, the river has been described in such a way as to lead us towards meaning (2)—that the river stands for human and social corruption and the city for an obscurity which is more than physical. The river is an important part of the description of London in chapter III. 'Through the heart of the town a deadly sewer ebbed and flowed, in the place of a fine fresh river' (pp. 28–9) is how it is first mentioned. At the conclusion of chapter VII, within a few pages of the first meeting on the Iron Bridge, the river is used as a metaphor for the people going in and out of prison as part of a description of Little Dorrit herself: 'Innocent, in the mist through which she saw her father, and the prison, and the turbid living river that flowed through it and flowed on' (p. 78). We must add, I think, that a river takes rather naturally a symbolic colouring; the image is sufficiently traditional for us to accept it without the expenditure of a great deal of energy.

When they first meet on the Iron Bridge, then, we will tend to have in our minds—not, perhaps, very clearly formulated—a sense of the river as suggesting the flowing of corrupted life and an impression of the city on either bank as labyrinthine and threatening. Far from clashing with a sense of the characters as autonomous beings, this will probably reinforce our sense of the perplexities in which they stand: Clennam is groping for some connection between the mysteries which he feels surrounding his own family and those which surround hers. He comes from a house which he believes to contain certain mysteries and which stands upon one bank and she from the Marshalsea, which contains other mysteries, and which stands upon the other bank.

Before their next meeting on the Iron Bridge Dickens develops the image of the river in the scenes at the Meagles's house, and at the conclusion of the meeting, when Clennam is puzzling about Little Dorrit's feelings, there is a substantial verbal echo in: 'his own associations of the troubled river running beneath the bridge with the same river higher up, its changeless tune upon the prow of the ferry-boat, so many miles an hour the peaceful flowing of the stream, here the rushes, there the lilies, nothing uncertain or unquiet' (p. 263).

To recognize the symbolic associations of the river, therefore, does not seem to me to run the reader into any danger of losing the sense of the whole by concentrating on a part. The river has from the beginning been given a symbolic significance (and, as I said, rivers take such significances more easily than many objects), and this is increased by specific verbal repetition. The significance is rather general; it does not demand a degree of elucidation which obliges us to concentrate on it to the exclusion of other elements in the passages.

But I think that when, moving on to meaning (3), we do become more specific, we are asking for attention to be withdrawn both from our sense of the characters as living beings and from our sense of the whole. The occasion of the first meeting is a concentrated one; in terms of the development of the plot and of the characters a great deal is happening: Clennam asks whether Little Dorrit has ever heard the name Clennam before; he is concerned about her fragility on a rough day; she is making excuses for her father's begging and explaining the high regard which others have for him; she talks about the Marshalsea and tells Clennam that the Barnacles seem interested in Mr Dorrit's case; Clennam learns of her fear that her father will discover she earns money. It is, in fact, one of the most closely-packed scenes between them. They are exploring one another's reactions and thus to gain the full effect of the scene we need to be alive to the answers which they give and to the possibilities of different answers. It is one of the scenes in which the reality of Little Dorrit is most clearly felt and this is because she is seen, in the space of a few pages, subject to a number of different feelings and causing a number of different feelings in Clennam. Thus we are obliged to pay attention to the ebb and flow of feeling. We cannot, I think, do so if at the same time we are speculating about the symbolic significance of the wilderness of steeples. The association 'steeples—bells—puritan upbringing—inhibition of feeling' is too tenuous, it requires the expenditure of too much mental energy, to coexist with the immediate sense of these people at this moment in a developing relationship. We can narrow down the argument to one sentence—the one in which the phrase occurs. Little Dorrit bursts out about the helplessness of her father, but she quickly recovers herself, because she is not accustomed to think about herself:

> He had but glanced away at the piles of city roofs and chimneys among which the smoke was rolling heavily, and at the wilderness of masts on the river, and the wilderness of steeples on the shore, indistinctly mixed together in the stormy haze, when she was again as quiet as if she had been plying her needle in his mother's room. (p. 99)

The steeples, in fact, are part of a distraction from the main drive of the action. There is no invitation to us to pause on them; if we do so, and call into our minds the associations which I summarized under meaning (3) we shall lose our sense of the forward movement, both in terms of the movement of the passage (and thus the novel) as a narrative whole and also in terms of the developing relationship between the two people. Here Dickens is surely using the steeples and the masts merely as given detail; they contribute to the verisimilitude of the scene, and that is all.*

The arguments which I have advanced against (3) apply with equal force against (4) unless it could be shown, as it can with some writers, that Dickens commonly works on us by precise but inconspicuous verbal echoes and that this fact sensitizes us to them. In fact Dickens's verbal echoes, normally, are extremely (sometimes painfully) obvious. The two uses of 'roaring streets' are separated by sixty-one chapters and, though the last sentence of a novel is one which we tend to read very slowly and which has great emphasis and where, since it is often in both senses the 'conclusion' of the book, we are right to expect every rift to be loaded with ore for which we must dig pertinaciously, the first

---

* In various places in the book, too, Dickens uses these details for a local heightening of emotional tension. When John Chivery sees the scene on a Sunday it is described as being more free from smoke than on weekdays (for Clennam, one must suppose, it would have been even gloomier on a Sunday). When Mrs Clennam crosses the river to tell her story 'the clear steeples of the many churches looked as if they had advanced out of the murk that usually enshrouded them and come much nearer' (p. 793). The view of the shipping suggests to old Nandy 'what he would do if he had a ship full of gold coming home to him' (p. 367). If we should endeavour to fit the whole of each scene into a consistent symbolic scheme we should certainly find it difficult. Nandy's dreams of fortune are innocent; commercial London as seen by Arthur Clennam (and, in general, by Dickens) is oppressive. There must be room in the book for both and any symbolic scheme must be loose enough to allow both.

occurrence is inconspicuous: 'Thus they emerged upon the Iron Bridge, which was as quiet after the roaring streets, as though it had been open country.' It would be quite unreasonable to expect the reader to treasure these two words for significances which might accrue to them later. It can only be recalled when the end of the book is reached or perceived at a second reading. Such a recall would require a feat of memory which is totally incredible. The kind of emphasis placed in the first chapter on the contrast of sunshine and shade is such that its recurrence in the last sentence is, quite possibly, recognizable, but 'roaring streets' asks no more to be carried in the mind than thousands of other phrases. At a second reading the observation is possible, but only, I think, if the reader is so intent on observing the recurrence (and the hundreds of similar echoes which I have not, myself, noticed) that he can have no attention left for other matters.

The echo is, of course, 'there'. But surely it is there because any writer, as he works at a book, will tend to have many words and phrases and constructions in solution in his mind (this phenomenon is not confined to novelists; all of us are likely when writing letters, say, to find that we have, in the common phrase, 'got a word on the brain'). But the fact that it is 'there' does not mean that it is helpful to recognize the fact. The kind of mental activity required for registering 'roaring streets' is not compatible with the kind needed for responding to the other aspects of the scene in which the words occur. This means that if we dig it out in the process of multiple rereadings and make a point of registering it thereafter we shall distort the response needed for the passage.

There is one interesting characteristic of interpretative criticism which can be seen in my examples from Little Dorrit. As the interpretation demands more from us, so it makes larger claims. Interpretation (1) asks for a modest degree of attention, while (2) and (3) demand increasingly more and (4) requires no less than total sensitivity to every turn of phrase in the whole of the novel. If we give these various degrees of attention, (1) merely says that the writing underlines the pathos of the relationship, (2) relates this pathos to other themes in the book, (3) interprets the nature of the pathos in specific terms which may somewhat alter our conception of the relationship of the two people on the bridge, while (4) proposes a minor but general interpretation of the whole novel which might involve modifications in our response in various places throughout its length. Thus, as the obviousness and certainty grow less and the severity of the demands on us grow more, the significance of the interpretation grows greater. I do not think that this is merely a freakish effect of this example. The effect seems common in interpretative criticism and presumably this is because the critic does not feel that the writer is justified in demanding total attention and total recall unless the reward is going to be commensurate with the effort required. No book, we feel, would call on us for such efforts except for some great end. In practice, of course, it is often a matter of the critic making great demands on us, and it is the highly selective nature of the attention which he is demanding which makes his interpretations sometimes seem plausible. The extremely close attention to detail and the extraction of symbolic significance from it requires such concentration that we have no attention left for other, apparently more elementary, aspects, which might otherwise make us doubt the rightness of such interpretations. The effect sometimes resembles hypnosis.

The examples which I have extracted for purposes of discussion from *Little Dorrit* are peripheral—that is, they are not directly concerned with the main structural symbols of the book. It might seem that when we are dealing with the central symbols there will be less need to guard against over-interpretation. I believe that this is not so. It is true that here, more than anywhere else, certain words, phrases, images will come with great ease to the writer and, since we are likely to be especially alerted to them, we will certainly be more likely to register them. But this is not to say that equal and unremitting attention is demanded to every occurrence of them. On occasions they may logically be 'there' and yet the degree of attention which they need may be very slight. The degree of awareness which is demanded and the extent to which we are justified in extracting what is logically 'there' is determined by the same criteria as I have suggested in discussing the Iron Bridge. This can be seen very clearly if we consider one central train of imagery in *Wuthering Heights*.

There are, in this novel, two clusters of basically antithetical images—related, naturally enough, to the two houses with their significant names of Wuthering Heights and Thrushcross Grange. They are given most clearly in a speech of Catherine which is one of the best-known passages in the book:

My love for Linton is like the foliage in the woods: time will change it, I'm well aware, as winter changes the trees. My love for Heathcliff resembles the eternal rocks beneath: a source of little visible delight, but necessary. (pp. 99–100: all page references are to the World's Classics edition)

These images and their relationship to the issues of the book are developed, and developed in ways which demand for their full effect something in the nature of a 'spatial' consideration—that is, a response which plays back over the book and enriches some passages by taking into account later ones. When Heathcliff on his return tells Nelly to take up a message to Catherine and her husband, it is thus that Nelly sees the threatened couple:

> They sat together in a window whose lattice lay back against the wall, and displayed, beyond the garden trees and the wild green park, the valley of Gimmerton, with a long line of mist winding nearly to its top (for very soon after you pass the chapel, as you may have noticed, the sough that runs from the marshes joins a beck which follows the bend of the glen). Wuthering Heights rose above this silvery vapour; but our old house was invisible; it rather dips down on the other side. (p. 114)

We feel a symbolic resonance in the garden trees and the recollection of Wuthering Heights which rises above the vapour from the stream but which is, from the viewpoint of the married couple, invisible. But the force is far greater and the interplay of imagery more complex when we look back to this passage from a later one. Just before Heathcliff's last meeting with Catherine and her death, Nelly is carrying Heathcliff's letter in her pocket, the letter which she has decided not to give to Catherine until Edgar Linton's return:

> Gimmerton chapel bells were still ringing; and the full, mellow flow of the beck in the valley came soothingly on the ear. It was a sweet substitute for the yet absent murmur of the summer foliage, which drowned that music about the Grange when the trees were in leaf. At Wuthering Heights it always sounded on quiet days following a great thaw or a season of steady rain. And of Wuthering Heights Catherine was thinking as she listened: that is, if she thought or listened at all; but she had the vague, distant look I mentioned before, which expressed no recognition of material things either by ear or eye. (pp. 193–4)

With no comment about a change of purpose on the part of Nelly, it continues: ' "There's a letter for you, Mrs Linton," I said, gently inserting it in one hand that rested on her knee.'

A 'spatial' reading and a willingness, in effect, to slow up one's reading so that the 'garden trees', the 'beck', the 'summer foliage' the 'great thaw' can yield up a full symbolic significance is justified—is, indeed, in any adequate reading demanded— because the two passages are closely related and because they are both crucial moments in the plot and in the relationships of the characters. Each is concerned with the central issue of the book, the irruption into the world of Thrushcross Grange of the feelings of Wuthering Heights; each comes at a moment of suspension of action. But we should be going far wrong if we went on, in an endeavour to explicate the effect of the imagery of the novel, to assume that the same objects will always bear the same symbolic charge or even that they bear any appreciable charge at all. They may, while remaining within the central symbolic pattern, carry a relatively light charge and demand less of what I have called a slowing up of our reading. Such is the case with the interchange between Nelly and young Linton Heathcliff when she is taking him to Wuthering Heights:

> 'Is Wuthering Heights as pleasant a place as Thrushcross Grange?' he inquired, turning to take a last glance into the valley, whence a light mist mounted and formed a fleecy cloud on the skirts of the blue.
> 'It is not so buried in trees,' I replied, 'and it is not quite so large, but you can see the country beautifully, all round, and the air is healthier for you—fresher and dryer. (pp. 253–4)

The trees certainly exist within the same symbolic pattern as they do in the previous passages which we have considered, but to dwell on them, to spend very long speculating on the light mist and so forth, would be to destroy the necessary effect of relatively speedy narration which is here in operation and which must exist throughout a large part of the book if the full impressiveness is to be given by such moments as the two pauses of suspense before Heathcliff's irruptions.

The opening of chapter XXIII, too, shows very clearly the recurrence of what is elsewhere of great symbolic significance. Nelly Dean is describing how she took young Catherine to meet Linton at Wuthering Heights.

> The rainy night had ushered in a misty morning—half frost, half drizzle—and temporary brooks crossed our path, gurgling from the uplands. My feet were thoroughly wetted; I was cross and low; exactly the humour suited for making the most of these disagreeable things. We entered the farmhouse by the kitchen way, to ascertain whether Mr Heathcliff were really absent; because I put slight faith in his own affirmation. (p. 291)

If we are intent on pursuing significances we can assert that the beck which sounds after rain has clearly been associated with the resistless power of passion, that the foliage of Thrushcross Grange can drown that music but that at Wuthering Heights it cannot be suppressed, that since young Catherine is fascinated by Linton Heathcliff it is appropriate that these brooks should come from the uplands and that it is also right that they should be temporary. If we discuss whether the significances are logically 'there' and can be justified as adding meaning, we shall have to admit them. But we shall be in danger of gaining these significances at the cost of distorting our response to the whole book. The narration at this point demands considerable speed; the opening of the chapter is part of a movement towards a happening for which we are waiting and the rhythm of the paragraph does not invite us to halt; the immediate associations with the brooks are practical—wet feet and annoyance. We may accept that Emily Brontë's mind in the act of creation worked within a certain field of imagery and that our own minds, responding, accept her vocabulary as appropriate. But to linger over this passage as long as we would over, say, the description of the scene just before Catherine receives Heathcliff's letter is to lose the variation of pace and tension, of density, which is essential for the total effect of this, or any other, novel.

'. . . the oneirocriticall masters, have left such frigid
Interpretations from plants, that there is little
encouragement to dream of Paradise itself.'

Sir Thomas Browne: *The Garden of Cyrus*

'All the same I think he [Zeno's psychoanalyst]
must be the only person in the world who, hearing
that I wanted to go to bed with two lovely women,
must rack his brain to try and find a reason for it!'

Italo Svevo: *The Confessions of Zeno*,
translated by Beryl de Zoete

7

Reinterpretation and misinterpretation

We guard against the over-interpretation of some parts of a novel—which may amount to a partial misinterpretation of the whole—by appealing to a sense of the total effect of the work, and we make this appeal sometimes against our own misplaced ingenuity or that of other readers and occasionally against misplaced ingenuity on the part of the writer himself. The criteria are much the same when we are faced by the necessity of choosing between two or more interpretations.

Naturally, we shall not choose between them unless we have to. Novels which allow us to hold simultaneously in our minds a number of coexistent interpretations are not uncommon. Probably the clearest case is Kafka's *The Castle* and it is one which shows with particular clarity, not only the possibility of multiple interpretations, but also the need not to exclude any of them. K.'s endeavour to find acceptance by the castle and to enter it is a metaphor which can be found appropriate to our lives in a number of different ways. It is a correlative for the situation of an individual who, in society, tries to find acceptance and a clear statement of his status, rights and purpose. But the bureaucratic nightmare in which this plight is presented also projects the struggle of the individual to accept himself and, in psychological terms, to resolve those contradictory impulses which are embodied in other people. Equally it stands for the plight of the Jew who feels himself excluded from a Gentile society. It expresses the situation of a man who seeks unambiguous knowledge of a transcendental order, for whom the Castle appears as the kingdom of heaven.* It can also be seen as an expression of doubt

* Whether we take the castle, in the religious sphere, to stand for some

about the status of any statement which includes the word 'meaning'. There is no question of our making an exclusive choice between these five interpretations; a claim that only one is valid leads to a damaging narrowness of response and is normally evidence only that the critic is imposing his own conviction that one such plight alone is meaningful. If we decide ultimately that the religious situation or the projection of the uncertainty of 'meaning' is the dominant one, this is largely because such an emphasis does not devalue the significance of the other interpretations, whereas an account of the book predominantly in terms of Kafka the neurotic or Kafka the Jew is in danger of doing so.

But there are possibilities of variant interpretations which do oblige us to choose because the two interpretations are incompatible, and, though it may be possible to carry two incompatible interpretations in one's mind for the space of a short poem, I do not believe that this can be done for a work as lengthy and requiring as many different kinds of response as a novel. Such a demand for choice is made by the incident of the burning of the codicil in *Little Dorrit*, which I have discussed briefly in chapter 5.

While we confine ourselves to the motives of the characters we are on sure ground: Little Dorrit asks Arthur Clennam to burn the codicil unread so as to save him from any pain which he might feel at the knowledge of his illegitimacy and so as to save Mrs Clennam from the shame of making the truth known; Clennam is prepared to burn it because he loves Little Dorrit and trusts her. So far, we may say, the situation is comparable with a similar one in *Middlemarch* where old Featherstone asks Mary Garth to burn one of his wills and a codicil. Here we are not aware of the contents of the two documents—though we discover shortly afterwards and are not surprised by what is revealed—but we know in general the motives of the people involved. Any uncertainty which we may have—as, for example, how far Featherstone is moved by spite and how far by a desire to make amends for previous harshness—takes its place within the constant speculation about psychological motivation which

Christian transcendence, or, as Erich Heller does (in my opinion rightly) for a perversion of the religious sensibility, makes no difference to the matter. A reader for whom, religiously, the Castle is a perversion will surely also feel that it is equally a perversion bureaucratically, psychologically, racially. He will also be likely to be dismayed in a different way by the erosion of 'meaning'.

is the essence of the book and contributes to our sense of the autonomy of the characters, an inability to regard them as totally comprehensible creatures of a plot. But the nature of Dickens's novel, its dependence on a symbolic structure, its far more determinist effect, obliges us to go farther than we might in a realistic work. We cannot leave a sense of choice as coming from autonomous characters; we are obliged to ask what is the significance of the incident within the total highly patterned structure of the novel. Little Dorrit's request is not only a matter of her choice; it is a continuation of a pattern.

It would, I think, be generally agreed that Dickens's intention seems to be to assert that Arthur and Little Dorrit can only be happy if there is complete trust between them, if all money claims are abolished in a relationship of love and if the unhappy past is put behind them. The burning of the codicil, then, functions as a pledge of love, a rejection of the power of money and an initiation into a happy marriage which takes them from the shadow of the Marshalsea into a world of freedom.

My reason for rejecting this and preferring to interpret the burning of the codicil as a destruction of the truth about sexual passion is that this reading seems to come closer to the total effect of the book, to what is achieved rather than what seems to be intended, and that the degree of coherence and predictability throughout the book obliges me to respond to the most logical interpretation. Quite simply, such a view fits in better with the essential sexlessness of Little Dorrit, her inability to function as a representative of that force of passion which, logically, could alone rescue Arthur from the paralysis of feeling which has been caused by its systematic suppression, and with the asexual, paternal, nature of Clennam's feeling for her. Moreover, the destruction of the codicil leaves him unenlightened about his mother; her deathly puritanism can still stand for him as a moral imperative, unaffected by any knowledge of its dubious roots. Significantly the idea of revelation of the truth as liberating has been very strongly established shortly before the scene of the burning. In the dispute between Mrs Clennam and Rigaud-Blandois the bringing to light of the truth about Arthur's father, Mrs Clennam's treatment of him and the roots of her oppression of Arthur have resulted in the (admittedly temporary) cure of her hysterical paralysis. The conception of the revelation of long buried truth as giving energy and release from paralysis has been unequivocally stated. Are we not, therefore, led to expect that the revelation may also release Arthur? The burning of the codicil is surely Dickens's unconscious admission that he cannot admit into his book the forces which Mrs Clennam has suppressed.

It is important for the critic who takes the view that I do here to realize exactly what he is doing. He is interpreting an action within the book in terms of the logic of its main development at a point at which the book is, by general agreement, weak. Tacitly, he is saying that, for reasons connected with Dickens's own peculiarities of mind, peculiarities which can be observed in passages to do with sexual love both in this book and elsewhere, he is unable to admit the logic of that structure which represents the deepest promptings of his genius. The reader, unhampered by these limitations (but subject, beyond doubt, to many others of which he is unaware), is in a position to observe that there can be seen, struggling against the local line of Dickens's narrative at this point, a more cogent logic which is marked by an incident which is ambiguous.

Reinterpretations need justification—normally the justification of observed ambiguity or contradiction—precisely because reinterpretation is for the critic so tempting an activity. It is always satisfying to believe that a greater man than oneself has not noticed what he is doing, and the act of reinterpreting part of a book (even more, the whole of one) is an activity in which the critic can easily seek compensation for his normally fairly humble role as honest middleman or industrious handmaiden. He can for a while enjoy the sense of apparent creative activity. But he always risks making a clever fool of himself.

Nowhere is this quasi-creative and often self-aggrandizing activity more common and more dubious than in total reinterpretations of novels in terms of some grand, omnicompetent, unitary explanation of all human behaviour, whether it be Marxist, Christian, Freudian, Jungian, or, like most literary critics' psychology, eclectic.* If a man cannot by his utterances

* To these I would add, as a variant on the psychological explanations, the interpretation of literature in terms of the repetitions of myths. Unless by saying that a certain character is a Prometheus figure or an Oedipus figure we imply that Prometheus and Oedipus are accepted symbolic figures within some system—unless, that is, we are making a claim in terms of some kind of depth psychology—we are only noting a similarity of plot or taking over an Augustan view that our culture must lean on that of Greece and Rome.

but speak forth the glory of God or exemplify the operations of the dialectic or reveal his own accommodation with his *anima* or his own Jocasta, then his apparent concern with Dorothea Brooke or Ursula Brangwen or a whale called Moby Dick is nothing but a screen behind which lurks some greater truth which the critic is determined to reveal.

It is, of course, quite possible for a critic who has certain beliefs to discuss a writer within this framework of ideas without feeling called upon to reinterpret the works. It would be possible to deduce from Dr Johnson's criticism of Shakespeare that Johnson was a Christian, but this is a very different matter from, say, the Christian interpretation of *D. H. Lawrence and Human Existence* by 'William Tiverton'. It is no coincidence that Tiverton's interpretation makes some use of psychological concepts of unconscious purpose, for psychological interpretations have, for the most part, been the ones which have involved most reinterpretation of the works themselves. This seems inevitable, given their emphasis upon unconscious motivation, as applied both to writers and to the writers' characters. Marxist interpretations, by contrast, tend to accept the books as they stand; they may ask us to change our valuations of the characters or to see this story as typical of a general situation; at the most they may speak in terms of a kind of simple allegory. We may agree or disagree with Lukács's view of *Anna Karenina* as a study of bourgeois marriage, but when we have taken from him what we can accept, it is not hard to throw the rest away and keep an unaffected novel which we have considered within a certain context, just as we may recognize that an actual human being is both an individual whom we know and a man who belongs to a certain class and fulfils a certain social role. But the essence of interpretations from the point of view of depth psychology lies in their claims that apparent motivation is not actual motivation; explicit statement is not total statement; nothing in a book can be taken at its face value.

Such psychological interpretations, if true at all, must be equally relevant to novels of all kinds (and, moreover, to all criticisms of these novels). But in practice symbolic novels are more often subjected to radical reinterpretations since they seem to operate in a manner which reveals more nakedly the fundamental conditions of their creators' minds, and the minds of those who respond to them, unhampered by the rationalizing and conscious observation of society or of the surface detail of human interaction. In effect what such criticism asserts is that all significant symbols which are to be found in a novel are public symbols, ones shared by the writer and all readers even before the book is written. I have suggested that in *Wuthering Heights* Emily Brontë has established the brook, whose noise can be drowned at Thrushcross Grange, as a symbol for the force of passionate affection; a psychoanalytically inclined critic would assert that she has succeeded in establishing this because brooks always are, unconsciously, symbols of this nature. A similar willingness to generalize a happening within a book can be seen in the very common transformation of meals into acts of communion; the central ritual of Christianity is often taken to represent the main cultural manifestation of this and all fictional eating is interpreted as symbolic communion of characters with one another.

There are certain characteristics of depth psychology of all kinds which make it virtually impossible to discuss whether, in any specific case, an interpretation is true, or what, in this context, we mean by 'true'. We are forced back, if we wish to talk in terms of truth, to questions of the basic truth or falsity of the entire theoretical system. These characteristics which make interpretations self-substantiating are those which are associated with the operations of the unconscious censor, with displacement, with transference, with the concept of compensation. One consequence of them is expressed succinctly, if somewhat inimically, in Professor H. J. Eysenck's *Sense and Nonsense in Psychology* in his account of some research by Calvin S. Hall: 'In his search of the literature [of psychoanalysis, that is] he found 102 different dream-symbols for the penis, ninety-five for the vagina, and fifty-five for sexual intercourse.' If the novelist's use of symbols is taken (as it usually is) as being akin to that of the dreamer, this gives the interpreter a degree of freedom which renders him practically immune to confutation. An attempt to differ raises at once the question of the validity of the whole conceptual apparatus. A similar freedom—amounting to an immunity from dissent unless the whole system is challenged—is expressed with great openness by Bernard C. Meyer, in his *Joseph Conrad: a psychoanalytic biography*, when he says: 'It is apparent that Conrad's voyeurism and exhibitionism were in themselves subjects of neurotic conflict. As a consequence these tendencies emerged either in covert fashion or in the form of their exact opposite.'

Few critics feel competent to preface any dissent which they wish to register with an interpretation by a full-scale discussion of the system within which the interpretation is made; many who may distrust the results of thoroughgoing psychoanalytic interpretation have an uneasy sense that, from time to time, they make unsystematic use of some psychological concepts—as I did when I spoke of Dickens's 'unconscious admission' that he could not introduce certain matter into *Little Dorrit*. A more promising line of approach, which does not oblige the critic either to assess the whole of a psychological system before he starts his proper work or puritanically to avoid insights which he may find helpful, is to concentrate attention on the effect which large-scale psychological interpretations have upon the books. A theoretical system may be untenable and yet yield some useful insights; a system may be true and nevertheless unhelpful. My conviction is that thoroughgoing psychological interpretations—which are normally basically either Freudian or Jungian—are unhelpful because they tend to replace one book by another.

Though, as I hope to show, this happens in practice, in principle it need not. It is possible to use an organized theory to demonstrate a pattern of largely unconscious conflicts and resolutions within a novel (and, for that matter, should we care for the task, within critical studies of that novel), but to regard this pattern as having an objective existence quite apart from our other responses to the book and thus requiring discussion of a totally different kind. Freud himself seems sometimes to have taken this view; but in practice this rarely occurs except in psychosociological discussions of bodies of work which are so bad that we have few responses to them but non-literary analytical ones. Such an approach has been used in discussing detective stories, thrillers and spy stories. Here the commentator is normally talking about books which other people enjoy and he assumes that they would talk about them in quite different ways and would, in fact, be unable to see the force of his arguments.

It is theoretically possible to go farther and to say not merely that two kinds of approach *can* be kept separate but that they *must*. This argument would assert that our responses to certain works are particularly powerful because they are symbolic of unconscious processes, but that it is essential for their effect that they should remain unconscious. In Conrad's 'Heart of Darkness', say, we are presented with a classic example of the Jungian 'night journey' but this knowledge should be kept private among psychologists lest, by becoming overt, it should spoil the effect which it ought to produce unconsciously. Similarly, we might say of Ernest Jones's famous interpretation of *Hamlet* that, by explaining Hamlet's behaviour so clearly in terms of the Oedipus complex, it spoils the effect of a play which depends for its force upon Hamlet's behaviour being puzzling. To clarify may be to spoil. This argument has great logical force; the psychologist is free to use novels as research material though the reader is unaffected by this research. But, in practice, this is not what happens; depth psychology is not normally left to the depth psychologists. They publish and others read.*

Psychological interpretations of works of literature are not, in any case, usually produced by psychologists and then read by straying critics. They are normally presented by psychologically-minded critics and there is no question of its being wiser not to speculate about unconscious sources and unconscious effects. These are precisely what we are invited to observe and the justification for the interpretations is that they explain literary works or deepen their effect. The terminology employed in presenting such interpretations reveals clearly the nature of the claim; we must all be familiar with such phrases as: 'what the book is really about is . . .', 'the deepest meaning', 'at the deepest level', 'the timeless realm of the unconscious', 'in the last analysis' (conducted, one cannot but feel, upon a heavenly couch). Very often we find a somewhat tendentious metaphorical use of 'surface'—the surface of a book is by definition superficial—and 'depth'—the depth of a book is profound; though not all critics who use this method are necessarily aware of the theoretical basis of their arguments, it is clear that the belief that

* The most extreme case of knowledge not remaining private comes, of course, with writers who are themselves familiar with psychoanalysis. How many deep readers have been taken aback as they read Thomas Mann by finding the author proffering them, with a polite smile, such a symbolic object as the pencil ('the little needle of hard, probably worthless lead came down as one loosened the screw') which Clavdia Chauchat gives to Hans Castorp? One inevitable effect of this is that a psychoanalytical interpretation of *The Magic Mountain* would be obviously ludicrous; the book is immune to any critical ingenuity of this kind.

what is unconscious is more significant than what is conscious, and that the critic's task is to draw the unconscious up into the light of consciousness, is an extension of the therapeutic methods of depth psychology. The critics are also assuming that the wider the references of any work the better, and that the more we are aware of the wider references the better; the claim for a general rather than a specific truth is often supported by a rhetorical re-naming of characters: Woman is a bigger word than Molly; Man is a more comprehensive word than any man's name; Eden has wider associations than any named country. Often, too, the appeal to depth psychology allows the critic to talk in terms which are vaguely but impressively religious; beneath the surface of a work which speaks of men and women and their relationships we are to feel the dark gods stirring. This, for example, is surely the appeal of Dorothy Van Ghent's description, in *The English Novel: form and function,* of one crucial event in *Lord Jim:* 'Jim's shocking encounter with himself at the moment of his jump from the *Patna* is a model of those moments when the destiny each person carries within him, the destiny fully molded in the unconscious will, lifts its blind head from the dark, drinks blood, and speaks.'

The effect of giving our attention to the 'deeper', more general, least conscious level of a work of literature, however, is not usually to add to that work another level of meaning; it is normally to direct attention away from the supposedly 'super-ficial' towards the supposedly 'profound'. The typical result of a psychological interpretation is to replace a complex, exact, specific metaphor for human experience by a general, unspecific, undifferentiated metaphor. It may be true (it may also not be true, but my argument does not oblige me to argue this) that the Mississippi of *Huckleberry Finn* and the African river of 'Heart of Darkness' both stand for the same unconscious psychological journey; but the more we regard this shared characteristic as the most significant feature the more we shall diminish the specific effects of the books and, incidentally, place them within a class of metaphors which includes many remarkably bad novels which involve journeys up and down rivers.

This replacement of a complex and specific metaphor by a general one can be most clearly seen in the special pleading which psychological critics use to smooth out those details which do not fit easily into the general myth. I do not know any interpretation based on depth psychology which avoids this and I have chosen for my examples of the process two critical interpretations which are interesting and often perceptive. It is not difficult to deal summarily with examples of gross nonsense or unhelpfulness—with a view of Conrad as a sado-masochistic, voyeuristic semi-impotent, repressed homosexual, or Jane Austen as an anal-fixated victim of constipation.* I prefer to discuss interpretations which do not seem to me to be negligible of writers who positively seem to demand interpretation—writers whose overt subject matter can easily seem like messages from the unconscious.

Newton Arvin, in his *Herman Melville*, offers a Freudian interpretation of *Moby Dick*, a work which, in its reliance on a symbolic structure and its frequent emancipation from the apparent order of logic, seems most to invite such an approach. He says:

> The Whale, in what looks like conscious malice, has reaped Ahab's leg away with his frightful, sickle-shaped jaw, and Ahab must now rely on a dead, artificial leg made of a Sperm Whale's jawbone. A kind of castration, in short, has been not only imagined and dreaded but inflicted . . .

After describing how, in a fall, Ahab has injured himself on his artificial leg, Arvin continues:

> A profound sexual injury is transparently symbolized here, and Ahab's 'ivory' leg is an equivocal symbol both of his own impotence and of the independent male principle directed cripplingly against him. It had been fashioned from the polished bone of a Sperm Whale's jaw, though not of course from Moby Dick's own: what, then, does Moby Dick himself, on this deep instinctive plane shadow forth? It would be easiest to say simply the father, the father who imposes constraint upon the most powerful instincts, both egoistic and sexual; the father also who threatens even to destroy the latter by castration and may indeed, in all but the literal sense, carry out the threat. On the deepest level, this is the oneiric truth about Moby Dick, but it is Melville with whom we have to reckon throughout, and for whom we have to remember how soon, and how overbearingly, the paternal role was played by Maria Melville. . . . (pp. 171–2)

* The first of these examples is an actual case; the second is my own fantasy, though, given her preoccupation with money, her dislike of the spendthrift and the repeated pattern of the holding back of feeling, her novels must surely have attracted the attention of such critics.

Arvin continues to deal with the problem of explaining why sperm whales are described in images which seem female as well as male (the whale's head as a womb from which Tashtego is delivered after falling in, as well as the whale's penis as a skin for his hunter) by showing that Melville's mother played a father's role, so that the images which might appear to conflict with the theory actually support it.

It is clear that Arvin, throughout this passage, is making an appeal to an authority outside the book itself, relating the precise imagery of the novel to a set of images which are taken as shared by us all: the form of words 'It would be easiest to say simply the father . . .' is a plain enough statement. Unless we started with certain convictions about a widely shared castration complex it would not be the easiest thing to say. Nor, unless we imported such a conception, would we need to have recourse to any knowledge about Mrs Melville's paternal role to explain the characteristics of the whale.

The effect of asserting that the whale-father/mother identity is the deepest truth is to distract attention from the actual effect of Melville's descriptions of the whale and the imagery with which it is associated. Moby Dick and whales in general are certainly associated with both male and female imagery; the great white whale is also specifically associated through its whiteness with all the colours of the spectrum, just as it appears both mild and malevolent. Surely the effect of this is to make us feel that the whale is ultimately unknowable, vast and mysterious beyond categorization. We may carve into it, anatomize sections of it, even grotesquely make use of the skin of its penis as a waterproof cloak, but we cannot know it all; we cannot catch it or destroy it and the farther we push our efforts to do so the greater is not only our courage but also our danger. This sense of the whale as vast, neutral, non-human, both apparently mild and apparently malevolent, is completely in accord with the legendary pattern which is indubitably present in the book—the legend of Faust. Ahab is explicitly likened to Faust; Fedallah is his Mephistopheles: 'The old man is hard bent after that White Whale,' says Stubb, 'and the devil there is trying to come round him, and get him to swap away his silver watch, or his soul, or something of that sort, and then he'll surrender Moby Dick' (World's Classics edition, p. 390). Like Faust, Ahab is warned from his quest by omens—the turning of the compass, the breaking of the log-line—and at the end he is destroyed amid appropriate imagery—the ship sinks 'to hell'. The frequent imagery of machinery—Ahab's humming which is like 'the mechanical humming of the wheels of his vitality in him' (p. 196); Ahab's own words: 'The path of my fixed purpose is laid with iron rails whereon my soul is grooved to run' (p. 204); Ahab's specifications to the Carpenter who is making him a new leg for a 'complete man' who is thought of in terms of technology—'chest modelled after the Thames Tunnel . . . no heart at all, brass forehead, and about a quarter of an acre of fine brains' (p. 559); all these place this Faust firmly within the line of thought where Faust has always belonged—that of our ambivalent feelings about man as scientist, technologist, exploiter of nature. The theme is an immense one and it cannot be said that in Melville's day or in our own it is other than central to our social, moral and religious experience. It includes, but is not confined within, our feelings about authority which Arvin expresses in terms of a fear of castration by the father. To suggest, as he does, that his interpretation is 'on the deepest level . . . the oneiric truth about Moby Dick' is to peer through a complex, minutely realized and specific metaphorical system to a 'deeper' (which surely is intended to mean not merely 'less conscious' but also 'more significant') metaphor which is both narrower and vaguer, more general and less precise.

My point about the loss of the specific in such an interpretation as Arvin's can probably be most economically put by a consideration of his treatment of the metaphor used to describe Ahab's accident. He says: 'The whale, in what looks like conscious malice, has reaped Ahab's leg away with his frightful, sickle-shaped jaw. . . . A kind of castration, in short, has been not only imagined and dreaded but inflicted.' This description is taken from chapter XLI:

> One captain, seizing the line-knife from his broken prow, had dashed at the whale, as an Arkansas duellist at his foe, blindly seeking with a six inch blade to reach the fathom-deep life of a whale. That captain was Ahab. And then it was, that suddenly sweeping his sickle-shaped lower jaw beneath him, Moby Dick had reaped away Ahab's leg, as a mower a blade of grass in the field. No turbaned Turk, no hired Venetian or Malay, could have smote him with more seeming malice.

The associations of 'reaped' and of 'sickle' are not what one would expect if they are to represent a castration (I doubt very much whether it would be possible to castrate a man with a sickle); they can only be made to serve if one is prepared to take any cutting action as a gelding, and ignore a good deal of the imagery of the passage. Their actual associations are with natural, even with peaceful acts, and they associate Ahab not with the castrated son but with man as a mortal creature, cut down like the grass. The malice is the malice such as men may impute to death, but it is only 'seeming malice'. Moby Dick can thus appear both malicious and peaceful, both beautiful and ugly, both male and female, can, in fact, always be described by contradictions because he is that 'Nature' which Bacon, near the time of the origin of the myth of Faust, wished to 'put to the question' but which, when thus racked, gives both useful oil and violent destruction.

Jungian interpretations often seem, at first sight, less radical in their effects on novels than Freudian ones because they tend to be less reductive and less schematic. But they, too, lead to decreased specificity and a blurring of precision. I consider here one which is far from mechanical by a critic to whom any student of Joseph Conrad must acknowledge a substantial debt— A. J. Guerard's interpretation in his *Conrad the Novelist* of 'Heart of Darkness'—a far more realistic work than *Moby Dick* but one which operates in part in terms of its symbols.

Guerard interprets Marlow's journey up the river towards Mr Kurtz as a 'night journey' and says:

> The approach to the unconscious and primitive may be aided by a savage or half-savage guide, and may require the token removal of civilized trappings or aids; both conceptions are beautifully dramatized in Faulkner's 'The Bear'. In 'Heart of Darkness' the token 'relinquishment' and the death of the half-savage guide are connected. The helmsman falling at Marlow's feet casts blood on his shoes, which he is 'morbidly anxious' to change and in fact throws overboard.

To this there is a footnote:

> Like any obscure human act, this one invites several interpretations, beginning with the simple washing away of guilt. The fear of the blood may be, however, a fear of the primitive towards which Marlow is moving. To throw the shoes overboard would then mean a token rejection of the savage, not the

civilized-rational. In any event it seems plausible to have blood at this stage of a true initiation story. (p. 40)

In general I do not think that it is possible to disagree with Guerard that 'Heart of Darkness' is the story of the initiation of Marlow; nor do I wish to deny that somewhere in the genesis of the story in Conrad's mind a part may have been played by his feelings about coming to terms with his own most obscure impulses, just as in the genesis of *Moby Dick* Melville's feelings about authority and his mother may have played their part. My intention is to show the limitations and distortions created by an endeavour to interpret the achieved works back to these obscure feelings expressed in the metaphorical systems of either Freudian or Jungian analysis. The desire to see 'Heart of Darkness' in terms of the Jungian archetypes certainly leads to a number of distortions which are surprising in a critic of Guerard's powers.

The helmsman, for example, must within this interpretation be considered as a guide. But Marlow's actual feelings about him are quite inappropriate to this role. He is described thus:

> He was the most unstable kind of fool I have ever seen. He steered with no end of swagger while you were by; but if he lost sight of you, he became instantly the prey of an abject funk, and would let that cripple of a steamboat get the upper hand of him in a minute. (Dent, Collected edition, p. 109)

Marlow's attitude to the helmsman is, in fact, precisely like his attitude to virtually all the other persons in the book up to this point—one of confident, somewhat detached, almost amused superiority. The whole movement of the book demands that, until he meets Mr Kurtz, Marlow should never have doubted his ability to master his feelings and his experiences and should never have questioned the straightforward and seamanlike virtues which he has brought with him to Africa.

Similar special pleading can be seen in the expression 'casts blood on his shoes', which gives a ritualistic impression which is in no way justified by the actual description of how Marlow, in the middle of the attack, while concerned with practical matters of navigation ('in another hundred yards or so I would be free to sheer off, away from the bank'), realizes that blood from the helmsman's fatal wound has soaked his shoes and socks. In the circumstances 'morbidly anxious' seems no more than a very reasonable expression of a desire to change them, tinged with the slightly ironic tone which has been characteristic of Marlow ever since he became involved with the squalidly rapacious exploiters of the Africans. Marlow, the only efficient man, the only one who has kept his head during the attack, maintains this ironic calm in the very next sentence to the one in which 'morbidly anxious' occurs:

> 'He [the agent] looked very dubious; but I made a grab at his arm, and he understood at once I meant him to steer whether or no. To tell you the truth, I was morbidly anxious to change my shoes and socks. "He is dead", murmured the fellow, immensely impressed. "No doubt about it", said I, tugging like mad at the shoe-laces. "And, by the way, I suppose Mr Kurtz is dead as well by this time." ' (p. 113)

Nor in the circumstances, does throwing the shoes overboard seem an 'obscure human act'; the lining of bloodstained shoes retains a permanent stain; most of us, if our shoes were soaked with blood from, say, a street accident of which we were a mere witness would probably throw them away. This is doubtless partly because we are more disturbed by bloodstains than by stains of paint or oil, but this is surely more concerned with fear of pain and of death than a desire to wash away guilt or reject the primitive. Nor does Marlow's comment that he is sending the shoes to 'the devil-god of that river' seem, in context, other than sardonically jocular.

'Heart of Darkness' is, as I have said, a far more realistic work than *Moby Dick*, even though its pattern of imagery and symbolism is very important, and we are surely not justified in pushing the more normal psychological reactions to the background in favour of more ritualistically symbolic ones. Guerard's *omnium gatherum* explanation in his footnote does, however, show very clearly the virtually untethered freedom which this kind of reinterpretation gives the critic; he admits the possibility of two incompatible interpretations— rejection of the savage or rejection of the civilized-rational. A less honest critic of Jungian tendencies, one cannot but feel, would have plumped for one or the other in the interests of a tidy theory, and would have left the alternative to a counter-dogmatist.

But the chief objection to this reinterpretation of the work is that, while leading us towards ambiguity and special pleading on behalf of a generalized theory expressed in a set of metaphors —'night journey', 'guide', 'relinquishment' and so forth—, it takes our attention away from what is specific and precise. One consequence of this is the virtual abolition within the story of any possibility of moral judgment. There is, in the description of the attack on the boat, an exceedingly powerful and very precise ironic point. Marlow assumes that the attackers are Kurtz's enemies and that they have probably killed him; the truth, as he later discovers, is that they are Kurtz's devotees and that they are trying to prevent Kurtz's enemies—the Europeans—from taking him away. Upon this is piled a further irony; at the sound of the steamwhistle which Marlow sounds: 'The tumult of angry and warlike yells was checked instantly, and then from the depths of the woods went out such a tremulous and prolonged wail of mournful fear and utter despair as may be imagined to follow the flight of the last hope from the earth' (p. 112). Marlow's sense of loss that he will, as he thinks, never talk to Kurtz is likened to 'the howling sorrow of these savages' and this is appropriate, because his initiation, when he meets Kurtz, is into a sense of sympathy with that with which he would have thought no sympathy possible. But it is a sympathy which he sees, by the end of the book, as a threat to the whole civilization which has produced the steam whistle which so frightens the savages—and the threat is produced by that civilization itself. Kurtz is not terrifying because he represents an archetypal primitive instinct. To make the night journey to that might well be considered morally most desirable. He is terrifying because, with his oratorical powers, his ability to fascinate the most unlikely people, his potential gift for politics 'on the popular side', his certainty that he comes from a master race, his one practical proposal in his report—'Exterminate all the brutes!'—and his ability to destroy Marlow's faith in the stability of society in the European capital, he prefigures with disturbing precision what was before long to be a specifically European, supposedly civilized, development.

If we could be content with saying (accepting for the moment that Jung's hypothesis of the 'night journey' as a feature of our unconscious or that Freud's theories about Oedipal conflict are true, are in some sense valid metaphors for human feelings) that 'Heart of Darkness' and *Moby Dick* may gain part of their force from unconscious hints of these unconscious traffickings of the mind, then we might do no violence to the books. But critics who adopt this method seem obliged to take our attention back from the achieved work to the unconscious promptings because they hold that our response to these is deeper, truer and more significant. A method of interpretation which offers so much is dangerously attractive, not least because it appears to offer a fusion of the individual and the general, the sense of expressing, in Johnson's words, 'sentiments to which every bosom returns an echo'. But its usual effect is not one of fusion but of replacement. It is not possible simultaneously to think of Marlow's helmsman as an initiating guide and an inefficient and patronized helmsman, nor of Melville's sickle as simultaneously a gelding knife and the traditional reminder that all flesh is grass. The supposedly 'deeper' interpretation replaces the supposedly more superficial and it does so, all too often, by overlooking the detail which is actually there and the actual resonances of the imagery, the sense of sharply realized and dense, unpredictable but coherent life, in favour of a scheme.

In the paragraph from that meditation on arcane interpretation, *The Garden of Cyrus*, which gives me one of the epigraphs for this chapter, Sir Thomas Browne says, as he feels the approach of night: 'We are unwilling to spin out our awaking thoughts into the phantasmes of sleep, which often continueth praecogitations; making Cables of Cobwebbes, and Wildernesses of handsome Groves.' My objection to the arcane interpretations of depth psychology is that when the critic offers to draw up the 'phantasmes of sleep' into the light of consciousness he does indeed very often make cables of cobwebs but the effect of this is all too often to replace wildernesses by handsome but all too systematically planted groves.

8

Entertaining ideas:
Crotchet Castle

Even before its first page, *Crotchet Castle* carries a number of labels which indicate what kind of book it is and how we are invited to read it. Lest we should overlook the significance of the title—that it concerns the stronghold of whimsical or perverse fancies—Peacock gives us two epigraphs about folly, one from Butler's *Miscellaneous Thoughts* and one, slightly misquoted, from de Sade. (The latter is akin to the paradox of the Cretan liar and I shall revert to it later when discussing the manner in which Peacock deals with ideas.) He then prefaces his first chapter with Captain Jamy's 'I wad full fain hear some question 'tween you tway' and adorns the chapter with five footnotes, three of which acknowledge his indebtedness to Horace or to Pope's *Imitation* of Horace, one gives a bogus anglicization of a Welsh name and the last recounts a medieval legend supposed to relate to an ancestor of one of the characters and compares it with a legend concerned with Luther.

The novel as a whole is faithful to these labels; it belongs quite clearly to that class of books which is commonly called the Novel of Ideas, a class to which belong the novels of Voltaire, Johnson's *Rasselas*, and an undeservedly neglected work from which Peacock may have profited, Robert Bage's *Hermsprong: or Man As He Is Not.** The chief characteristic of these works is

---

* Robert Bage's *Hermsprong: or Man As He Is Not* was first published in Dublin in 1796. There seems to be no evidence that Peacock had read it, though it would appear most unlikely that he had not. It appeared as volume XLVIII of Mrs Barbauld's *The British Novelists* in 1820 under the title *Man As He Is Not; or Hermsprong*, though she gives the correct title in her introduction, where she says of the novel: 'Hermsprong is democratical in its tendency. It was published at a time when sentiments of that nature were prevalent with a large class of people, and it was much read.'

that the focus of our interest is on the ideas expounded or considered by the characters rather than on the relationships or feelings of those characters.*

Crotchet Castle is not a book which stands in need of exegesis or interpretation. The kinds of question which confront us when we think about it are concerned with the nature of the pleasure which we take in it—or the dissatisfaction which it provokes—as compared with those caused by other novels. In practice, this usually amounts to discussing why it should be presented in the form of a novel at all.

This is, indeed, a fundamental question. Obviously the appeal of this and of similar books is largely akin to that of occasional essays—both in the way in which we respond to the ingenuity, originality or viability of the ideas presented (or the opposite of these qualities) and in the way in which we carry away from our reading a sense of the personality of the writer rather than of his characters. It is, of course, true that all novels give us a sense of the presence of the writer—no less when he claims, formally, to have withdrawn from his created world than when he stands in it, addressing us—but our relationship with Johnson or Voltaire, Peacock or Bage is far more akin to our relationship with, say, Montaigne, than it is with Tolstoy or James or Lawrence.

Why, then, should the writer adopt the form of the novel rather than that of the occasional essay? Or, to phrase it more usefully, how does our response to novels of ideas differ from our response to essays? The tempting suggestion that the writer casts his essayist's ideas in the form of a novel because he thinks he will more easily find a public will not stand up as an explanation. Novels of ideas are not aberrant bastard forms in an age of fiction; they were there before fiction became the most popular prose form. The impulse to dramatize the clash of ideas and the desire to read such dramatization is deepseated. The dialogues of Plato bear witness to it.

An actual scrutiny of our response suggests that the key to the appeal of such works, like that of 'Imaginary Conversations', lies in the status of the ideas themselves. They are not normally ones of striking originality, of specialized application or of com-

---

* See the next chapter for discussion of novels in which ideas play a large part but in which this interest does not exclude concern for the characters themselves.

plex theory. They are essentially ideas which gain their significance as part of a total attitude—the attitude of the man who is depicted holding them. Most frequently they are either the great commonplaces, as in *Rasselas*, or crotchets and doxies, as in Peacock's works, or, as so often in Voltaire, *idées reçues*, or the orthodoxies of the opposition in conflict with received opinions, as in Bage's *Hermsprong*. The men and women who hold the ideas are not developed characters, but the ideas, to give their full effect, must be conceived as parts of total attitudes. Novelists of ideas are paying tribute to the fact that ideas in all their purity cannot exist outside the pages of treatises; in life they are those parts of a complex attitude which can be formulated in general terms. Such novels also give scope for what we might call mock trials by experience. If ideas in isolation are less 'real' than ideas as held by men, so those notionally held by men are less 'real' than those ideas which have been tested by experience. Thus Johnson can suggest the weakness of certain forms of Stoicism by showing the effect of his daughter's death on the Philosopher ('they discourse like angels, but they live like men'), Voltaire can confront Candide with the Lisbon earthquake, and, at a much lower level of seriousness, Peacock can show that, confronted by Captain Swing's mob, theorizers unite in resistance.

Our response to this is less to investigate an idea than to imagine what it would be like to hold it. In novels of ideas we may be said to entertain ideas; the festive metaphor is appropriate because the ideas are frequently not those with which we normally spend every day. Our vicarious enjoyment, indeed, is often the enjoyment of entertaining somewhat outrageous ideas, or of holding successively a number of incompatible ones. In this promiscuity, such novels correspond to that argumentative and dialectical process by which we are often said to 'make up our minds'.

Such a form involves an inevitable tension. We have to grant some credence to the characters who hold the ideas, but we have only a sketchy feeling of their existence; they are commonly types, and if they turn into individuals who engage our feelings so that we care more about them than about their ideas the novel will fail because the emphasis on formulatable notions will begin to seem unnatural. The commonest obvious kind of failure in the contemporary form of the novel of ideas—science fiction (or, as its practitioners often prefer to call it, speculative fiction)—

comes from the writers' desire to equip their characters with plausible and significant sexual relationships. In Peacock the need for a point of equilibrium is very clearly seen in *Melincourt,* when Captain Forester is searching for his abducted love, Anthelia. If we take his feelings as seriously as we would those of, say, Angel Clare when he is looking for Tess or Dmitri Karamazov for Grushenka, we will be outraged that he is always ready for a good speculative argument. But if we lose all sense of him as Anthelia's lover, then we lose the sense of a connection between his views and his feelings, and this will damage the novel because one of Peacock's points in *Melincourt* is that hypocrites can pretend to convictions but only practice shows which convictions are sincere. We are called upon to give just so much credence to Captain Forester's love as will establish this point, but no more.

When, for example, the assault by robbers on Folliott is described in chapter VIII of *Crotchet Castle*—'One of them drew a pistol, which went off in the very act of being struck aside by the bamboo, and lodged a bullet in the brain of the other'—we have no sense of real danger to Folliott from his armed attackers nor of the real death of one of his assailants; the man must die so that Folliott can defeat two attackers and so that, when the body disappears, he can reflect, 'Oh, the monster! . . . he has made a subject for science of the only friend he had in the world', in this remaining true to the main principle of characterization in the novel—hobby horses.

Minor inconsistencies of characterization, like stereotyped relationships, are of little moment in *Crotchet Castle;* Mr Crotchet himself is allowed to assert in his argument with Dr Folliott about his Venuses that the statues are there:

> To be looked at, sir; just to be looked at: the reason for most things in a gentleman's house being in it at all; from the paper on the walls, and the drapery of the curtains, even to the books in the library, of which the most essential part is the appearance of the back. (*The Novels of Thomas Love Peacock*, edited by David Garnett, p. 697)*

This is not 'in character'; Mr Crotchet is not a man to be sceptical about gentlemen's houses; he has worked too hard to acquire one and to fill it with the right inanimate and animate

* Hart-Davis. 2nd edition corrected 1963.

contents. But the inconsistency, which might be severely damaging in some novels, is here no more than a minor blemish. The joke is apt at this point and there is only Crotchet available to make it; its effect, combined with other signs of width of view in Crotchet, is to blur our picture of him. In a world of monomaniacs he is the one who, possessed of no crotchet of his own, has least character, for character in this book normally depends upon the possession of a characteristic idea. Most of the characters are rightly defined by their names and Peacock takes care, when the names are not immediately definitions, to provide explanatory etymologies.

There is one exception to this primacy of ideas over feelings, for Peacock provides a Romantic love story. Susannah Touchandgo, deserted by young Crotchet, settles in pastoral fashion with the Ap-Llymrys. Merionethshire—'the land of all that is beautiful in nature, and all that is lovely in woman', Peacock's tribute to the county where he met his wife—is a nineteenth-century forest of Arden and the cult of the picturesque provides Peacock with an acceptable version of the pastoral. Mr Chainmail's sight of Susannah on the ruined castle is worthy of Gilpin's description of the Wye or Mrs Radcliffe's account of Borrowdale.*

> The folds of the blue gown pressed by the sea breeze against one of the most symmetrical of figures, the black feather of the black hat, and the ringleted hair beneath it fluttering in the wind; the apparent peril of her position, on the edge of the mouldering wall, from whose immediate base the rock went down perpendicularly to the sea, presented a singularly interesting combination to the eye of the young antiquary. (p. 729)

* Peacock's interest in the various arguments about the picturesque and the beautiful is shown in *Headlong Hall*, where he sides with Sir Uvedale Price against Payne Knight in his satire on Mr Milestone, who wants the 'glorious achievement of polishing and trimming the rocks of Llanberris'. His own descriptions of mountain scenery are normally couched in the vocabulary of the picturesque; the Aberglaslyn Pass is 'sublimely romantic' and the Llanberis Pass, unpolished by Mr Milestone, is described thus: 'a narrow and romantic pass, through the middle of which an impetuous torrent dashed over vast fragments of stone. The pass was bordered on both sides by perpendicular rocks, broken into the wildest forms of fantastic magnificence.' Miss Touchandgo's retreat would thus seem more artificial to modern readers than to Peacock himself, though it is always difficult to decide how far the picturesque vision of late eighteenth- and early nineteenth-century travellers was recognizable by themselves as an enjoyable cult.

Frequently Peacock shifts the picturesque associations towards the operatic, the mode of the picturesque which was probably most agreeable to him, and, I suspect, most viable for us. When Mr Chainmail first sees his love: 'Her apparel was rustic, but there was in its style something more *recherché*, in its arrangement something more of elegance and precision, than was common to the mountain peasant girl. It had more of the *contadina* of the opera than of the genuine mountaineer' (p. 728).

It is appropriate, therefore, not only that she sends her father, with a kiss, the song 'Beyond the sea, beyond the sea', but also that Mr Chainmail collects from Merioneth the lengthy ballad *Llyn-Y-Dreiddiad-Vrawd, the Pool of the Diving Friar*, both fine examples of good bad poetry, adequate performances for the kind of opera in which the *contadina* and her fellows might appear, though inferior to what Peacock, who once asserted in a review that 'There is nothing perfect in this world except Mozart's music', knew to be possible.

The pastoral is complete with the comic rustic swain, Harry Ap-Heather, and when it is time for the heroine to leave the pastoral world, as all heroines of pastoral must, this is achieved by her confession of her ignoble origins as the daughter of a moneylender and Mr Chainmail's acceptance that, despite the fact that in the days of Richard I her father would have been plucked by the beard in the street, 'she is, according to modern notions, a lady of gentle blood'. Thus are we returned to the artificial world of crotchets.

The love story fulfils a number of functions in the novel. It is part of the intellectual game and a mild satire on artificial modes, but it is sufficiently charming to remind us of those ranges of feeling which the rest of the book ignores. Thus it simultaneously points to the artificiality of the novel's main mode and slightly tempers it. Without it, *Crotchet Castle* might seem too monotonous; in a less pastoral form the feelings would break the mould. Its most important function, however, is that the conclusion of Mr Chainmail's courtship allows us to feel that the novel has reached some conclusion. The termination of the pastoral and the consequent final gathering at Chainmail Hall, with its succession of songs, provides just enough formal resolution to satisfy our demand for a sense of completeness, though the obviously factitious nature of the ending and the brisk 'Conclusion' assert that it is as contrived as the book demands.

This ending is particularly necessary because the basic principle of the novel is non-resolution. This is manifested in the first really effective stroke in the book. We are introduced to Mr Crotchet—originally Ebenezer Mac Crotchet—and the joke (not a very good nor very acceptable one) is at his expense as a partly Scottish, partly Jewish financier masquerading as an English gentleman. Peacock continues:

> . . . he seemed to himself to settle down as naturally into an English country gentleman, as if his parentage had been as innocent of both Scotland and Jerusalem, as his education was of Rome and Athens.
>
> But as, though you expel nature with a pitchfork, she will yet always come back; he could not become, like a true-born English squire, part and parcel of the barley-giving earth; he could not find in game-bagging, poacher-shooting, trespasser-pounding, footpath-stopping, common-enclosing, rack-renting and all the other liberal pursuits and pastimes which make a country gentleman an ornament to the world, and a blessing to the poor; he could not find in these valuable and amiable occupations, and in a corresponding range of ideas, nearly commensurate with that of the great king Nebuchadnezzar, when he was turned out to grass; he could not find in this great variety of useful action, and vast field of comprehensive thought, modes of filling up his time that accorded with his Caledonian instinct. (pp. 651–2)

This is a felicitous stroke, formally effective and a welcome re-assurance that we are not being asked simply to acquiesce in anti-Scotticism and anti-semitism. Rapid reversals and the pairing of opposites are Peacock's method for much of the book. The *tenson* which Dr Opimian praises in *Gryll Grange* was obviously close to Peacock's heart (though we might believe that a *joc partit* would have been even closer*). The beginning of chapter VII, 'The Sleeping Venus', is typical: Mr Chainmail is paired with Mr Skionar, Mr Henbane with Dr Morbific, Mr Philpot with Mr Firedamp, Mr Toogood with Sir Simon Steeltrap. Mr Crotchet has no partner and so Dr Folliott, who has been debating with Mr Mac Quedy, tears himself away so that there can be a set-piece argument between them, even, as I have said, at the expense of giving Mr Crochet comments which are out of

* Garnett's note on p. 779 of his edition defines it thus: 'If the challenger to such a duel of couplets chose the subject he had to offer his antagonist the choice of attacking or defending the proposition and undertake to take the other side whichever it might be. This was a *joc partit*.'

character. Temporarily silenced by farcically falling from his chair in horror at Mr Crotchet's willingness to allow his daughter to sit naked for a sculptor, Dr Folliott is allowed to win in battle against the footpads in the next chapter.

Most of the characters are allowed to score some good points and these, though appropriate to the circumstances, are frequently effective even when detached from them. Captain Fitzchrome's response to Dr Folliott's assertion that Mr Crotchet is a 'highly respectable gentleman': 'Good and respectable, sir, I take it, mean rich?' (p. 664), provides us with the typical pleasure of the epigrammatic, and his description of the man who 'has a rotten borough, for the sake of which he sells his daughter, that he may continue to sell his country' (pp. 726–7), with its emphasis on circularity and its implications about priorities, is a more developed example of the same mode. Peacock, for the sake of the pleasure of succinct wit, gives talents with no sparing hand. To Mr Touchandgo's undoubted financial gifts is added the verbal dexterity which permits him to write to his daughter from America: 'The people here know very well that I ran away from London, but the most of them have run away from some place or other; and they have a great respect for me, because they think I ran away with something worth taking, which few of them had the luck or the wit to do' (p. 720).

There are also passages of more sustained verbal play, of which the most entertaining is probably chapter VI, 'Theories', in which Mr Mac Quedy endeavours to read a paper which begins 'In the infancy of society . . .' and is never permitted to continue, being constantly interrupted by the pet ideas of the others and the interruptions of Dr Folliott who finally ends the possibility of prepared papers by threatening to read the first half of the forthcoming Sunday's sermon.

Typically, 'Theories' ends with Folliott's conclusion that 'you can scarcely find two to agree on a scheme, and no two of those can agree on the details', with Mr Trillo's song in praise of wine —the stimulant farthest removed from the sphere of pure ideas, and the last words: 'The schemes for the world's regeneration evaporated in a tumult of voices.' Nobody is allowed to win because all must be ready for debate next day. Peacock defines the situation well:

> In this manner they glided over the face of the waters, discussing everything and settling nothing. Mr Mac Quedy and the

Reverend Doctor Folliott had many digladiations on political economy: wherein, each in his own view, Doctor Folliott demolished Mr Mac Quedy's science, and Mr Mac Quedy demolished Doctor Folliott's objections. (p. 715)

This permanent lack of resolution is both possible and inevitable because all ideas are presented as crotchets, notions, doxies. Several of them are first introduced thus in the description given to Captain Fitzchrome by Lady Clarinda, a self-confessed cynic, who accepts the Captain's praise for her observation by informing him that she is writing a novel. Often the reduction of ideas —some potentially serious—to the status of crotchets is achieved by abbreviating them to their simplest terms. The explanations given for the disappearance of the Captain, after he has left them to wander in the mountains, is the clearest case of this *reductio ad absurdum*:

> After the lapse of a day or two, the Captain was missed, and every one marvelled what was become of him. Mr Philpot thought he must have been exploring a river, and fallen in and got drowned in the process. Mr Firedamp had no doubt he had been crossing a mountain bog, and had been suddenly deprived of life by the exhalations of marsh miasmata. Mr Henbane deemed it probable that he had been tempted in some wood by the large black brilliant berries of the *Atropa Belladonna*, or Deadly Nightshade; and lamented that he had not been by, to administer an infallible antidote. Mr Eavesdrop hoped the particulars of his fate would be ascertained, and asked if any one present could help him to any authentic anecdotes of their departed friend. The Reverend Doctor Folliott proposed that an inquiry should be instituted as to whether the march of intellect had reached that neighbourhood; as, if so, the captain had probably been made a subject for science. Mr Mac Quedy said it was no such great matter to ascertain the precise mode in which the surplus population was diminished by one. Mr Toogood asseverated that there was no such thing as surplus population, and that the land, properly managed, would maintain twenty times its present inhabitants: and hereupon they fell into a disputation. (p. 718)

Thus Mr Crotchet's ambition, declared in the second chapter, cannot be fulfilled: 'The sentimental against the rational, the intuitive against the inductive, the ornamental against the useful, the intense against the tranquil, the romantic against the classical; these are great and interesting controversies, which I should like, before I die, to see satisfactorily settled' (pp. 660–1). Instead of any settling his guests offer him an anthology of the devices whereby conclusions can be frustrated. Dr Folliott puts his finger on the besetting sin of all peddlers of nostrums when he objects to 'premises assumed without evidence, or in spite of it; and conclusions drawn from them so logically, that they must necessarily be erroneous' (p. 660). But he is himself the grossest offender against any rational procedure of argument. The others may orate without listening to their opponents, but Folliott has more varied ways of aborting logical discussion. He turns off arguable statements by scoring points which make rational discussion unlikely:

> MR MAC QUEDY. . . . Laughter is an involuntary action of certain muscles, developed in the human species by the progress of civilization. The savage never laughs.
> THE REV. DR FOLLIOTT. No sir, he has nothing to laugh at. Give him Modern Athens, the 'learned friend', and the Steam Intellect Society. They will develop his muscles. (p. 663)

He does not confine his sabotage to arguments in which he is himself taking part; when Chainmail and Mac Quedy, arguing about the virtues of the Middle Ages, appear to be getting closer than usual to propositions which might admit of rational clarification, he shifts the ground of argument: 'Gentlemen, you will never settle this controversy, till you have first settled what is good for man in this world; the great question, *de finibus*, which has puzzled all philosophers' (p. 713). His favourite evasion is the closure imposed by the approach of food, which none of the characters is likely to resist, or an appeal to social duties and pleasures:

> THE REV. DR FOLLIOTT. . . . There, sir, is political economy in a nutshell.
> MR MAC QUEDY. The principles, sir, which regulate production and consumption, are independent of the will of any individual as to giving or taking, and do not lie in a nutshell by any means.
> THE REV. DR FOLLIOTT. Sir, I will thank you for a leg of that capon. (p. 658)

To his other tactics he adds, as we might expect, lively misrepresentation of his opponent's case. When the rioters appear outside Chainmail Hall in the last chapter he appears to argue rationally, but slides out of answering Mac Quedy's counter argument by combining misrepresentation with the assertion that there is no time for further argument:

> THE REV. DR FOLLIOTT. It [the riot] is the natural result, Mr Mac Quedy, of that system of state seamanship which your science upholds. Putting the crew on short allowance, and doubling the rations of the officers, is a sure way to make a mutiny on board a ship in distress, Mr Mac Quedy.
> MR MAC QUEDY. Eh, sir, I uphold no such system as that. I shall set you right as to cause and effect. Discontent increases with the increase of information. That is all.
> THE REV. DR FOLLIOTT. I said it was the march of mind. But we have no time for discussing cause and effect now. Let us get rid of the enemy. (p. 754)

To this passage Peacock adds a footnote which indicates just how far I have been using Folliott as a scapegoat for evasiveness of which his creator is guilty. The footnote is to Mac Quedy's 'Discontent increases with the increase of information' and runs:

> This looks so like caricature (a thing abhorrent to our candour), that we must give authority for it. 'We ought to look the evil manfully in the face, and not amuse ourselves with the dreams of fancy. The discontent of the labourers in our times is rather a proof of their superior information than of their deterioration.' *Morning Chronicle: December 20, 1830.*

We can only assume from this that Peacock was unable or unwilling to see that the *Morning Chronicle*'s interpretation was arguable and that he was using Folliott to suppress it. Critics have often been at pains to assert that Peacock's views are not identical with those of Folliott, and it is true that they are not identical in all points (Folliott is worsted in the argument about the Venuses, for example), but normally Peacock uses him as a device for preventing the exploration of ideas which other characters expound—often in caricatured form—but which he is unwilling to treat seriously.

Folliott stands for 'moderation' or 'good sense'. He, more than any other character, is associated with food and drink, the things farthest from pure ideas, the things about which there can be no argument, and, though we could envisage the monotonous truncation of argument by food and drink as savage criticism, we are not likely to do so in *Crotchet Castle*. Moreover, in so far as he has crotchets—and he has an advantage over the other characters that his crotchets are plural and our sense of his identity comes more from a feeling of his physical presence —they are ones with which the book as a whole invites us to sympathize. His constant appeals to the classics are echoed by Peacock's footnotes, so that what we might take as pedantry becomes part of an air of erudition which permeates the whole book. Similarly, his hostility to the 'march of mind' receives backing when the book's conclusion turns out to be the rout of the mob by all the male characters except Mr Philpot, who is drunk, Mr Toogood, who is imprisoned in a coat of mail, Mr Trillo, whose harping is inspiriting the warriors, and Mr Crotchet, who is too cowardly.

It is true that other characters express arguments which are not confuted, but, though there is no intellectually formulated resolution of conflicting ideas, we cannot, even in so loosely constructed a novel as *Crotchet Castle*, remain in a state of total suspension of judgment. A dominating mood is established, largely through the agency of Folliott, who plays the largest part in the book, frequently brings disputes to a close, and ends by proposing the entertainment which rounds off the story, and this mood functions as a non-logical resolution of intellectual conflicts. Though many arguments are unresolved, we do not feel that all issues are genuinely open. Many have been closed by suggestions that 'a leg of that capon' or 'a wine-glass, full of claret' should terminate discussion, and finally the others follow Folliott in battle and rejoicing.

Non-logical resolutions are not uncommon in novels of ideas. The dialectical method, combined with the fact that their authors are unlikely to be original thinkers who can produce a convincing new synthesis of conflicts, normally lead to a close which satisfies us by changing the terms of the argument. In periods of general shared agreement within society about religious or moral or social values, the writer can rely on agreed certainties as his points of reference, as Johnson does at the conclusion of *Rasselas*. Some novelists may succeed by conveying a sense of emotional conviction; Bage's *Hermsprong* convinces us not only because he applies logic more ruthlessly to received social judgments than was common (so that he often seems to be speaking for a logically based but socially suppressed subversiveness) but also because he writes with real passion. Peacock has no comparable intensity of feeling and his conception of 'good sense' and 'moderation' does not have that confident validity which Johnson could assume for his Christian assumptions.

We should have been prepared for this by the second epigraph, a misquotation or adaptation from the Marquis de Sade:

> Le monde est plein de fous, et qui n'en veut pas voir,
> Doit se tenir tout seul, et casser son miroir.

In practice such an attitude means that, all men being fools, there is no reason for changing anything. As in the paradox of the Cretan liar, which it resembles, we cannot even believe the man who utters it. No certainty is attainable and thus no argument for change can be taken seriously and there can be no reason for disturbing the *status quo*. Belief in the epigraph is bound to lead either to total nihilism, as de Sade himself would suggest, or, more commonly, to a frivolous and reactionary complacency. Nowhere is this more clearly displayed than in chapter VIII, 'Science and Charity', in which the Charity Commissioners discover that Folliott, albeit unknowingly, receives one pound per annum which should go towards the upkeep of an almshouse, now ruined. By depicting the Commissioners as comic bureaucrats, Peacock (who is pursuing his vendetta against Brougham, who was largely responsible for setting up the commissions) directs attention away from an indubitable misappropriation of a public fund and towards the ineffective stupidity of those who discover the misappropriation. To Folliott's question: 'I wonder who pays them for their trouble, and how much?' the parish clerk answers: 'The public pay for it, sir. It is a job of the learned friend whom you admire so much. It makes away with public money in salaries, and private money, in lawsuits, and does no particle of good to any living soul' (p. 707). It thus comes to seem unworthy of notice that Folliott will presumably continue to receive the charitable pound per annum. In some novels we might be prepared to accept this simply as a picture of bumbling bureaucracy, but *Crotchet Castle's* demand that we should be intellectually alert forces us to recognize the perennial strategy of defenders of the *status quo* whereby corruptions sanctified by time are justified on the grounds that reformers are often comically ineffective. The objection to this strategy, in this context, is not primarily that it is politically shoddy, but that it discredits intellectual activity and implicitly disparages all ideas.

This, in a novel of ideas, is a crucial weakness. So much which we demand from other novels seems irrelevant to our judgment of works like *Crotchet Castle*, but if the focus of our interest is on intellectually formulated ideas then we cannot abrogate our intellectual awareness.

We do not ask that the ideas should be original or up-to-date or even true. That some of the eccentric crotchets which are mocked, like Mr Firedamp's proposal for abolishing malaria by drainage, have proved good practical advice is interesting but not very important. What we do ask is that an idea, when presented, should be given its due.

It is true that our pleasure in novels such as *Crotchet Castle* may come, as I have said, from vicariously holding outrageous ideas or holding a series of incompatible ones; but we demand, whatever our intellectual flights, that we never lose the sense of intellectual energy. There are, of course, ideas which invite frivolous treatment (and, at the time when this novel was written, Mr Firedamp's proposal must have seemed one), but we need to feel that behind the frivolity stands intellectual rigour in reserve; otherwise the frivolity asserts itself as a judgment on the writer rather than on the ideas. Moreover, sudden intellectual reversals are ineffective unless we have entertained one idea long enough to want to mobilize our intellectual energies in its defence. In *Crotchet Castle* we recognize some ideas which are potentially serious and we are disappointed when they are transformed into abbreviated parodies of themselves and hustled quickly away, with the verdict going to complacent prejudice masquerading as sensible moderation. Peacock allows his characters to present a wide variety of ideas, and some passages in the book—Lady Clarinda's picture of the enclosing landlord, Sir Simon Steeltrap, for example—sound radical enough. But in the long run we shall say of Peacock what Lady Clarinda says of Folliott: 'He is of an admirable temper, and says rude things in a pleasant, half-earnest manner, that nobody can take offence with.' I have described *The Way We Live Now* as showing the erosion of conventional orthodoxy by experience; *Crotchet Castle*, despite its incidental felicities, shows apparent openness of mind eroded by basic frivolity. Peacock entertains ideas but he does not take his guests seriously enough. The pleasure in this, though genuine, is limited and self-limiting.

'James's critical genius comes out most tellingly in his mastery over, his baffling escape from, Ideas; a mastery and an escape which are perhaps the last test of a superior intelligence. He had a mind so fine that no idea could violate it.'

T. S. Eliot

'I confess that, for my part, I am rather glad to find ideas anywhere. They are not very common; and there are a vast number of excellent fictions which these sensitive critics may study without the least danger of a shock to their artistic sensibilities by anything of the kind.'

Sir Leslie Stephen

9

Novels of ideas and ideas in novels

'Novels of ideas' are generally thought of as a very special form of fiction and not just as one end of a continuum which extends from, say, *Crotchet Castle* and *Rasselas* at one end to a farther end where we find those works which least stimulate us to think about propositions which can be formulated and discussed out of context. It is worth while considering, in terms of our response to them, why they seem so special a kind of fiction because this throws some light on a more generally significant issue—the relationship between formulatable ideas and other elements in novels in general.

What distinguishes novels of ideas from other kinds of fiction is certainly not the quality nor the originality nor even the frequency of their ideas. It is hardly worth saying that George Eliot manifests an intelligence far beyond anything shown by Peacock; there are more solid ideas in Dostoevsky's *The Possessed* (*The Devils*) than in *Rasselas*. Yet nobody is likely to refer to *Middlemarch* or *The Possessed* as novels of ideas. What distinguishes this particular form is far more the particular way in which we are invited to respond to the ideas and the extent to which this response is developed almost in isolation from other responses.

I have said in the previous chapter that the novelist of ideas, in choosing this form, is paying tribute to the fact that ideas do not exist in a vacuum but are held by men as part of their total attitude towards their experience; the works, in thus making us feel that the ideas propounded are held by people, differ in their effect from theoretical essays, though they closely resemble essays, such as those of Montaigne and Lamb, where the writer is revealing his personality rather than arguing a case. But the characters are allowed to achieve their individuality only to a very limited extent. They are never allowed to arouse feelings which might take attention away from the ideas which are the novelist's first concern. The tendency for the characters to be lay figures is particularly shown in the minor characters; they often exist only to give a central character some necessary intellectual exercise; we might often say that they are embodiments of the cases which provoke causistry. A charmingly extreme example of this occurs in *Hermsprong*. Hermsprong, together with Miss Campinet and Miss Fluart (Bage, like so many writers of novels of ideas, gives his characters names whose oddity seems designed to underline their lack of normal plausibility) sets out to visit Mrs Marcour, the recently bereaved widow of a French naval officer, thus demonstrating his good heart. On the way he tells them part of the story of his life and this develops into an anecdote about European unwillingness to accept Red Indian religious legends while not boggling at Balaam's ass and Eve's serpent, and then into an argument with the two ladies about filial and marital obligations. Chapter LIII ends: 'This long conversation had been interrupted at Mrs Marcour's and afterwards renewed. I thought it useless to mark the interruption.' Such a summary dismissal is an extreme case, but characters always have to take second place to ideas. If they do not, as we shall see, the balance of the book is destroyed.

Not only are we asked in a novel of ideas to adopt a different attitude towards characters but we are also asked to be satisfied by a very different kind of resolution of the feelings aroused by the story. Like all novels—indeed, like all works of art—a novel of ideas must give us some sense of shape and of completeness; some resolution must be achieved. But here this resolution seems always to be either deliberately factitious or else achieved by changing the terms of discussion so thoroughly that argument is cut short. The explanation of this is surely that once a novelist has set us to speculate about ideas he has invited us to engage in a kind of mental activity which will probably refuse to be limited by the structure of the book. Johnson's praise of Shakespeare—so true of most works of literature—that the end of the work is 'the end of expectation' is not likely to be earned by a work which encourages free speculation.

Peacock solves this problem of bringing a novel of ideas to a conclusion by his pastoral love story; only a relationship which we recognize as highly artificial can coexist with the equally artificial debate form of the rest of the book and only an obviously conventional ending of this kind can bring matters to a close.

A consideration of *Rasselas*—an infinitely better work than *Crotchet Castle*—should make clear just how restricted is the freedom of action of the novelist of ideas. We can see most clearly both that he cannot give his characters more than a very little individuality and also that even the existence of a shared belief in a conclusive and transcendental doctrine only allows him to bring the work to a close by asserting the inconclusiveness within the book of that very principle of argument which has seemed central to its nature.

In chapter IV of *Rasselas*, while the Prince is still imprisoned within the Happy Valley, he daydreams about the world outside and finds one dream, in particular, surprisingly effective. 'One day, as he was sitting on a bank, he feigned to himself an orphan virgin, robbed of her little portion by a treacherous lover, and crying after him for restitution and redress.' He starts up and pursues the imaginary villain until he is brought up short by the foot of the mountain, where he inveighs against his enclosure. One lesson which the reader might draw from the book—indeed, Rasselas himself might have drawn it—is that such imaginary confrontations are as valuable a training in self-exploration as the majority of the meetings which take place once the Prince escapes from the valley. Few, admittedly, are as novelistic as this, but they involve as little of the accidental, as little of the untidy stuff of reality. Johnson normally adheres to the principles which Imlac expounds to Rasselas: 'The business of a poet . . . is to examine, not the individual, but the species; to remark general properties and large appearances . . . he must consider right and wrong in their abstracted and invariable state.'

We are not called upon to feel for those with whom, in other kinds of novel, we should inevitably sympathize. When we read: 'In a short time the second Bassa was deposed. The Sultan, that had advanced him, was murdered by the janissaries; and his successor had other views, and different favourites', we take the Bassa and the Sultan as lay figures, necessary properties to illustrate a thesis about power. The philosopher's daughter must die, not so that we can be moved by her father's suffering, but so that Johnson can end his chapter with the kind of measured sentence which carries so much of the weight of conviction of wisdom throughout the book: 'The prince, whose humanity would not suffer him to insult misery with reproof, went away, convinced of the emptiness of rhetorical sound, and the inefficacy of polished periods, and studied sentences.'

There is, however, one passage in the book where Johnson comes close to rousing interest in characters and feelings which would be immediate rather than illustratively theoretical—the kidnapping of Pekuah. Here he is on the brink of damaging the effect of the book and we realize that if he goes a step farther the structure of balanced and antithetical wisdom will be destroyed. We have very little sense indeed of the individuality of Pekuah, nor of her mistress, Nekayah, but the situation is so straightforwardly threatening that even this degree of intrusion into the book of normal human pains and dangers is enough to make Imlac's measured comments verge on the smug. His judgments in the following passage are no different in tone from his commentary throughout the book, nor are they less rational, but the context makes us judge them differently:

> 'Consider, princess, what would have been your condition, if the lady Pekuah had entreated to accompany you, and, being compelled to stay in the tents, had been carried away? Or how would you have borne the thought, if you had forced her into the Pyramid, and she had died before you in agonies of terror?'
>
> 'Had either happened,' said Nekayah, 'I could not have endured life till now: I should have been tortured to madness by the remembrance of such cruelty, or must have pined away in abhorrence of myself.'
>
> 'This, at least,' said Imlac, 'is the present reward of virtuous conduct, that no unlucky consequence can oblige us to repent it.'

Such a judgment might justly be made in retrospect by a detached observer; made by a man who is involved in the happenings— and even the minimal arousing of our sense of the characters as people is sufficient to change Imlac's role very slightly—it is surely smug and unfeeling about Nekayah's grief.

Peacock, in a basically frivolous novel, can introduce his pastoral love affair without disrupting the total effect. Johnson so convinces us that he is deeply and seriously concerned with ideas that even the slightest hint of real feeling in his characters

166

presents a threat to the security of effect. His freedom of action is quite extraordinarily limited.

The conclusion of *Rasselas* also indicates just how far novels of ideas differ from other kinds of fiction. It would be completely fatal to most novels to change the terms of judgment at the end, even if there were enough social agreement about what beliefs are true to make doing so intellectually reputable. Even death-bed conversions have to be plausible within our conception of the converted character's nature throughout the book. But the sudden change of terms in the last pages of *Rasselas* is virtually unprepared and it makes much of what has gone before psychologically implausible—or it would do so if we had been thinking in terms of psychological plausibility, if we had been considering the characters as feeling beings. Johnson appeals to a religious sense which has previously played no part in the book: ' "To me," said the princess, "the CHOICE OF LIFE is become less important. I hope hereafter to think only on the choice of eternity." '

They prepare to return to Abyssinia. Religion, here brought forward as an absolute value, has not previously been presented as a possibility; had it existed, for example, some comfort might have been possible for the bereaved philosopher. But we have not felt enough for his sorrow to resent his being cheated. Our interest has been in the ideas of the book, to which justice has been done in their own terms; we do not complain at a sudden access of supernatural wisdom. The novelist of ideas, though he cannot afford to engage our feelings with his characters, can afford to introduce ideas as he will. Other works of fiction are self-contained; novels of ideas are not. Despite formal gestures towards resolution, we are not bothered by the sudden introduction of new attitudes. In these works we can move out freely to new ideas which have not been announced earlier in the books; we cannot move towards a deeper imaginative participation in the experience of the characters who embody or speculate about ideas.

One extreme consequence of our lack of response to the characters as feeling beings is that such books can, and often do, deal with experiences which may be too disturbing or painful for other forms. Sometimes writers seem to tackle such subjects as a way of sharpening their questions and sometimes because they are obsessed by such horrors and hope to exorcise them and sometimes, no doubt, for a mixture of these two reasons which we cannot disentangle. Voltaire's precisely cool style alone enables us to contemplate what he describes in *Candide*:

> Old men, crippled with wounds, watched helplessly the death-throes of their butchered women-folk, who still clasped their children to their bloodstained breasts. Girls who had satisfied the appetites of several heroes lay disembowelled in their last agonies. Others, whose bodies were badly scorched, begged to be put out of their misery. Whichever way he looked, the ground was strewn with the legs, arms, and brains of dead villagers. (*Candide*, chapter III, translated John Butt)

> Candide was flogged in time with the anthem; the Basque and the two men who refused to eat bacon were burnt; and Pangloss was hanged, though that was not the usual practice on those occasions. (*Candide*, chapter VI)

The effect is eventually farcical, totally intellectual. A modern novel of ideas, Nathanael West's *A Cool Million*, first published in 1934, achieves its purpose in the same way:

> As time went on, the riot grew more general in character. Barricades were thrown up in the streets. The heads of Negroes were paraded on poles. A Jewish drummer was nailed to the door of his hotel room. The housekeeper of the local Catholic priest was raped. (Penguin Modern Classics, p. 167)

The effect of the book is well exemplified in the speech made at the end by the Fascist dictator who has used the simple hero, Lemuel Pitkin, throughout, and who now finds it useful to convert him posthumously into the Horst Wessel of American Nazism:

> '. . . although dead, yet he speaks.
> 'Of what is it that he speaks? Of the right of every American boy to go into the world and there receive fair play and a chance to make his fortune by industry and probity without being laughed at or conspired against by sophisticated aliens.
> 'Alas, Lemuel Pitkin himself did not have this chance, but instead was dismantled by the enemy. His teeth were pulled out. His eye was gouged from his head. His thumb was removed. His scalp was torn away. His leg was cut off. And, finally, he was shot through the heart.
> 'But he did not live or die in vain. Through his martyrdom the National Revolutionary Party triumphed, and by that

triumph this country was delivered from sophistication, Marxism and International Capitalism.' (p. 176)

There are situations of accumulated mass suffering which may perhaps best be dealt with in intellectual terms; a more overtly emotional response would overwhelm us. The bitter hilarity of West, as of Voltaire, ensures that our intellectual understanding of their themes remains unblurred.

To sum up—the speculative frame of mind which is demanded by novels of ideas does not allow us to have more than the slightest of concerns for the characters as feeling people (though it does demand that they are people enough to convince us that the ideas do not exist within a vacuum) and it does not allow us to feel that the novel has reached a conclusion, a resolution within the terms of the book. We will always abandon the person for the idea and we will always reserve the right to go on speculating outside the scope of the novel in a way which would be totally destructive of the effect of any other kind of novel; and we will do this with a good conscience because it is the writer's obvious intention that we should do so and because it is the nature of ideas to make us do so. But if we move in the other direction—towards concern for the emotions of the characters or towards the need for a resolution within the terms of the book we rapidly destroy the effect of the work. All novels, as we have seen and as I hope to show at greater length in my last chapter, are held in balance between conflicting pulls and achieve much of their effect from this sense of tension. The particular characteristic of novels of ideas is that the balance is especially precarious because the very nature of ideas—that, unlike any other element in novels, they are discrete and detachable—means that any disturbance of the balance will tend to make our response not a literary one at all. Novels of ideas do not form a continuum with other kinds of novels but with 'imaginary conversations', occasional essays, polemic and learned essays.

Nevertheless ideas—formulatable propositions—are not confined to novels of ideas. But when we encounter them in other works we take up an essentially different attitude towards them; on those occasions when we do not, I think it can be shown either that we are misreading the book or that the work is flawed.

All novels, in that they present an area of imagined life,

permit us to make generalizations which we may formulate as ideas. Sometimes these generalizations are drawn from the whole work and express its bearing; very often critics speak as if they are crystallized in statements either made by the writer *in propria persona* or given to a character to express. Such an approach to novels is, of course, very common in popular, unsophisticated discussion. D. H. Lawrence is, for many people, the man who said we should have more sexual experience and have it more abundantly; William Faulkner is commonly talked about in terms of his ideas about the culture of the American south. But this is not confined to unsophisticated readers. It is difficult to describe the effect a novel has on us—not least because the reading of it is a lengthy process and a description which would do full justice to the experience would be similarly lengthy, complex and even diffuse. We have, therefore, to simplify and, since we usually want to formulate our judgments relatively briefly, we tend to express our judgments in terms of that which is most easily formulatable: ideas. We know—or we should know—that we are simplifying, but it is the rare critic who can convey to his readers just how far his account is a simplification, indeed a translation of the work into quite other terms. This happens in part because much of the effect of novels is very simple and elementary, having to do with wanting to know what happens next and with allowing our feelings to be affected by fictitious people and happenings in a way which may look extraordinarily naïve. Either fearing to seem naïve, or assuming that his readers will take this naïve level of response for granted, the critic does not mention it. If, for example, we read through the volume on Dostoevsky in the series *Twentieth Century Views* it is easy to forget that the critics are discussing novels which take some time to read and tell stories about people who have relationships with one another; they tend to present philosophic statements as the meanings of the books. There is, moreover, one rhetorical device which is extremely tempting but which is also misleading about one's intentions. Having summed up, in full knowledge (one hopes) that one is simplifying, it is tempting to buttress one's argument with some well-chosen words of the writer which support one's summing up. (Frequent appeals to Hardy's President of the Immortals provide what is probably the clearest example of this.)

In the actual complicated experience of reading novels, though, we are not normally tempted to extract the ideas and speculate about them out of context. Appeals are, of course, made to our experience of life or our knowledge of history, but we are not asked to fix our attention on general propositions; our focus is within the book itself. When, in the first chapter of *Middlemarch*, George Eliot says of Dorothea and Celia Brooke: 'Young women of such birth, living in a quiet country-house, and attending a village church hardly larger than a parlour, naturally regarded frippery as the ambition of a huckster's daughter', she is making a comment which, expressed as it is in such general terms, could provide the starting point for sociological discussion of the attitude of different social classes to conspicuous display; we would treat it so if we were given it in isolation—pointing out the pejorative intention of 'huckster's' and producing facts about the close links between land and trade in the eighteenth and nineteenth centuries. But, early though the sentence comes in the book, George Eliot has already established her tone and interested us in the Misses Brooke. We cannot, therefore, consider the sentence in isolation; it is a part of the narrator's tone and part of the characterization of the girls. It tells us something about their plainness of dress and a good deal about their social attitudes; 'huckster', we feel fairly sure, corresponds to their feelings—especially to Dorothea's. Applying the sentence thus to them, we do not pursue speculations outside the context.

The same is true of general conclusions which we may draw from a novel and express in the form of brief ideas. Of *Middlemarch*, for instance, it is often said that it shows that as we sow so shall we reap. This is a reasonably perceptive statement about the book, but a highly simplified one, and we do not approach the generalization in the same way as we approach Peacock's generalizations about the irreconcilability of crotchets. We do not feel obliged to produce examples of the wicked flourishing like green bay trees and of accidental, arbitrary disasters. We see it rather as an inadequate, but basically justified, way of indicating our residual feeling after the experience of reading a work which has engaged our feelings in many ways and which is deeply imbued with the Protestant consciousness. It is no accident that it is a biblical quotation which has been chosen to express this feeling. The biblical overtones are necessary; if we were to rephrase it as 'our fates are determined by our previous actions' it would lose most of its force. Here, as so often in summings up of novels, the formulation of the idea refuses to be separated from the tone of the book.

The difficulty of separating ideas from their context and the danger, if we try to do so, of misrepresenting the books is true even of novels which make much greater play with formulated intellectual propositions than *Middlemarch*. *A Portrait of the Artist as a Young Man* is a very clear case because here we find a section of the book—the lengthy discussion of aesthetics—which often has been discussed in isolation.

The *Bildungsroman* or *Kuenstlerroman* is not a common form in English, but Joyce's novel is an example. Stephen is an intellectual; the novel is concerned with his development; Joyce has to make his intellectual convincingly intelligent; Stephen has to define the nature of his rejections and his acceptances in intellectual terms. The long discussion with Lynch is thus a necessary part of the novel, a necessary part of Stephen's progress. But, since the novel is autobiographical and Stephen's formulations of aesthetic theory are known to be Joyce's own formulations, and thus of some interest not only in their own right but also in terms of Joyce's artistic development, this part of the book has often been discussed without reference to its context. To think of it in this way, however, severely limits its effect within the book and has also, I believe, led to some misconceptions even of Joyce's own ideas.

By the time we reach this section we are interested in Stephen; we have seen him undergoing a large variety of experiences and working out the terms in which he will live. We recognize the ideas as his ideas and the manner of their presentation as his manner. It is typical of Stephen that he uses his Jesuit training to express his acceptance of a way of life which involves rejecting the Jesuits and that he presents his argument with a kind of contemptuous dandyism, an affectation of arrogant certainty ('Aristotle has not defined pity and terror. I have.') to a man who is clearly in no position to oppose the arguments adequately, a man who will be left behind like the other students when Stephen follows his new path. Formally we respond to it as a passage of sustained affirmation after a passage of disjointed rejection. We cannot overlook that the starting point for Stephen's theory, the misquoted tag from Aquinas' *Summa Theologica*—'*Pulcra sunt quae visa placent*'—has already been used by him in his rather weary conversation with the English convert dean of studies, the man 'ungraced by aught of saintly or of prelatic beauty', who has asked 'When may we expect to have something from you on the aesthetic question?' Nor can we fail to relate the life that Stephen is rejecting—Moynihan's juvenile obscenities, MacCann's peace testimonial, Davin's nationalism, a life which appears dreary and provincial—to the fact that Stephen's theory is one which emphasizes the transcendence of the ordinary—'The mind', he says, 'is arrested and raised above desire and loathing' in an aesthetic experience; his proclamation of faith is for the need 'to press out again, from the gross earth or what it brings forth, from sound and shape and colour which are the prison gates of our soul, an image of the beauty we have come to understand—that is art'. The theorizing leads us on, too, to the moment when despondency can fall again upon Stephen when, after Lynch says, 'Your beloved is here', Stephen's 'mind, emptied of theory and courage, lapsed back into a listless peace'. In its context the passage is not at all self-contained; it is a part of a forward movement.

Nevertheless the passage has often been discussed in terms of its ideas with little concern for context, and it is certainly possible to use it as the starting point for an interesting discussion, apt to certain aesthetic claims, though the speculations which we enjoy could have been started equally well by some other text (just as, if we chose to isolate George Eliot's sentence about the taste of hucksters and the taste of ladies we might have an interesting discussion which could have been started by any number of other texts). But the passage is one which has led many critics astray and produced many puzzles and misunderstandings. This is, I think, because numerous critics have not recognized the absolute necessity of either taking it completely out of context or completely in context. They have tended to mix up Stephen's ideas *qua* Stephen's ideas with Stephen's ideas *qua* Joyce's ideas, and both with the expression of ideas which can be considered without relation to any person or character.

Nowhere has confusion been greater than in discussion of the words with which Joyce concludes his description of the progress from the lyric via the epic to the dramatic: 'The artist, like the God of creation, remains within or behind or beyond or above his handiwork, invisible, refined out of existence, indifferent, paring his fingernails'. This has been widely taken as an assertion that art and morality are unconnected, that the artist has no concern with morality, and much ink has been spilt either asserting that Joyce (that creator of great humane masterpieces) is a typical modern writer in advocating this view, or (more intelligently) puzzling over the apparent contradiction between this and Stephen's own desire to forge the uncreated conscience of his race and our sense of Joyce as a writer whose work has a clear moral bearing. I do not think that, in or out of context, the passage bears the meaning commonly given to it. Stephen expresses himself somewhat ambiguously so that we are not sure how far he is thinking of an historical sequence and how far of a hierarchy of forms, but what he is describing is essentially a process whereby the artist withdraws *in propria persona* from his work until, in the dramatic form, his feelings are present only impersonally as a part of the whole work. Stephen is not suggesting that epic writers make moral judgments and that dramatists (or novelists using dramatic methods) are morally neutral. But the manner in which Stephen's ideas are expressed, in sentences like 'The aesthetic image in the dramatic form is life purified in and reprojected from the human imagination. The mystery of aesthetic, like that of material creation, is accomplished', has led unwary critics astray because the images which cluster round the idea of detachment are so strong as to suggest that here is the emotional centre of the argument. In context there is no problem about the phraseology and the images which Stephen chooses. He is describing a technical method; he is also brooding about art as a way of transcending the daily particulars which so weigh upon him. His grandiose words require no explanation if we set them beside such a sentence as: 'The life of his body, ill clad, ill fed, louse-eaten, made him close his eyelids in a sudden spasm of despair.'

In brief, we can read the discussion on aesthetics as an exposition of certain attitudes towards aesthetic questions, and if we do so the links which we make will be between these propositions and arguments outside the book—between, say, these theories and those of Lessing. In this case it will be irrelevant whether the words are Stephen's, or anonymous. But in this case we have virtually ceased to read this book; an extract or a summary would do as well. Or we can read the passage as part of the novel and then the links will be between these propositions and other parts of the book. But if we blur the distinction between these two ways of reading the passage we are likely to misread both the aesthetic theory and the novel. It is only in novels of ideas proper that we do not need to distinguish between two different ways of responding, because these novels are so unresolved and their characters are so generalized that when we return from the speculations and arguments set going by the novelist's formulation of ideas, but not controlled by him, we shall not disrupt the books.

It may be objected that I am making too rigid a distinction between different ways of reading and, in particular, that I am speaking as though there are clearly recognizable entities within novels called 'ideas' which are different from other kinds of statement. Though it is convenient to talk about 'ideas' as a way of indicating certain kinds of statement, the important matter has to do with different kinds of response. But, it may be asked, do not writers who are in no way likely to be called novelists of ideas, novelists whose works have a complex organization and whose characters are highly developed fictional beings, continually make statements which provoke us to speculate? Am I not suggesting that our response to novels is much simpler, much more uniform than in fact it is?

Certainly our response to fiction is very complicated. Fiction is, compared with, say, string quartets, a very 'impure' art, and much of the effect of the greatest fiction comes from a sense of tension between conflicting demands.* The tension between what I have earlier called 'lifelikeness' and 'shape' is not an inherently unstable one. The conflict between our interest in verisimilitude of character, which involves a just acceptance of the contingent and the accidental, and our demand for form— the conflict, in Nostromo, say, between our imaginative participation in the feelings of Don Carlos Gould and our awareness of him as a manifestation of the symbolic pattern of enslavement to silver—is not by any means necessarily disruptive. Both find their field of activity within the novel; both are contained, in a successful work, within what we might call a provisional or hypothetical or detached frame of mind—both the result (Coleridge's formulation can hardly be avoided) of a 'willing suspension of disbelief for the moment'. Both take their place

---

* In chapter X I develop this idea. It is enough to indicate at this point, I hope, that one vital task of the critic is to distinguish, when he is discussing what James called 'loose and baggy monsters', between that looseness and bagginess which may be harmful to the effect of unity and that looseness and bagginess which may be a vital, structural principle.

within our feelings about novels as metaphors and not as documents. Our feelings about characters are akin to those which we have for real people, for example, but if they ever grow too much like them—if we lose our sense of detachment and start to identify our feelings with individual characters—we shall find that our emotions will swamp our awareness of the total plan of the book or make us unwilling to accept it. We shall resemble those who send flowers to the BBC when television characters die.

Similarly, our feelings about ideas, beliefs, generalizations in novels are akin to our feelings about them in daily life. But if the sense of the provisional—the sense that they exist primarily within the context of the book as part of its total metaphorical statement—weakens, they, too, will destroy the total effect. Moreover, the feelings roused by ideas are particularly likely to be disruptive; the speculative or argumentative frame of mind is hard to accommodate because it tends so easily to move outwards from the novel. Ideas are very portable. The novelist may provoke speculation or argument, but he cannot easily control its development. And once he has provoked us to argue, to bring evidence from outside the novel to bear on issues within it as part of a direct argumentative process, where will we stop?

Fortunately such incitements to argument are often so disposed in novels, otherwise unified in their effect, that they are isolated. The 'Prelude' and the concluding paragraphs of the 'Finale' of *Middlemarch* would surely be disruptive of the novel were they not so eminently forgettable. When George Eliot asserts, in the 'Finale', 'A new Theresa will hardly have the opportunity of reforming a conventual life, any more than a new Antigone will spend her heroic piety in daring all for the sake of a brother's burial: the medium in which their ardent deeds took shape is for ever gone', it is hard not to start arguing with her— the 'for ever' has such a tone of dogmatism that we feel impelled to wonder whether, perhaps, simple pieties of family still may, and still do, conflict with the orders of the state. Since, however, we do not think of Dorothea as a St Teresa throughout the book, our disagreement does not spread beyond the tendentiousness of this section.

There are, however, writers whose works seem always in danger of provoking a disruptive response. Earlier I suggested that unsophisticated discussion of D. H. Lawrence is conducted largely in terms of detachable ideas. It must be admitted that, though this is inadequate to his best work, he cannot be acquitted of responsibility for such misreading. Much which seems unsatisfactory in as good a novel as *The Rainbow* appears to come from a change of tone from a dense complexity of realization to a thinner argumentativeness. This is very clear, for example, when Lawrence analyses Skrebensky's state of mind thus:

> He could not see, it was not born in him to see, that the highest good of the community as it stands is no longer the highest good of even the average individual. He thought that, because the community represents millions of people, therefore it must be millions of times more important than any individual, forgetting that the community is an abstraction from the many, and is not the many themselves. Now when the statement of the abstract good for the community has become a formula lacking in all inspiration or value to the average intelligence, then the 'common good' becomes a general nuisance, representing the vulgar, conservative materialism at a low level. (Penguin edition, p. 329)

The tone of this, which contrasts strikingly with what comes before and after, is the tone of argument; the sentences are articulated as if for a debate—'therefore', 'Now'—and the language is at a high (and rather hackneyed) level of abstraction —'the highest good of the community', 'lacking in all inspiration or value', 'the average intelligence', 'at a low level'. We can hardly avoid wishing to argue this as a general case, and, whether we agree with it or not, the effect will be to weaken our sense of Skrebensky as a man and, more damagingly, to encourage us to treat as general propositions, advanced for refutation or confirmation, other parts of the book where such an attitude is inappropriate. It is important to emphasize that the harm in such passages as this is done regardless of whether we agree with the argument or not. It is the change in the nature of the response demanded which is damaging, not the possibility of our differing with the author. Dickens's view of the administrative system of England in *Little Dorrit* is highly tendentious—indeed, propagandist. But we are not disposed to check it against historical evidence because the opinions have been absorbed into the complex symbolic scheme of the book, a scheme which has room for the farcical, the emblematic, the verbally extravagant. The Circumlocution Office never appears as part of an argument which we are tempted to confute; it is part of Dickens's consistent vision of England.

A similar absorption of potentially controversial material within a dominant tone so that we yield it provisional assent can be seen in A *Passage to India*. Forster's tone is a complex one which accommodates a wide range of feelings: the opening chapter establishes the coexistence, within an ironic vision, of the grotesque, the beautiful, the muddled; above all, we are made aware of the proximity of the unrelated, huddled beneath a vast sky. Though in the next chapter Forster comes very close to his characters, we never, throughout the book, lose our sense of this ironic vision nor of a vastness which may at any moment dwarf the individuals. Consequently Forster can generalize, comment, appear dogmatic, even address the reader directly in a manner whose very old-fashionedness is part of the ironic detachment ('Visions are supposed to entail profundity, but—Wait till you get one, dear reader!') and yet preserve the provisional acceptance by his readers of the world which he presents. The dominant mood of the book—of irony confronting muddle—makes it possible for us, without feeling obliged to argue, to accept such apparently dogmatic statements as:

> A community that bows the knee to a Viceroy and believes that the divinity that hedges a king can be transplanted, must feel some reverence for any viceregal substitute. At Chandrapore the Turtons were little gods; soon they would retire to some suburban villa, and die exiled from glory.

or:

> The police inspector, for instance, did not feel that Aziz had degraded himself by reciting, nor break into the cheery guffaw with which an Englishman averts the infection of beauty.

On the few occasions when we sense that we are being led into an argumentative frame of mind it is not because the statements are any more tendentious or the generalizations any more questionable, but because the characteristic tone is missing. When Forster says: 'No one, except Ronny, had any idea of what passed in her mind, and he only dimly, for where there is officialism every human relationship suffers', this seems to me a weakening of the grip of the book; this is not because I disagree with the statement—indeed, I agree with it wholeheartedly—but because Forster is here saying succinctly what elsewhere in the book is projected in a complex and ironic fashion which ensures that what is said is experienced within the total fictional experience.

It should be clear, from the examples which I have given of those occasions when novels are in danger of disruption because of a shift of tone to the argumentative or the speculative, that it is a danger to which the best novelists are prone. Some of the very greatest are perhaps in most danger. Of these Tolstoy is probably the most striking. His strength lies in his extraordinary power of making us believe what he says; he often has only to assert for us to believe. He gains this in large measure from our sense that he is interested in everything, that he is the least narrow of novelists. But this vast range of interest, this potentiality for sympathy with everybody and this sense of deep and passionate involvement with all aspects of life sometimes manifests itself as direct concern by the writer with ideas, beliefs, theories. This is, of course, most clear in *War and Peace*, where the argumentative historical sections, were they not so easily detachable from the rest, would present considerable problems. For if we are led to argue about the significance of human decisions in historical happenings, can we avoid arguing similarly about those matters which we must accept because Tolstoy tells us that they are so? If we start disputing Tolstoy's conception of Napoleon, may we not at least conceive the possibility of disputing his conception of Nicholas Rostov? Tolstoy himself was aware that the detachable nature of the theoretical disquisitions was an advantage. His comment is disarming; he spoke approvingly of those readers who were, he thought, in the majority who,

> 'when they come to the historical, and especially the philosophical arguments, will say, what again! How dull!—and will look and see where the argument ends, turn over the pages and go on reading. This sort of reader is the one who is dearest to me. His criticism I value most of all.' (Quoted in R. F. Christian: *Tolstoy's 'War and Peace'*, p. 56)

The clearest example in his works, however, of the relationship between what we admire and what we may regret is in *Anna Karenina*. In this novel one of the main structural elements is the contrast, manifested in a variety of ways over many hundreds of pages, between the essentially centripetal relationship of Anna and Vronsky and the essentially centrifugal relationship of Kitty and Levin. Anna and Vronsky narrow their interests and relationships until finally Anna has excluded most of her life, and, since Vronsky has not narrowed his quite so much, she kills herself in a sense of emptiness. Kitty and Levin are taken out to wider and wider concerns; they become absorbed in family affairs, they become part of widely extended family lines, they spend much of their time thinking about other people and other things. The paradox, both psychologically convincing and structurally powerful, is that, by thinking less about their relationship, they make their marriage more secure, while Anna and Vronsky, by thinking about their relationship more and more, make it less secure. Tolstoy shows us Levin, therefore, as a man who will reach out increasingly to explore more and more ideas, and one strength of the book is that he can make this involvement real because he was himself the kind of man for whom this kind of involvement was central. Inevitably, it seems, this concern for theories, ideas, beliefs, is not always digested within the book. There are times when ideas are attributed to Levin but we feel that they are there because Tolstoy himself is interested in them. The summary disposal of the concert and the aesthetic criticism in Part VII, chapter V, for example, is surely Tolstoy's verdict, and it is unfortunate because the thinness, the cursoriness of the treatment incites us to start arguing. But if Tolstoy's insatiable interest sometimes breaks the tone of the novel these minor flaws are a small price to pay for the triumphs. We do not praise the greatest novelists for their control nor because their detachment is never endangered; we praise them for their comprehensiveness, for a width of response which carries its own dangers.

We might draw a parallel here with the way in which many nineteenth-century novelists become involved with the characters which they create. They tended to be much more naïve about their characters than twentieth-century novelists; nobody now, I imagine, would in his last illness ask for his own fictitious doctor, as Balzac is said to have done. One mark of this relative lack of sophistication is the last rounding-off chapter of so many novels, which assumes that we have become so interested in the characters (and so has the novelist) that we cannot bear not to be told what happens to them after the novel is really over. The effect is now sometimes comic and usually disconcerting. This, we say, is taking the characters out of the unity of the novel, and implying a non-literary feeling for them. A necessary detachment is missing. But without an interest so intense that at times it distorts the unity of the work, we feel fairly sure, the writers would not have had the energy which creates the characters within the book.

Such flaws—whether of excessive directness of empathy with fictitious characters or excessive directness of speculation about ideas—are flaws and to suggest otherwise is to underrate the potentialities of fiction. But they are the flaws of strength and it seems that in fiction, unlike some other arts, only minor works are flawless.

'Without Contraries is no progression.'
William Blake: *The Marriage of Heaven and Hell*

IO

Tense and baggy monsters

Each novel is a unique metaphor which arouses, controls and directs a multitude of responses which are often potentially conflicting. Each novel is a resolution of clashes, an accommodation between different kinds of interest. The categories which I have used provisionally and for convenience in this book are useful because a number of different kinds of accommodation have proved relatively common and recognizable. But these categories are never more than generalizations about kinds of resolution; any novel worth serious discussion presents itself to us as a state of tension in which the parts, the kinds of interest manifested by the writer and called out in the reader, the kinds of energy generated as we read, are in a state of potential conflict. Any accommodation is a necessary restraint of one kind of energy for the sake of some other kind of energy.

The *locus classicus* for such a view of the balanced unity of a novel is James's much quoted passage from *The Art of Fiction*:

> I cannot imagine composition existing in a series of blocks, nor conceive, in any novel worth discussing at all, of a passage of description that is not in its intention narrative, a passage of dialogue that is not in its intention descriptive, a touch of truth of any sort that does not partake of the nature of incident, and an incident that derives its interest from any other source than the general and only source of the success of a work of art— that of being illustrative. A novel is a living thing, all one and continuous, like every other organism, and in proportion as it lives will it be found, I think, that in each of the parts there is something of each of the other parts.

This has justly been taken as the most cogent expression of

opposition to that critical method which organized discussion of novels in terms of their component parts. In this context it is impossible to dissent from it. But I think that the context has changed; we are not now likely to encounter critical works which have as their chapter headings 'Characters', 'Plot', 'Style', and so forth. (We are perhaps more likely to find doubts expressed about the propriety of speaking, even to the extent that James does, of 'parts' and reservations about his use of 'illustrative', which seems to imply that there is something other than the novel itself which is being illustrated by the novel.) I believe that what needs to be emphasized now is that James's formulation, excellent though it is, does not do sufficient justice to that sense of conflict within novels—to the feeling that much of their energy comes from a sense of tension between conflicting pulls.

This metaphor of tension is often used and we tend to give it ready assent, but it is perhaps not always taken seriously enough. It is tempting, but misleading, to accept the metaphor and to have at the back of our minds a model of the perfect novel in which all the parts are in a state of tension with one another but in which this tension produces a state of perfect balance. What I want to suggest is that one of the sources of power in good novels comes from a constant sense of interests, fascinations, obsessions which threaten this balance, and that this implies that even in the greatest novels (perhaps especially in the greatest novels) the threat is sometimes successful.

Some of the conflicting forces within novels are inherent in any artistic endeavour—between diversity and unity, for example —and some come from the extreme impurity of novelists' (and most readers') impulses. By this I mean that many of the greatest novelists have not had it in mind only to create a unified work of art; they have wanted, as Tolstoy did in the last part of *Anna Karenina*, to persuade us of political or social truths, or as George Eliot did in *Middlemarch* to document a way of life.

Nostromo provides an excellent example of the kind of conflict which is inherent in any novel which offers to deal with a large theme. Conrad sees certain principles working themselves out in the history of his fictitious South American republic and certain psychological and moral laws which appear inherent in human nature and which take a particular form because of the specific social circumstances of Sulaco. He chooses, to present the principles and to act as one of the main structural features of the book, a number of repeated images or *motifs*. The most important is the story—introduced apparently casually into the first, seemingly purely descriptive, chapter—of the treasure seekers on the waterless promontory of Azuera who, the local inhabitants say, found the treasure but haunt it—'rich and hungry and thirsty'. The image is repeated frequently in the novel as a way of linking the fates of most of the main characters; they are all 'rich and hungry and thirsty'. But the principles are manifested in the lives of individual characters in whom we are required to be interested and who will generate no interest if they are seen only as puppets created to prove a case. They are—they must be —individualized. The situation is, in fact, just like that which we confront when we think of actual history. Opinions may vary about the accommodation which Conrad achieves; some readers will feel at times that the individuals are subdued to the pattern, some will feel that the pattern is in danger of being lost because of the development of the individuals. The point which I am anxious to make is that one of the sources of strength in the book comes from a recognition, conscious or not, that the conflict is there. We respond to the experience of Conrad grappling with a vast and diverse mass of material and bringing it into some sort of order. The energy of the book comes from a sense of intellectual effort. And this satisfaction could not exist if we were not aware of the possibility of failure and of the impossibility of total success.

A somewhat different conflict is perceptible throughout Dickens's best work—a tension between our sense of the unity of the book and our awareness of the local felicities—felicities which are often in danger of seeming irrelevant and opportunist. Dickens's later works are often justly praised for their greater unity, but—quite apart from the pleasure which we take in local exuberance of fancy—we surely feel such a sense of Dickens's greatness because the unity results from holding together energies which are trying to fly apart.

I have already, in chapter 9, discussed the conflict which is set up between two kinds of response when the novelist shows himself seriously interested in ideas which demand discussion in their own right, and I have suggested that this kind of conflict is often a particularly disruptive one. But here, again, it needs to be said that much of the power of the greatest novels comes from an awareness of the possibility of disruption. I do not believe, for example, that the 'Grand Inquisitor' chapter of *The Brothers Karamazov*, however detachable it may appear, disturbs the poise of the book, but I do believe that the overwhelming force of the novel comes in part from a sense that it could do so but that Dostoevsky has triumphed by holding together the most apparently contrary energies.

Nowhere, of course, does the presence of an interest which might disrupt the novel's balance and unity seem so clear as in the great nineteenth-century writers' concern with the presentation and development of characters in detail and in depth, in season and out of season, often apparently for their own sake. Few readers bother about this; bother is the province of critics and they draw support from James's strictures on 'leaks in the form'. It is certainly true that the great Russians, in particular, make us feel that there is more in their characters than is needed by the plot or the theme. James's practice is the opposite of this and his dislike of fluid puddings is thus inevitable. But it is surely true that his practice results in a diminution of the tension which yields energy. If we consider such a character as Dr Prance, in *The Bostonians*, we find that our praise ends in a limiting judgment. Dr Prance seems to me to be one of the best observed minor characters in one of James's most successful novels. One can have nothing but admiration for his deft presentation of the 'little doctoress' and for the subtlety with which he thereby suggests a further way of judging the urges which bedevil Olive Chancellor and of enforcing a revaluation of Verena Tarrant's famous 'innocence'. One ends by saying that she performs her role to perfection. She does just as much as she has been put there to do. Within James's scheme it would be unthinkable that she should do more and any suggestion of it would produce a leak in the form. But this *is* a limiting judgment; it leaves us with a sense of restriction, a sense that she is being used by James, a sense of the abrogation of freedom. And this is a judgment about the kind of form which James has chosen.

By contrast, the sense, in other novelists, that their characters transcend their functions is a perception about the form of those novels. Our sense in Tolstoy, for example, that the characters contain more possibilities than are used up in the book creates a vast penumbra of possible alternative relationships and happenings. Justice is done to the accidental and it is from this that our sense of the credibility of the happenings comes. George Eliot was irritated by suggestions that Dorothea Brooke might be going to marry Lydgate, but the effect of *Middlemarch* depends, as Barbara Hardy shows so well in *The Novels of George Eliot*, upon the sense of alternative possibilities—of which this marriage is one. The irritation is understandable; speculations about whether the right hero will marry the right heroine hardly do justice to novels of this scope; but the sense that things might be different, not only for a few people but, by a multitude of slight changes radiating outwards, for the whole of society is central to George Eliot's view. Nor is this confined to George Eliot. We might say, briefly, that one of the most powerful effects of many of the major novels of the nineteenth century is of a form—a plot or pattern of relationships and happenings—which occurs within a density of created experience which implies the possibility of alternative forms.

The greatest novels—those which we feel to be the best metaphors for life—are usually the ones where we feel the greatest tensions, where the risks are greatest. We feel when we are reading Tolstoy, Dostoevsky, Dickens, Stendhal, Proust, Joyce, that our imaginative participation in the experience of the characters is in danger of swamping our sense of the whole, necessary pattern; that our sense of local exuberance and inventiveness is in danger of destroying our sense of forward movement; that our sense of the urge to formulate beliefs of general validity is in danger of changing our response into one of argument and non-literary speculation; that our awareness of the possibility of the accidental happening is in danger of breaking a structure which relies upon the conviction that what happens is inevitable. It is for this reason that the greatest novels are nearly always long novels.*

Inevitably, as I have said, there must be occasions when the tension between different kinds of interest, different kinds of response, breaks down. Novelists who have the intellectual energy and emotional commitment to their subjects from which

---

* There are novels which achieve their effect by a deliberate clash between different—even, apparently, contradictory—modes. The most obvious example of this is probably *Moby Dick*, where the prefatory 'Etymologies' and 'Extracts' alone should be enough to prepare us for this. In rather different ways *Ulysses* and *The Magic Mountain* produce the same effect. When the possible contradictions of response are thrust forward as consciously as they are in these novels the risk of disintegration is less.

major works spring are the kind of men who know the truth of Blake's proverb of Hell—'You never know what is enough unless you know what is more than enough.' Paradoxically, such breakdowns of tension—such pullings away of novels from their centres of gravity—often contribute to the general success of the novels, without ceasing themselves to be flaws. Our necessary sense of Levin's (and Tolstoy's) passionate concern for beliefs is strengthened by those passages where Tolstoy's didactic aims come to the fore; our sense of Joyce's striving towards the unification within one book of the most diverse material is reinforced by effects (of repeated imagery of organs of the body, precious stones and so forth) which are in themselves inert and pedantic; our sense of George Eliot's profoundly intelligent understanding of human nature is confirmed by her unwillingness to leave her characters, which causes her to feel that we will, at the end, accept, as we might for actual people, a summary of what happens to them after the book might seem to be over.

But such flaws only have this incidental value as proofs of strength when we feel that they grow disproportionate against very strong pulls from other concerns. Forster's *Howard's End* is a novel in which some elements seem disproportionately important but in which little tension is generated. A pattern is there, a concern for shape and an interest in ideas, but nothing like enough justice is done to the characters; they fit into their pattern too easily; they do not fight against it. Many picaresque novels, likewise, lack tension because we feel that there is too little sense of form tugging against the sprawl of reminiscence—though in the best examples of this form tension is normally created by a tough intellectual interest in society.

I think that sufficient attention has not generally been paid to the effect of tension between different kinds of energy within novels because we have not paid sufficient attention to what is probably the most basic of all the conflicts within fiction—that between the novel as object and the novel as process. A novel is both a created object to which we look back and an experience which we undergo. If we are to give an adequate account of it we must do justice to both. To say that a novel is a created object is, of course, a metaphorical way of putting it. What we actually grasp is a recollection of a temporal process, of a series of experiences, of responses to imagined situations, of progress from one point to another. Some of these we remember very clearly, about some we are a little vague. According to what we take to be the main drive of the novel we shall have concentrated our attention more at some points than at others, according to what critical school has influenced us we shall have been alert to notice certain things rather than others. However good we are as readers, we shall not remember everything and as we reflect upon the novel some parts of it will seem linked together and become reinforced and others, unsupported, will tend to slip away. From what we remember we construct a whole which we think of as 'the novel' and which we talk about in terms of some abstraction, in terms of 'plot', 'imagery', 'structure', 'characters', 'theme'. One characteristic of this view of 'the novel' is that we know it all; we know the end when we remember the beginning.

But we also have—or ought to have—a recollection of what the process of experiencing the book was like. We remember that we were surprised at some points, in suspense at others, that we wanted to hurry on in some sections and to linger in others, that sometimes our temporary expectations were fulfilled and sometimes they were frustrated.

This awareness of the process of reading, the sequence of experiences, is what we tend to forget in critical discussion. This is just as well if it is irrelevant—like the impossibility of reading without interruption—but much of the process is far from irrelevant.* Variations of tempo, of degrees of attention, of memorability, are all elements of the novel, and so are surprise, suspense and frustration. Such variations may, of course, result from the wandering attention of a fallible reader or, like the sagging of interest in some of the middle parts of A la Recherche du Temps Perdu, from the novelist's lapses. But they may be an inherently valuable part of the book. In 'Heart of Darkness', for example, immediately after the attack on the river steamer we

* I think we must exclude from critical discussion the almost certain fact, for example, that we have interrupted our reading several times and taken it up again, sometimes in mid-happening, in a somewhat different frame of mind. We must exclude this because different readers will have been interrupted at different times and we will have tried not to let this affect our response to the book. But, though we cannot take this into account in our judgments (just as we cannot take into account the idiosyncrasies of different readers and thus have to assume a perfect reader and a perfect reading), we ought not to forget that it happens and that it is one of the peculiar characteristics of the reading of novels and lengthy poems. Music, the other art which takes place in time, is not usually treated thus. We do not leave the concert hall or lift the needle of the gramophone halfway through a movement and return to the symphony twenty-four hours later.

find a disruption of the orderly progression of the story. Marlow begins to hint, to leap ahead, to tell his listeners things which do not belong at this point in the narration. The effect of this is to make us feel that, once he has described the removal of the last obstacle to his meeting with Mr Kurtz, his memory of Kurtz suddenly overwhelms him with an intensity which makes it impossible for him to contain it within an orderly sequence of narration.

Much of what we call the 'shape' of a novel is given by these variations in degree and kind of attention, by relaxations and tightenings up. The structure of *The Magic Mountain* is often and rightly described in terms of opposing intellectual concepts and *leit-motifs* and of the increasing illumination appropriate to a *Bildungsroman*. But it is also created by the alternations between the different kinds of attention which it demands— alternations between tough wrestles with physiology and politics and chemistry and the very different kind of attention (involving a different speed of reading) which we give to Hans Castorp's relationships with his fellow inmates of the International Sanatorium Berghof. As we ourselves sink into intellectual strenuousness in the section called 'Research', for example, with, like Hans, a heavy book resting on our chest or stomach (for, though doubtless not as heavy as Hans's volume on 'the properties of protoplasm', *The Magic Mountain* is nevertheless quite weighty), slowing down our reading speed (for the matter with which we and Hans grapple is indubitably tough), leaving behind for the moment Settembrini's appeal for a return to the flat land, we feel the full perilous fascination of Hans's stay on the magic mountain.

The extraordinarily effective narrative technique of *The Brothers Karamazov*, too, accounts for much of the effect of the book. Dostoevsky's characteristic device, used again and again, is to pursue a scene between two or more characters who are hammering out some issue until, just as they are approaching a resolution, they are interrupted by another character who brings other concerns with him—only to be interrupted in his turn, after he has changed the course of conversation or action, by the irruption of yet another character and another set of feelings. This overlapping method not only gives the novel its headlong pace but also builds up the sense of complexity, of the inseparability of all the emotions in the book and, further, produces in the reader a feeling of nervous tension, even sometimes of nervous irritability, which predisposes him to feel with the Karamazovs.

There are various reasons why we tend in discussion to pay too little attention to the process, the experiences which we have undergone. One is that we feel that many of the most important experiences are so elementary that they can be taken for granted. It is a characteristic of the discussion of fiction that we only mention some of its most fundamental qualities if something goes wrong. We may mention a lack of involvement, but we do not usually think it worth saying that a good novel holds our interest; yet the holding of our interest is one of the most vital qualities which any novel—any novel whatever—must have if it is to succeed. Perhaps we can take this for granted, but what is taken for granted is often forgotten or underrated. Who would know, from the whole body of criticism of *Ulysses*, say, that one reason why we go on reading it is because we want to know what happens next? Who, then, realizes that in a novel which does not immediately satisfy our urge to know, a very important part of the effect is a tension between wanting to know and trusting the writer enough to allow him for the moment to frustrate us?

The clearest example here, I think, occurs in *Nostromo*. One of the most impressive parts of that novel is the section in which we are frustrated in our natural desire to know whether help arrives in time to save Gould and his allies from the revolutionaries. We greatly underrate Conrad's achievement if we forget that, in moving forward in time and learning 'what happens next' through Joe Mitchell's boring reminiscence, we have a sense of being cheated of our expectation of a big rescue or failure scene, and then rewarded by the recognition that Conrad is showing us that it does not really matter whether help comes in time or not; the real defeat has already taken place. Perceiving this, we find our sense of one kind of anticlimax transformed into a far more significant climax which is both formal and emotional. And we must remember, too, that when we undergo this experience we have an acute sense of tension between our interest in the fate of the characters and our interest in the completion of a pattern of values and symbols and judgments.

Those who do most of the talking about novels—critics and teachers—have other reasons, too, for paying little attention to the elementary, the fundamental, the qualities which are often shared by great novels and by vast numbers of others. There is a tendency not to want to bore readers or listeners with what they may be expected to notice for themselves and to spend time on more interesting and original perceptions. Often one develops a line of thought, with the book providing evidence. This line of thought may be good, even true, and one may not be suppressing what does not fit in with one's case. But it is hard not to take as read those responses to the book which are not related to this line of thought. The effect of this—particularly for an unwary reader or one who tends to accept one's viewpoint—is to exclude from discussion parts of the novel which contribute (possibly at a lower level of concentration) to its total effect. The minute-by-minute or chapter-by-chapter changes, the slight surprises, the local exuberances, the temporary bafflements or agreeable illuminations can easily disappear from our discussion. Accounts of novels usually make them seem a lot thinner than they are; and when we look at our notes we are sometimes surprised just how little of the book we actually talk, or write, about.

But mostly the reason is that it is hard to talk about novels except at some level of abstraction. The satisfactory plot, the credible character, the symbolic pattern can be described, defined, extracted for discussion. The process of minute-by-minute response can only be experienced by rereading or partially recollected by reminding ourselves and others of it.

Many of the other tensions of which I have spoken are clearly related to this conflict between the novel as achieved object and the novel as process, because many of them are tensions between the sense of the whole and the experience of the part. We need a kind of double vision when we think of novels. We need (I propose to be as elementary as I can—that is, as elementary as most great novelists have been, which is a lot more elementary than most of us feel happy to be when we function as critics) simultaneously to hope when reading *Nostromo* that Mrs Gould will not be too unhappy and to will her to be as unhappy as the pattern of the book demands. We need to remember that we willed desperately that K. should find some way of talking, if not to the Prince, at least to Klamm, and simultaneously to assent to the iron necessity of the fable which prevents him from doing more than wait in Klamm's carriage, the one activity, he is assured, which will prevent Klamm from coming. We need to feel the rightness of Stavrogin's suicide and assent to the last paragraph of *The Possessed*—'The verdict of our doctors after the post-mortem was that it was most definitely not a case of insanity'—and simultaneously to remember vividly our state of bafflement for most of the first half of the novel. We need to understand Ivan Karamazov's story of the Grand Inquisitor as part of the structure of defining beliefs of the novel and simultaneously to recollect our total absorption in Ivan's story, so that for most of the time that we were reading it we virtually forgot everything else. We need to remember the exhilaration of Dickens's description of Lord Lancaster Stiltstalking who, as The Noble Refrigerator, 'shaded the dinner, cooled the wines, chilled the gravy, and blighted the vegetables', and simultaneously place this recollection within an unexhilarating pattern in which the Barnacles and their like do chill and blight feelings.

When I say that we need to do this I am, of course, aware that to a very large extent we do actually achieve it. Even the most unsophisticated reader can perform feats of complicated response which it would baffle us to describe. But, as I have said, most accounts of novels suggest something so much thinner than the books themselves. We can never stress too much the complexity, the density, the energy of major novels, the sense which they give us of often contradictory forces kept in precarious balance. And at the present time, I suspect, what we most need may be a reminder of some of those most basic, most apparently obvious qualities of fiction. Novels, as I said at the beginning of this book, may be seen as metaphors for human life and one of the most important elements in our response to metaphors is the knowledge of how to 'take' them, so that we do not pursue unwanted associations. In metaphors as lengthy and as complicated as novels the possibility of failing in this can be very great. Some of the ways in which novelists see to it that we read aright, that we do not pursue undesirable lines of thought, rely upon very simple and basic responses. Perhaps these can be taken for granted, but I do not think that in discussion of fiction at the moment it is safe to assume that the elementary will not be forgotten. At every critic's shoulder, perhaps, there should be that reader whom Tolstoy said was dearest to him, saying 'I wonder what's going to happen next?'

Index

Accidental, the:
  in realistic novels, 56, 61–2, 106–7, 186–7
  relative lack of in *Little Dorrit*, 116–17
  in *The Castle*, 117
  absence of in novels of ideas, 165
Argumentative tone: disruptive effect of, 176–81
Arvin, Newton: *Herman Melville*, 138–41, 142
Austen, Jane: 59, 67, 80, 138
  Emma, 56
  Pride and Prejudice, 48, 49, 57, 107
Authorial narration:
  complex function of, 48–55
  implications of absence of, 68, 72–3
  possibly misleading effect of, 77
  in Trollope, 14–17, 20, 21, 24–5, 28–29, 36–41
  in Dickens, 86–7, 93–8
  in Dostoevsky, 190–1
  in Mann, 190

Bage, Robert: *Hermsprong*, 147, 148, 149, 158, 164
Balzac, H. de: 46, 55, 60, 180
Beckett, Samuel: 9, 79, 111, 117
Bildungsroman: 172
Blake, William: 182, 188
Booth, Wayne: *The Rhetoric of Fiction*, 70, 71
Borges, J. L.: 'Pierre Menard, Author of Don Quixote', 82
Bowen, Elizabeth: 82

Brontë, Charlotte: 10, 58
Brontë, Emily: *Wuthering Heights*, 2, 8–9, 10, 45, 85, 105, 108, 123–6, 134
Browne, Sir Thomas: *The Garden of Cyrus*, 128, 145

Categories of novels, necessarily provisional: 2–3, 4–5, 11, 183
Cervantes: *Don Quixote*, 5, 82
Characters:
  autonomy, necessity for sense of, 116–18, 120–1
  relative lack of sense of in symbolic novels, 89, 105, 116–17, 131
  novelists' obsession by, 180–1, 186
  presentation of, in realistic novels, 48–55, 67, 70, 130–1, 186–7
  in 'impersonal novels', 68–70, 73–76, 78–83
  types in novels of ideas, 149–51, 153–4, 164–7, 169
Chekhov, A. P.: 77
Christian, R. F.: *Tolstoy's 'War and Peace'*, 179
Coincidences:
  damaging nature in *Felix Holt*, 68
  function in Dickens's work, 90
Coleridge, S. T.: 175
Conrad, Joseph: 58, 68n, 69, 111, 138
  'Heart of Darkness', 118n, 136, 137, 141–5, 189–90
  Nostromo, 59–60, 175, 184–5, 191, 192
  The Secret Agent, 49
  Lord Jim, 137

Defoe, Daniel: 49
Dickens, Charles: 9, 69, 105, 185, 187
    Great Expectations, 90
    Little Dorrit, 11, 46–7, 85–102, 105,
        108, 109–10, 113–23, 130–2, 135,
        177–8, 193
Dostoevsky, F. M.: 89, 111, 170, 187
    The Brothers Karamazov, 1, 49,
        150, 186, 190–1, 193
    The Possessed (*The Devils*), 163, 193

Eliot, George: 46, 48, 55, 62, 71, 77, 83,
    163, 188
    Felix Holt, 68
    Middlemarch, 49–54, 58–9, 60, 61,
        62–4, 65, 67–8, 106, 130–1, 133,
        171–2, 173, 176, 184, 187
Eliot, T. S.: 162
Eysenck, H. J.: *Sense and Nonsense in
    Psychology*, 134

Faulkner, William: 74, 76–7, 111, 170
    'The Bear', 141
    The Sound and the Fury, 74, 75–6,
        82
Fielding, Henry: 67
Firbank, Ronald: 9
Ford, Ford Madox: 69, 72
Forster, E. M.: 56
    Howard's End, 188
    The Longest Journey, 117n
    A Passage to India, 77, 178–9
Freud, Sigmund: see Psychology,
    depth: interpretations in terms of
Frye, Northrop: 5, 105

Garnett, David: 150, 153n
Gautier, Théophile: 44
Golding, William: *The Inheritors*, 74
Guerard, A. J.: *Conrad the Novelist*,
    141–5

Hardy, Barbara: *The Novels of George
    Eliot*, 187
Hardy, Thomas: 58, 150, 170
Harvey, W. J.: *Character and the
    Novel*, 3
Heller, Erich: 130n
Hypnosis: resemblance of some criti-
    cism to, 123

Ideas, Novels of: 2, 11, 147–81 *passim*
    working definition of, 147–8
    nature of appeal of, 148–9, 163–4

status of ideas in, 148–9, 158, 160,
    163
function of characters in, 149–51,
    164–7
appropriateness for painful sub-
    jects, 167–9
critical standards appropriate to,
    158–60
non-resolution, principle of intel-
    lectual, 153–7, 169
resolution, non-intellectual, 152,
    157–60, 164–5, 167
Ideas in novels: 11, 147–81 *passim*
    their nature in novels of ideas, 148–
        149, 163
        in *Crochet Castle*, 155, 157, 160
        in other kinds of novel, 169–81
    temptation to extract them from
        context, 170, 172–5
    potentially disruptive effect of, 164,
        169, 172–5, 176–81, 186
Interpretation: (see also Overinterpre-
    tation; Re-interpretation; and
    Symbols), 11, 105–26 *passim*
    demanded by symbolic novels, 105,
        108–9
    of *Little Dorrit*, 85–102 *passim*, 112–
        115, 118–20
    of *Wuthering Heights*, 123–5
    criteria of convincingness of, 108–
        109, 116–18
Illusionist fallacy: 70–1, 72
Impersonal novel: 70–7, 78–83
    problem of choice of language in,
        81–3

James, Henry: 55, 61–2, 65, 67, 68n,
    71, 76, 111, 148, 175n, 186
    The Art of Fiction, 183–4
    The Bostonians, 186
    The Portrait of a Lady, 48
    What Maisie Knew, 81
Johnson, Samuel: 44, 59, 66, 70, 106,
    133, 164
    Rasselas, 147, 148, 149, 158, 163,
        165–7
Jones, Ernest: 136
Joyce, James: 70, 77, 187, 188
    *A Portrait of the Artist as a Young
    Man*, 55, 172–5
    Ulysses, 5, 71–2, 73, 80, 82, 115–16,
        137, 187n, 191
Jung, C. G.: see Psychology, depth:
    interpretations in terms of

Kafka, Franz: *The Castle*, 104, 117, 129–30, 192

Lamb, Charles: 163
Lawrence, D. H.: 66, 133, 148, 170
  The Rainbow, 176–7
Lukács: Georg: 3, 46, 133
Lowry, Malcolm: *Under the Volcano*, 79

Mann, Thomas: 111
  The Magic Mountain, 136n, 187n, 190
Maturin, C. R.: *Melmoth, the Wanderer*, 39, 41
Melville, Herman: 111
  The Confidence Man, 9
  Moby Dick, 1, 2, 9, 45, 105, 108, 133, 138–41, 142, 143, 144–5, 187n
Metaphors, the nature of: 5–10
Metaphors, novels considered as: 5–11, 83, 102, 106, 137, 183, 187, 193
Meyer, Bernard C.: *Joseph Conrad, a Psychoanalytic Biography*, 134–5, 138
Misinterpretation: 2, 4–5, 9, 10–11, 129–45 *passim*
  (See also Interpretation; Over-interpretation; Reinterpretation; Names, significance of; Psychology, depth, interpretations in terms of)
Montaigne: 148, 163

Naïvety of great novelists: 179–81, 192–3
Names, significance of: 15, 39, 41, 94, 115
'Novel, the': misleading nature of term, 1–2

Opening chapters, their function: 85–86
Over-interpretation: (See also Reinterpretation and Misinterpretation), 11, 105, 108–26 *passim*, 129
  criteria of, 116–18
  need for criteria of, 109–12
  invited by writer, 115–16
  application of criteria to *Little Dorrit*, 112–23
  to *Wuthering Heights*, 123–6

Peacock, Thomas Love:

Crotchet Castle, 11, 147–60, 163, 164–5, 166, 171
  Melincourt, 150
Picaresque novels: 188
Picturesque, the: 151–2
Plot: see Structure
Process, novel as: 49–54, 112, 117–18, 125–6, 188–93
Proust, Marcel: 8, 77, 78, 187
  A la Recherche du Temps Perdu, 5, 57, 189
Psychology, depth, interpretations in terms of, 132–45

Realism, realistic: 2, 3, 4, 6–8, 11, 13–83 *passim*
  definition of, 45–7
  the accidental in, 56, 186–7
  autonomy of characters in, 59, 60, 116, 186–7
  fallacies concerned with 'depiction', 47–8
  function of description in, 48–55
  dialogue in, 67, 70
  progressive nature of convention, 67–8, 71
  structural problems in, 34–6, 48, 55–65
  as a term simultaneously true and useless, 78–9
Reeve, Clara: *The Progress of Romance*, 2–3
Reinterpretation: (see also Interpretation; Over-interpretation; and Misinterpretation), 11, 99–102, 129–45 *passim*
  need for justification of, 132
  temptations of, 132
  Marxist, 132–3
  Christian, 132–3, 134
  in terms of depth psychology, 132–145
    of *Moby Dick*, 138–41, 144–5
    of 'Heart of Darkness', 136, 141–5
Richards, I. A.: viii, 5
Richardson, Dorothy: *Pilgrimage*, 73, 74
Robbe-Grillet, Alain: 78
Romances: (see also Symbolic novels), 2–3, 4, 5, 8–9, 105–6

Sade, Marquis de: 147, 159
Sarraute, Nathalie: *Portrait d'un Inconnu*, 79, 80

Scott, Sir Walter: 56
Ivanhoe, 1
Shakespeare, William: 6, 8, 10, 133, 136
Solipsism of impersonal novel: 78–83
Stephen, Sir Leslie: viii, 45–6, 162
Stendhal: 55, 77, 187
Le Rouge et le Noir, 47
Sterne, Laurence: Tristram Shandy, 1, 78
Stream of consciousness: 68–83 passim
Stone, Harry: 69
Structure:
 in realistic novels, 48, 55–65, 67–8, 77, 180–1, 186–7
 in The Way We Live Now, 34–6, 60–1, 65
 in Anna Karenina, 179–80
 in Nostromo, 184–5
 in impersonal novels, 78–80
 in Little Dorrit, 88–91, 93
 in novels of ideas, 164–5, 167, 169
 in Crotchet Castle, 149, 152–60
Surprise, suspense: (see also Process, novel as), 189, 191
 Trollope's avoidance of, 36–7
Svevo, Italo: The Confessions of Zeno, 128
Symbols, symbolism:
 Critics' urge to discover, 2
 Trollope's avoidance of, 85–6
 in realistic novels, 106–8
 in symbolic novels, 105, 108–26 passim
 psychological views of, 134
 Dickens's use of in Little Dorrit, 86–102 passim, 109, 112–23, 130–132
 Emily Brontë's use of in Wuthering Heights, 123–6
Symbolic novels: 11, 85–145 passim
 definition of, 105–6
 function of symbols in, 105, 108–26
 most subjected to interpretation, 133–4

Tension:
 inherent in novels, 183–93
 energy generated by, 185–6, 187–8
 weakness caused by lack of, 186, 188

greatest in greatest novels, 187
created by our response to ideas, 176–81, 185–6, 187, 188
between lifelikeness and shape, 55–56, 58–65, 175–6, 180–1, 184–5, 187
between unity and local felicities, 185, 187, 188
between technique and subject matter, 72–7
between characters and ideas in novels of ideas, 149–51, 164–7, 169
between novel as process and novel as object, 188–93
Thackeray, W. M.: 77
Tiverton, Brother William: D. H. Lawrence and Human Existence, 133
Tolstoy, Leo: 7, 46, 54, 55, 58, 60, 62, 77, 83, 148, 179–80, 186–7, 188, 193
Anna Karenina, 48, 49, 61, 64–5, 107–8, 116, 133, 179–80, 184
War and Peace, 179
Trollope, Anthony: 55, 62, 72, 77, 82, 83
The Way We Live Now, 11, 13–42, 45, 59–61, 62–5, 77, 87n, 97, 106–107, 160
Autobiography, 40
Letters, 40
The Belton Estate, 29
Is He Popenjoy?, 36
John Caldigate, 27, 29
Twain, Mark: Huckleberry Finn, 137

Van Ghent, Dorothy: The English Novel: Form and Function, 137
Voltaire: 147, 148
Candide, 149, 168, 169

Watt, Ian: The Rise of the Novel, 1–2
West, Nathanael: A Cool Million, 168–9
Woolf, Virginia: 56–8, 70, 77, 78, 80, 81n, 82

Zola, Emile: Le Roman Expérimental, 46